COURTS OF LOVE, CASTLES OF HATE

DEDICATED

To the Languedoc and its castles,
from Aguilar to Usson,
in whose courts the troubadours sang.
Hard walking up the steep unpaved tracks
But the empty halls serenade an unforgotten past,
whether Miraval, Saissac or Tuchan,
or, most of all,
Puivert whose musicians still look down today.

Surely the greatest glory of Occitanian civilisation – that which made it known throughout Europe – was the troubadours. They started writing their lyrics around the time of the First Crusade (1095) and continued even through the period of catastrophe and decadence until about 1295
(A. Bonner, *Songs of the Troubadours*, 1973, 14)

COURTS OF LOVE, CASTLES OF HATE

TROUBADOURS & TROBAIRITZ IN SOUTHERN FRANCE, 1071–1321

AUBREY BURL

THE HISTORY PRESS

First published in the United Kingdom in 2008 by The History Press
Cirencester Road, Chalford, Stroud, Gloucestershire, GL6 8PE

British Library Cataloguing in Publication Data.
A catalogue record for this book is available from the British Library.

ISBN 978 0 7509 4536 3

Typeset in Photina MT.
Typesettting and origination by
The History Press
Printed and bound in England.

Contents

MAPS

Acknowledgements

There are many people to be thanked for their help in the writing of this book: Sarah Bond for Browning's good poem about Jaufré Rudel; Arthur Brown of Ash Bank Photography for the pictures of Burlats and Die; Peter Dale for his translations of Dante and Villon, and his reminder of Swinburne's better poem about Rudel; Aurélie Friedel (Lilet) for the photograph of the statuette of the countess among the commemorative fountains at Die; Peter Meadows for details about Byrthnoth, the Battle of Maldon and the memorial in Ely Cathedral; to Michelle and colleagues at Jessops Photography for their diligent preservation of a damaged film; and to Arthur Brown for restoring the images, and to the Information Office at Tamworth for guidance to the statue of Ethelfleda near the castle.

Birmingham University Library and the Society of Antiquaries of London assisted with background material, as did numerous custodians of courts and castles throughout the Languedoc.

The writing of this musical-cum-martial history was greatly eased by the advice and encouragement of Jim Crawley, Sarah Flight, Hilary Walford and Mary Critchley of Sutton Publishing at a time of considerable change for them.

As always, my thanks go to Judith, my wife, who accompanied me on explorations in Languedoc and elsewhere and encouraged me to search for elusive compact discs of troubadours and trobairitz, even long-forgotten trovéres, discs lurking in diverse places like the Musée du Moyen Âge in Paris; and the souvenir shops of widespread French abbeys and cathedrals.

And finally, of course, my gratitude and appreciation goes to those melodious singers of long ago. Their songs can still be heard. Faintly.

Introduction

Troubadours: Language: French, Occitan – and Obscene!

They were all different. 'I shall write a song about nothing at all,' laughed Guilhem of Poitiers. 'I am heartbreakingly in love with a far-off woman,' pined Jaufré Rudel, 'although I have never seen her.' Some troubadours sang of love's joy, others of its pains. Others not of love at all. 'I chant of battles, blood and booty,' proclaimed Bertran de Born. More romantically, some serenaded their hostess, occasionally too persuasively for the dangerous jealousy of her husband. They were all different, even the women troubadours, the *trobairitz*.

One woman grieved at laws that forbade her to wear *vel ni banda* (pretty veil or silken wimple). Another mourned that her lover had abandoned her

car ieu non li dormei m'amor
because I would not sleep with him.

For two and a half centuries in the south of France fine courts and castles enjoyed the music of the troubadours as they entertained audiences in the medieval age of chivalry.

Chivalry did not always mean chastity. It is a general belief, but a mistaken one, that troubadours sang of pure, courtly love, a dispassionate belief in honourably polite behaviour by men towards the woman that they adored, a remote and unattainable goddess.

Such a platonic ideal was both extolled and frequently disregarded. Troubadours, whether nobly born or commoner, had the natural urges of later poets such as the Elizabethan Christopher Marlowe when he translated an elegy of Ovid:

I cling'd her naked body, down she fell,
Judge you the rest: being tir'd she bade me kiss;
Just send me more such afternoons as this.
(Ovid, Elegy V, 24–6, 'Lying with Corinna', 24–6)

A few years later John Donne wrote:

Full nakedness, all joys are due to thee,
As souls unbodied, bodies unclothed must be.
(Elegy XIX, 'To His Mistress going to Bed', 33–4)

But four centuries earlier the troubadour Arnaut Daniel had sung:

Del cors li fos non de l'arma . . .

Would I were hers in body, not in soul!
And that she lets me, secretly, into her bedroom.
(*Lo ferm voler* . . . 'The Firm Desire, 13–14')

The passion is there, but it is not coarse. It may not be chaste, but it is respectful, and this is true whether of French-writing *trouvères* of northern France or of troubadours composing in the 'langue d'Oc' of the south. Exceptions to their seemliness are few.

Most troubadours composed their songs and poems in the Romance language of Occitan in southern France (Fig. 1). It was similar to French, but there were differences, sometimes considerable, of vocabulary and spelling. In this book the custom is to quote short extracts, often one line, from the original 'Oc' followed by a full translation in English.[1]

For readers wishing to hear modern renderings of the medieval words and music, Appendix One lists compact discs of troubadour music known to the author. It also contains the names and songs of the individual musicians.

Despite the above protestations of respectful wording in this book, there must be a warning for readers offended by obscenities: Chapter Four contains profanities, some so socially unacceptable that neither their modern forms nor their classical roots are included in the majority of dictionaries, whether English or Latin.

The justification for the inclusion of such language is that the subject of that chapter, the earliest-known troubadour, Guilhem, 9th Duke of Aquitaine and 7th Count of Poitiers, intentionally used it to avoid ambiguity about his meaning. The expletives were, however, infrequent, occurring in only two of his eleven surviving songs.

As noticed above, later troubadours frequently shared his amorous enthusiasms but expressed them in terms that would have been entirely acceptable to a Victorian afternoon tea party.

A note has to be added about the names of troubadours. In an age when literacy was uncommon, when there was no standardisation of language and when local dialects were prevalent, much spelling was phonetic and inconsistent.

As an example, one singer had a surname variously spelled: Mareuil, Marolh, Maruelh, Marueill, Marvoil and five more alternatives. To avoid such contradictions names here generally follow today's French translation of the original *Vida*, the biographical 'Life', written by medieval chroniclers.

In their 1973 *Biographies des Troubadours*, the editors, Boutière and Schutz, updated the old Occitanian Árnaut de Maroill to the now-accepted Arnaut de Mareuil. Similarly, Savaric de Malleo of Chapter One became Savaric de Mauléon; and the Duke of Aquitaine and the Count of Poitiers of Chapter Four, once recorded as Guilhem, lo Coms de Peitieus, is now Guilhelm of Poitiers.

Map 1. Regions of the Occitan language.

Map 2. Major cities, towns and regions in southern France.

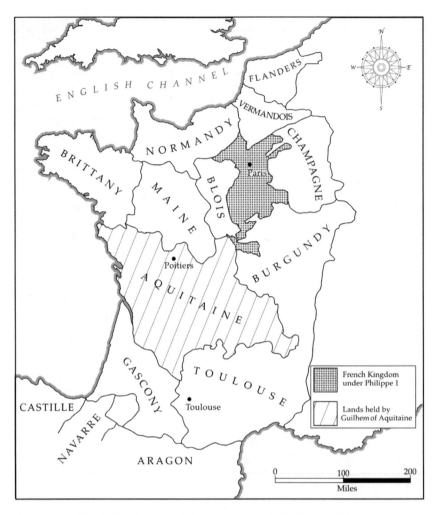

Map 3. Lands of the Count of Aquitaine and the King of France.

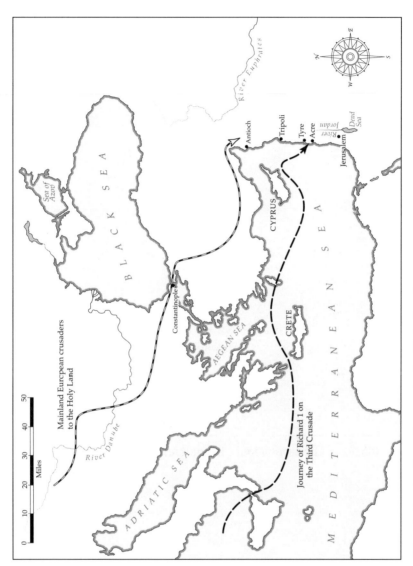

Map 4. Routes from France to the Holy Land.

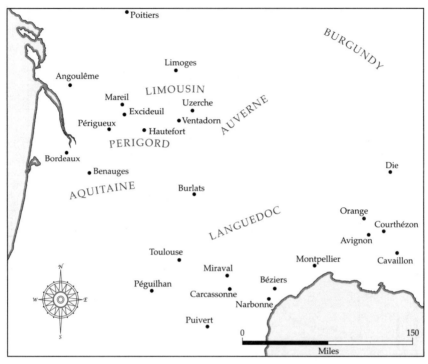

Map 5. Places of the troubadours in the Languedoc and Provence.

ONE

We consider that marital affection and the true love of lovers are wholly different and arise from entirely different sources

(Ermengarde, Viscountess of Narbonne. Bk 2, Ch. VII, 171)

A woman who under the excuse of a mistake of any kind seeks to preserve an incestuous love is clearly going contrary to what is right and proper.

(Eleanor, Queen of England. Bk 2, Ch. VII, 170)

The two quotations come from: Andreas Capellanus, *De Arte Honeste Amandi*, 'The Art of Courtly Love', *c.* 1180.

The Art of Courtly Love

The French love courts [*cours d'amour*] have attracted the most scholarly attention. A number of misconceptions used to exist about this institution, until it became clear that these courts were not real legal sessions but social events that were especially popular with women.
(J. Bumke, *Courtly Culture* . . ., 2000, 408)

The judges were all of high nobility and they were all women. There was Eleanor, Countess of all Aquitaine, former wife of King Louis VII of France. There was her daughter by him, Marie, Countess of Champagne. There was Adèle, third wife of Louis VII; and Eleanor's niece, Isabelle of Vermandois, Countess of Flanders, whose mother was Eleanor's sister. There was the learned Ermengard, Viscountess of Narbonne. There was even a circle of ladies in Gascony, each one of good birth.

All of them, it was believed, were discriminating judges of the quality of the poems sung to them by importunate troubadours at tribunals in the courts of Poitiers, Troyes, Narbonne and elsewhere. The courts debated the answers to questions posed by the singers: which gifts it was seemly for a lady to accept from her would-be lover; whether love could exist between a man and his wife; whether jealousy was permissible between unmarried lovers; whether a man could truly love two women at one same time.[1]

The ladies were undisputed arbiters of courtly behaviour, presiding over the Courts of Love, seats of poetical judgement. Such assizes, however, were the late-twelfth-century literary creations of Andreas Capellanus, who claimed to be the resident chaplain of Marie of Champagne at Troyes. Between 1182 and 1186 he was a clerical witness to seven charters. As one was signed by Marie herself, it is probable that he was telling the truth about his position.

Capellanus flattered the Countess of Champagne, complimenting her on her artistic sensitivity, and improving the praise by including the names of other great ladies, all of them relatives, friends and intimates of Marie.

Descriptions of their attractive courts were given in his manuscript *De arte honesti amandi* (On the Art of Honourable Love), also known as 'De amore livres tres' (The Three Books of Love). In this it followed the pattern of the three books of the Roman poet Ovid's *Ars Amatoria* (The Art of

Love), Books I–II for men, Book III for women, a cynical manual of sexual seduction, considered by the *Encyclopaedia Britannica* as 'perhaps the most immoral book ever written by a man of genius'.[2]

Follow my advice, wrote Ovid in the last decade BC, and no man would fail to entice a woman to bed.

> *Posse capi; capies, tu modo tende plages . . .*

> Girls can be caught – and that you'll catch her if
> You set your schemes right . . .[3]

Technique was the secret. Dress well, be courteous, attentive, give modest presents and reach the inevitable goal by patient, calculated stages. Ovid was almost unconcerned about the pleasurable final act. Advice on bedroom gymnastics was as succinct as the words that Frank Sinatra was to sing two thousand years later, 'Just take it Nice'n Easy'. 'Relax', advised Ovid.

> *Crede mihi, non est veneris properanda voluptas.*
> 'Believe me, Love's height of pleasure must not be hurried'

and

> *Sed neque tu dominam veils maioribus usus*
> 'Take care not to cram on full sail and outrace your mistress'.[4]

Behind its alluring words, *Ars Amatoria* advocated the adulterous pursuit of married women, using serving-girls and intermediaries as assistants. In this Ovid was following a tradition of earlier Roman poets, Catullus, Tibullus and Propertius among them, who had wooed and won the consent of highly born wives to discreet adultery.

Capellanus' three books became extremely popular in medieval France as a hilarious satire. There had already been enthusiasms for Virgil and Horace, but the thirteenth century was *the aetas Ovidiana*, 'the Age of Ovid', and it was from Ovid that Capellanus framed the structure of his own book.[5]

It had a similar basis but an entirely different and moral interpretation of love, in which the lady had complete sovereignty over her lover. Troubadours had to pay court to a well-born wife, but 'with a lover undertaking to serve his married, and therefore enticingly unavailable, mistress'.[6]

The second of his three books contained twenty-one letters posing questions of the behaviour of women towards their suitors. Predictably, the greatest number of challenges, seven, were solved by Marie. Of the others, five problems received answers from Ermengard, three each from Eleanor and 'the Queen', Adèle, two from Isabelle, and one from the group of ladies in Gascony.

The final book listed the thirty-one definitive Rules of Love, beginning 'Marriage is no excuse for not loving' and concluding with 'Nothing forbids one woman from loving two men nor one man by two women' and in between were twenty-nine pronouncements that, despite Andreas' clerical status, would not have been approved of by his Church.

Pure love, he said, 'goes as far as the kiss and the embrace and the modest contact with the nude lover, omitting the final solace'. Mixed love, however, included copulation and gets its effect from every delight of the flesh and culminates in the final act of Venus . . . it too is true love and it is praiseworthy, and we say it is the source of all good things. 'It would be improper . . . to claim as a sin the thing from which the highest good of this life takes its origin'.[7]

Even though he had taken holy orders, Capellanus claimed that he had the right to make physical love. 'So if I ask any woman to love me, she cannot refuse me on the pretext that I am a clerk.' He even boasted of his insidious serpent's tongue that persuaded an attractive nun that she should submit to his advances. Luckily, perhaps hypocritically, maybe fearing divine retribution, or even simply lying, he added that, just in time, he quelled his lustful insanity 'and with a great effort' resisted the temptation to seduce her.[8]

The social status of other women decided how they would be treated by followers of the code of courtly love. A knight should invariably be courteous and submissive to ladies of quality. Females of the bourgeoisie would usually receive respect. But, should the man take a liking to some peasant woman, he should condescend to praise her, then, 'when you find a convenient place, do not hesitate to take what you seek and to embrace them by force . . . use a little compulsion as a convenient cure for their shyness'. Ovid had said much the same.

Vim licet . . .

It's all right to use force – force of *that* sort goes down well with
what in fact they love to yield
they'd often rather have stolen. Rough seduction
delights them, the audacity of near-rape
is a compliment . . .[9]

Capellanus never advocated treating a high-born lady so brutally. Decorum forbade it. His writings were popular and widely read, but, although their treacherous arguments were persuasive, his Courts of Love were fictional. In Capellanus the descriptions of courts were evocative with their good food and wine, service, warmth, laughter and love. The courts were real but they were not court-rooms.

Yet they were accepted as realities until late in the nineteenth century because of a book of 1575, *Les Vies des Plus Célébrès et Anciens Poètes Provensaux* (Lives of the Most Famous Old Poets of Provence), by Jean de Nostradamus, brother of the famous astrologer and self-proclaimed prophet. The *Lives* was an uncritical medley of traditional biographies, guesswork and deliberate deception. He claimed it was based on a manuscript by a monk, Moine des Îles d'Or, but his name, 'Cybo de Gennes', was actually an anagram of the name of one of his brother's friends.[10] His book was worthless. Yet for centuries it was given credence.

One reason was that it was apparently confirmed by a poem of Geoffrey Chaucer's, 'The Court of Love'. Chaucer certainly knew about Capellanus and courtly love. His *Troilus and Criseyde* similarly sang the joys and pains of love. He had been to France on several occasions, four times in 1377 alone, and in 1359 he had been captured near Reims during an invasion by Edward III, finally being ransomed for the sum of £16.00, less than was paid for the release of Sir Robert de Clyntone's warhorse.[11] From Chaucer's knowledge of French society it was entirely credible that the poem 'The Court of Love' described a court of judgement or poetical tribunal that he had seen.

It did not. The poem, which once existed only as a single manuscript at Trinity College, Cambridge, was no more than a pastiche, a sixteenth-century imitation in competent Chaucerian style, and its contents showed that the anonymous writer knew the books of Capellanus. Until the verses were exposed as spurious, the Courts of Love remained credible.[12]

For Capellanus it is probable that his invention of a poetical Court of Love derived from a traditional form of verse that had long been used by troubadours. It was the *tenson*, a debate or argument on some point of love between two troubadours who, if they could not agree, referred the unresolved question to an independent judge.[13] One *tenson* concerned a contemporary of Andreas, the nobleman Savaric de Mauléon.

He was a great lord, the seneschal or steward of Poitou, holding many castles in the service of John, king of England.[14] In 1206 he successfully defended one at Niort against Philippe-Auguste of France. For his loyalty he was granted lands in England despite having briefly supported John's nephew, the rebellious Arthur of Brittany, being captured with him at Mirabeau and imprisoned in the deadly 'no food or water' Corfe castle in Dorset. He escaped.[15] Arthur was murdered.[16]

De Mauléon lived at the midpoint of the troubadour period, an age of 250 years that began five years after the Battle of Hastings and declined and disappeared twenty-five years before the Battle of Crécy in 1346.

The intervening 250 years began with a birth. The first great troubadour, William of Poitiers, was born in 1071. The period ended with a death. The great Italian troubadour Dante Alighieri died in Ravenna on September 1321.

The tradition of courtly love began in Poitiers but it soon spread southwards into that land of sunshine, song and east, Occitania, 'region of *Oc*' (Fig. 1).

In France two different words had developed from the Latin *hoc ille*, 'yes', the corrupt northern French *oui*, and the purer southern *oc*, from which the Languedoc gets its name, 'the langue d'Oc'. It was spoken in France but it was not French.

In England the first line of a poem by the troubadour Bernart de Ventadorn would be translated as: 'When the fresh grass and leaf appears . . .', but in France the lines differed:

Occitan	French
Can l'erba fresch'.lh folha par	Quand l'herbe [est] fraiche, et la feuille parait

They are similar but not identical. A linguistic parallel can be made between two English medieval poets, Geoffrey Chaucer and William Langland, fourteenth-century contemporaries who were both composing their masterpieces, *The Canterbury Tales* and *The Vision of Piers Plowman*, around 1380. Chaucer's Prologue begins with lines that even in the original spelling are understandable today;

Whan that Aprillë with his shourës soote
The droghtë of March hath percëd to the roote

Whereas Langland begins clearly enough:

In a somer season. whan soft was the sonne

but only five lines later becomes incomprehensible:

Me byfel a ferly. of fairy me thougte

meaning, 'I chanced upon a wonder of enchantment as it seemed to me'.

In England the vernacular varied almost unintelligibly from region to region, north, south-east, south-west. For Chaucer, a Londoner, the dialect was East Midlands, but Langland, a Shropshire man from Cleobury Mortimer, wrote his poem in the dissimilar patois of the West Midlands.

'A northern and southern man, meeting by chance, or for business, would resort to French because the dialects were mutually incomprehensible, as much in diction as in accent.'[17]

From similar parochial contrasts in vocabulary people from northern France considered the 'langue d'oc' barbaric and fit only for effete southerners. But the troubadours used it and sang it in tens of thousands of musical verses over a boisterous quarter-millennium of years.

It was boisterous because it was two and half centuries of turmoil during which the baron and troubadour Savaric de Mauléon lived, fought and loved. There were constant wars between England and France over French territory extending from Normandy and Anjou in the north, through Aquitaine, down to Gascony in the south-west, wars that involved English kings from Henry I to Edward III.

The same centuries saw eight crusades to the Holy Land. De Mauléon himself went on the indecisive Fifth Crusade in 1219.[18] Between those crusades there was a lesser but just as brutal crusade in the south of France, the early thirteenth-century Albigensian Crusade that smashed castles and razed towns as the Catholic Church ponderously crushed the blasphemous cult of the Cathars, a persecution that saw military suppression followed by religious cruelties as the Inquisition imprisoned and tortured heretics in their scores and burnt hundreds more alive, cleansing their flesh of sins.

The troubadour centuries were times of national and personal loyalties. Loyalties were transitory. They were guided by ambition, power, wealth, advantage. There were humiliations, treacheries, assassinations.

It was an elusive epoch when there were no objective historians, only partisan chroniclers and credulous biographers of the wandering singers. One was about Savaric de Mauléon describing him as 'a mighty lord of Poitou' and 'Above all did he delight in generosity, and chivalry, and love and jousting, and singing, and playing, and poetry, and feasting, and spending money'. The 'Life' or *vida* was written by another troubadour, the long-lived, much travelled Uc de Saint-Circ, who was probably the author of several other anecdotal lives.

Among the many contradictions of that knightly age Savaric de Mauléon was a triple chameleon, white as a famous troubadour, green as a frustrated lover, red as the militaristic employer of a powerful army of mercenaries and crossbowmen whom he could hire out to considerable financial advantage.

Like many French noblemen he opposed attempts by feeble French king after king to increase the royal dominions and gain control over the estates of barons with loyally pugnacious armies. It was self-interest that caused de Mauléon to support England against Philippe-Auguste, Philip II, in John's claim to be lord of many regions in France including Aquitaine, a vast area of 16,000 square miles that stretched from the River Garonne northwards to the River Loire, and westwards from Burgundy to the Bay of Biscay. Aquitaine covered a third of France.

De Mauléon also helped John more locally in the Languedoc south of Aquitaine. The king asked him to assist Raymond VI, Count of Toulouse. To John family honour was involved. Raymond was married to John's sister, Joan.

The count was raising an army to fight the leader of the Albigensian Crusade, Simon de Montfort. As an inducement Raymond sent 100,000 gold *livres* to de Mauléon, who 'promised his ready and willing help, whether anyone else liked it or not'.[19]

In early September 1211 a formidable host laid siege to the crusaders' weakly manned, crumbling walls of the town of Castelnaudary some miles west of Carcassonne. De Montfort was absent. But, instead of attacking the pitiful garrison, Raymond VI entrenched his enormous army on a nearby hill and contented himself with bombarding the town with a trebuchet. The missiles reached the targets, but the hastily chosen stones were brittle and crumbled harmlessly against the walls.

The tactic was characteristic of the Count. He was generously considered an irresolute man by some writers, but a more trenchant term would be 'coward'. There was no onslaught or battle until far too late after de Montfort had arrived with cavalry and reinforcements. The armies met at Saint-Martin-Lalande and, despite much individual courage, the Toulousians were overcome.

As always de Mauléon fought bravely. As the crusaders charged into his men he shouted, 'Stay calm, my lords, don't move. No one take down or fold his tent, or you are all dead men!'[20] It was futile. Because of Raymond's customary indecision defeat and retreat were inevitable.

The young Cistercian monk Pierre des Vaux-de-Cernay, who wrote a triumphant Catholic history of the Albigensian Crusade, the *Historia Albigensis*, rejoiced at the victory but expressed venom at the vile opponent who had had the effrontery to bring paid mercenaries to fight the crusaders.

With our enemies came that most deprived apostate, that iniquitous transgressor, son of the Devil, servant of the Antichrist, Savary de Mauléon, more evil than any heretic, worse than any infidel, assailant of the Church, the enemy of Christ. O most corrupt of mortals – or should I say himself a mortal infection – I speak of Savary, who, villain unredeemed, shameless and senseless, rushed against God with neck down, and dared to assault the holy Church of God! Prime mover of heresy, architect of cruelty, agent of perversity, comrade of sinners, accomplice of the perverted, a disgrace to mankind, a man unacquainted with manly virtues, devilish – himself the devil incarnate![21]

Despite the vilification of which he was unaware, and losing the battle, de Mauléon did not lose reward. He continued to support the count until they quarrelled in 1212 during a protracted siege at Penne d'Agenais. He demanded a further 10,000 gold crowns as money due to him. Raymond VI refused. De Mauléon, man of action, kidnapped the count's youngest son and demanded a ransom. Raymond left for Bordeaux to intercede with John, only to return a month later and pay de Mauléon 'a large sum'.[22]

From 1215 to 1216 de Mauléon and his mercenaries were in England supporting John against an alliance of barons. In October that year, crossing the perilous tides of the Wash, the king just escaped death but lost his baggage-train, royal treasure and precious relics. At Newark he contracted dysentery and died. Savaric de Mauléon was appointed one of the executors of the king's will and was probably one of the cortège that escorted the king's body to Worcester. He later attended the coronation of Henry III. He was so often in England that some called him English. Jean de Nostradamus did, 'gentilhomme, anglais'.[23]

Warrior, diplomat, crusader, opportunist – to the modern mind it might seem improbable that he could also have been a famous troubadour, but his biographer confirmed it. He also wrote that his misguided subject was helplessly in love with a coquette, a teaser of men's passions, a woman who hinted of many favours but delivered none. Such false temptresses are not unknown. The Roman poet Catullus had been sadly acquainted with one. A rival bitterly described her:

In triclinio Coa, in cubiculo nola.

in the dining-room a delight in translucent Coan silks.
in the bedroom an impregnable fortress.

The epigram was clever. *Coa* was not only an island but also a pun on 'coitus'. *Nola* was a walled city that resisted a siege by Hannibal. The word was also another pun on *nolo*, 'no sex'.[24]

Savaric de Mauléon was to be tortured by a similar unrewarding tantalus, an promising but unsatisfied romance. He and Catullus were not the only poets to suffer the frustrations of sexual denial. In 1619 Ben Jonson told William Drummond of Hawthornden that John Marston, the playwright, 'lay diverse tymes with a woman, who shew him all that he wished except the last act, which she would never agree unto'.[25]

Later the same century Andrew Marvell wrote his most famous poem 'To his Coy Mistress', of which these lines are extracts:

Had we but world enough, and time,
This coyness, lady, were no crime.

    .   .   .   .   .

But at my back I always hear
Time's wingèd chariot hurrying near,
And yonder all before us lie
Deserts of vast eternity.

    .   .   .   .   .

. . . then worms shall try
That long-preserved virginity,
And your quaint honour turn to dust,
And into ashes all my lust:
The grave's a fine and private place,
But none, I think, do there embrace.

    .   .   .   .   .

Now let us sport us while we may . . .

How successful his plea was Marvell did not reveal. Nor is the 'mistress' known. Perhaps she was a woman from Hull, from Italy, or from Spain – or maybe simply no one particular lady, just an imaginary, reluctant lover.

Just as many of Catullus' most explicit poems are still excluded from many sixth-form school texts, so Marvell's 'indecent' masterpiece was omitted from Palgrave's respectable *The Golden Treasury of Songs and Lyrics* of 1861.[26]

Quite differently, Savaric de Mauléon's *tenson* about his unattainable but flirtatious minx has been printed many times. It survives. So does the castle in which the temptress lived.

Today, from Bordeaux the A62 toll motorway or *péage* runs several miles eastwards to the ramparted village of Cadillac by the Garonne river. From there a tortuous country lane twists three miles northwards to Benauges and its half-ruined castle, walled, with two heavy twelfth-century bastions. De Mauléon would have known them. So would the two other admirers of the seductive but obstructive lady, Guilhelma, the young and attractive wife of Pierre de Gavaret, Viscount of Benauges.

Unattainable the viscountess may have made herself but she enjoyed the compliments, the yearning glances, the small but in very good taste gifts, the attention and she had no intention of allowing these pleasures to

end. The flirt and *femme fatale* arranged an assignation for both Savaric de
Mauléon and his rivals, Elias Rudel of Bergerac and Jaufré Rudel of Blaye, a
namesake of the well-known troubadour who had died around 1170. Her
scheme was heartless and ingenious.

Some sympathy is possible. Little is known abut Guilhelma except her
name, how old she was, at what age she married, her relationship with her
husband. Most alliances between well-born families were for the benefit
of the man. His arranged wife was expected to bear children, preferably
boys. Some girls wedded as young as twelve, although sexual intimacy was
normally delayed for two or three years. 'The age of fifteen is taken as the
watershed year for marriage and conjugal relations.'[27]

At the time of de Mauléon and the Rudels, Guilhelma may have been
no more than eighteen or nineteen years of age but possibly already with
children. She may have been bored with a loveless marriage, actively
disliking an uncouth husband. An anonymous female troubadour, a
trobairitz, was candid about hers:

Coindeta sui! si cum n'ai greu cossire

>   *I am lovely*
> and so my heart grieves
> about my husband whom I neither love nor desire.
> I'll tell you why I am so amorous
>   *I am lovely*
> for I am small and young and fresh
>   *I am lovely*
> and should have a husband who gives me joy
> with whom I could play and laugh all day.
>   *I am lovely*

In a *rondeau* by an unnamed northern French woman troubadour, a
trouvère, another unsatisfied wife devised her own solution: '*Soufrés, maris,
et sin e vous anuit . . .*', she sang:

> *Be patient, husband, and may it not irk you.*
> *Tomorrow you will have me and my lover will tonight*
>   I forbid you to speak one word of it.
> *Be patient, husband, and do not move*
>   The night is short, soon you will have me again,
>   When my lover has had his pleasure.
> *Be patient, husband, and may it not irk you.*
> *Tomorrow you will have me and my lover will tonight.*[28]

Not all married men were so meekly compliant. Guilhelma's own may have been one of the dangerously possessive ones. She was famed for her beauty and she may have wanted some enjoyment without the dangers of an unwanted pregnancy. If so, it was only by selfish deception that she planned a rendezvous with all three of her admirers.

Several weeks before that intended meeting invitations by word of mouth were delivered by her personal messenger. The men were asked to attend her on the same day, the intentional company of three men together being sufficient to remove the danger of her reputation being smeared by malicious tongues. But at each destination the messenger hinted that the summons was really intended for that man alone, the others being invited merely to deflect suspicions of favouritism. The argument was believed because each anxious, would-be lover wanted it to be sincere.

Theirs were not casual acceptances of a visit to a neighbour. In days of poor roads, dangerous outlaws and travel on horseback with a retinue of armed men and baggage-wagons the journeys were long, maybe no faster than some 10 miles a day. Both Blaye and Bergerac were 40 miles from Benauges, Blaye to the north, Bergerac to the east. For de Mauléon in Poitou it was more than 100 miles of country to cross and it would have been several, uncomfortable days before he arrived.

The tryst was stage-managed and its setting was contrived. The four, three men, one woman, were arranged round a table to which servants brought refreshments, delicacies and wines. Elias faced Guilhelma. Jaufré and Savaric were on either side of her, sitting as close as they dared.

Guilhelma had prepared for their coming. Her face had been carefully made up, powdered with an added whisper of saffron for its fragrance to blend with her fastidiously selected perfume. Her long hair, hanging artfully down her back, had been brushed, combed, parted in the middle, and framed in a delicate circlet of gold and silver.

Her pointed, tight-fitting shoes with ornamented buckles were made of the finest leather. Jewelled rings glittered on her fingers. Her golden necklace was studded with minute gems.

From her shoulders hung a scarlet woollen mantle trimmed with the fur of black squirrel and lined with cloth as white as snow on high mountains. Under the mantle she wore a long, trailing, provocatively shaped brightly coloured gown, 'peacock dresses', grumbled clergymen, of the most delicate ecru silk from Damascus, silk so sheer, almost diaphanous, that it seemed to swirl and ripple round her like a translucent sea of green.

The three suitors were bewitched by the vision of almost unworldly loveliness that smiled on them. Centuries later the Stuart vicar, Robert Herrick, in his 'Upon Julia's Clothes', enthused:

Whenas in silks my Julia goes,
Then, then, methinks, how sweetly flows
That liquefaction of her clothes
Next when I cast mine eyes and see
That brave vibration each way free,
O how that glittering taketh me!

And Guilhelma played her three men as though the warrior-trained knights were musical instruments, her eyes gazing at Elias, eyelids slowly closing in invitation, an enticing glance to the side, a demure downwards look as though she had been too bold. He was magnetised.

What he did not know, could not see, was that below the table her hand was reaching Jaufré's, touching, stroking, gently squeezing, a sudden embarrassed withdrawal before returning to his bewitched fingers.

Savaric was unaware of eyes or hand. It was against his foot that hers rested, nudging, brushing, resting lightly upon it, moving up and down so lasciviously suggestive, so intimate that he realised in startled ecstasy that the final favours had been promised. It was a farce without laughter, a contriving, self-centred minx and three joyfully gullible dupes.

There was never a need for that medieval Salome to lose her seventh veil. Her victims had already lost their heads.

It was only after they had left the castle in triumphant mood that one of them bragged of Guilhelma's promise. Her eyes proved her affection, boasted Elias. Anyone could look at anything retorted Jaufré, but her hands were not forced to hold his. Hands are commonplace, replied Savaric, but feet do not have independent minds, they obey the commands of their owner.

The arguments went on without any agreement, although it was de Mauléon, a well-known troubadour, and generous patron of troubadours, who was more skilful with words. The others protested at his advantage and when he remained adamant about the superiority of feet over eyes and hands the two demanded to be represented by other troubadours who could argue their claims in a poem of debate, the *tenson*.

Jaufré chose Gaucelm Faidit from distant Uzerche, a poor singer, unsuccessful gambler, a corpulent glutton married to a lovely prostitute who rapidly also became fat, but he was prolific in the composition of beautiful melodies and had as his patron the noble Marie de Ventadorn.

Elias selected an obscure troubadour, Uc de la Bacalairia, today's La Bachéllerie, 30 miles south-west of Uzerche. He was little known but courtly, skilful and well taught.[29] Savaric de Mauléon and the two fashioned the *partimen*. It had a strict rhyme scheme for its thirteen-line stanzas, a bb a cc dd eee ff, and just as strict a rule that each line should contain the same number of syllables as the first, eight. Each troubadour had to follow that construction. It began with a challenge by Savaric in the first stanza:

Gaucelm, tres jocs enamora
Gaucelm, Uc, three love-games occurred

Partisc a vos et a N'Hugon

And which is best is asked of you.
Choose two you prefer. After two
Then I shall champion the third.
A lady had three men who yearned
To gain favours she always spurned.
Sweetly, kindly she gave replies
That mingled hands and feet and eyes.
Her bright eyes charmed the man she faced,
One by her had his hand embraced,
The third, her foot by his was placed.
Consider well! Choose two. Let me
Defend the last one of the three.

In the second stanza, adhering to the same rigid pattern, Faidit stated that the 'richest gift is received by that lover upon whom those fair eyes fix their faithful gaze'. Handshakes were commonplace and there was no love revealed by an accidentally adjacent foot.

Uc de Bacalairia disagreed, arguing that Gaucelm had made an ill-judged choice because eyes look everywhere and on everyone, 'but when the white and ungloved hand softly presses that of its lover, then truly does love proceed from the ground of the heart'. He supposed that de Mauléon would argue for the foot, but Uc could not support him in that either. Feet were a long way from the heart.

Savaric did argue for the foot, but after negative stanza after stanza it was agreed that in despair the problem should be referred to that noblest of arbiters, Marie of Ventadorn and two other ladies. The verdict has not survived.[30]

There is a grace-note. According to a centuries-old story, friends of de Mauléon, deeply concerned about his infatuation, almost obsession, with the evasive Guilhelma, told him of an equally attractive, much more obliging young noblewoman in Gascony, perhaps one of the sixty poetry adjudicators mentioned by Capellanus. She may have been Mascarose de la Barthe, Countess of Armagnac. La Barthe, near Auch and some 90 miles south of Benauges, would much later become famous for its Haut-

Armagnac brandy, different from cognac but just as strong and of a distinctively fine flavour.

From the reports the beautiful, young Mascarose was apparently very willing to share both her charms and her body with such a renowned troubadour, and she arranged a rendezvous for Savaric to come to her, no doubt at a time when her husband was away and when she could rely on the discretion of her servants and ladies-in-waiting.

Grapevines were as communicative then as today, and gossip of the assignation reached Guilhelma, who was taken aback and alarmed at the news of such a dangerously compliant rival. Instantly she sent loving words to Savaric, pleading that he come secretly to her on, by no coincidence, the precise date of the meeting already accepted for Mascarose, promising him that he should have everything, all, that he had desired for so long.

It is written that the bewildered de Mauléon discussed his problem with a visiting Provost of Limoges, who firmly advised him to reject Guilhelma, who was merely jealous and, as always, would prove unyielding. Also, it would be discourteous to reject the generosity of the other lady. But the obstinate Savaric ignored him and persisted in his unfulfilled longing until he died on 27 July 1233.

The story could be fantasy, a romantic whim of frustrated love created by some troubadour as he wandered around the courts of the Languedoc. But it is unlikely. The story was vouched for by Uc de Saint-Circ. He, personally, had delivered Guilhelma's false invitation: *e sapiens per ver que* ieu . . .

Know of a truth that I . . . was the messenger that went there [from Guilhelma to de Mauléon] and delivered those messages to him.[31]

And, as Saint-Circ left the service of Guilhelma to be a follower of Savaric de Mauléon, who became his patron, the statement is probably trustworthy. It is known that Uc wrote the *vida* of de Mauléon and of the most brilliant of troubadours, Bernart de Ventadorn. He said so. It is likely that he wrote many other 'Lives'.[32]

He has his own *vida* and it shows how many troubadours became troubadours, capable men who found conventional ways of making a living incompatible with their own inclinations:

Aquest N'Ucs si ac gran rens de fraires majors de se . . .

Uc's older brothers wanted him to be a cleric. They sent him to school in Montpellier but while they thought he was studying religion he was learning about the songs troubadours sang, *cansos, sirventes, tensons, coblas,* and he read about great men and women of the past. For a long time he wandered, poor, in Gascony, on horseback or on foot, until the Count of Rodez and the Viscount of Turenne encouraged him in his vocation. At last he came to the viscountess of Benauges.[33]

The *vidas*, Uc's and those of other unidentified authors, are a medley of proper biography, geographical itineraries, guesswork, errors and exaggerations. Yet they are invaluable as the only records surviving of itinerant singers and their performances from court to court. They are also invaluable as a counterbalance to the idealistic 'Courts of Love' that Andreas Capellanus portrayed.

A casual reading of their lyrics suggests that a troubadour singing to his lady pleaded for nothing more unseemly than platonic friendship, an idealistic courtship so distant that the woman remained a 'distant, haughty and superior figure'.[34]

From the knowledge of the far less idyllic aspirations towards Guilhelma by Savaric and the Rudels, however, it was often far from a spiritual relationship that they wanted and she opposed. Nor do the *vidas* of troubadours invariably argue for purity and chasteness. One of the first troubadours, the early twelfth-century Cercamon, was explicit. He longed for something more corporeal than worship from afar.

Qu'eu non puesc longjamen estar

for I cannot stay away much longer
and live, or be cured elsewhere,
unless I have her next to me,
unclothed, to kiss and embrace
within a curtained room.[35]

Chaste worship is not what all of Uc's *vidas* suggest, and it was probably not what Capellanus intended. So far from his *Art of Love* being a scholarly exposition of the purity and seemliness of courtly life, it more probably lampooned it as 'an elaborate intellectual joke'. Audiences chuckled at its sly ambiguities. It is insincere, a satire on conventional courtly love. It was very popular.[36]

In the troubadours' treatment of women their poems were the antithesis of the poetry that had been composed before them. In ages earlier than the late eleventh century, women, unless they were martyred saints or obsequiously servile wives, were seldom mentioned. The background to the ballad was the battlefield not the boudoir. There were no Boudicas – except perhaps the early tenth-century Ethelfleda, 'Lady of the Mercians'.

TWO

THE POETRY OF MEN

Then Taillefer, minstrel, knight, his heart afire,
proud on his mighty steed, sang to inspire
the great Duke with that epic of heroic fate,
of gallant Roland, Charlemagne the Great,
of Oliver and warriors at his side
who rode to fight at Roncevalles. And died'.

(Wace, *Roman de Rou*, III, ll. 8013 ff.)

Before Troubadours: War-Songs, Wanderers and Wives

The minstrel boy to the war has gone,
In the ranks of death you'll find him . . .

(Thomas Moore, 'The Minstrel Boy')

In any calendar of notable dates, AD 1071 was not one of the more memorable years. In the battle of Manzikert a late Roman emperor, Romanus Diogenes IV, was defeated by the Seljuk Turks, who went on to take Syria, Palestine and the Holy City of Jerusalem, events that resulted in eight successive military Christian crusades. The cathedral of St Mark in Venice was finished. And in Venice the innovation of a two-pronged fork was introduced, revolutionising manners of eating.

But 1071 was also the year in which Guilhem, 7th Count of Poitou and 9th Duke of Aquitaine was born. He was the first of the troubadours.

There had been more dramatic years before and afterwards. The coming of the Millennium, 'the Year of our Lord', *Anno Domini* 1000, believed to be exactly 1,000 years after the birth of Christ, had been dreaded as the arrival of the Last Judgement and the end of the world. Nothing happened. In 1066 the Battle of Hastings saw the defeat of the Saxon king, Harold Godwinsson, and the victory of William of Normandy, an event that changed the history of England. In 1075, with the assistance of French masons the cathedral of St James of Compostela, was completed and became the persistent destination of thousands of pilgrims from all over Christian Europe.

Closer to the poetical theme of this book, in 1074 Omar Khayyam, famous Sufi philosopher and mathematician, was appointed to reform the old Persian Calendar. He had already composed his celebrated *Rubaiyat*, 'robaiyats' of hundreds of four-line verses, that was to be paraphrased almost eight hundred years later in one of the finest English poems through the elegantly elegiac quatrains of Edward Fitzgerald's own version of the *Rubaiyat*.

Fitzgerald's work had inevitable imperfections of translation that were patronisingly criticised as 'a mid-Victorian poem of his own from an ill-understood classical Persian text' by Robert Graves, a far better poet but a much less musical one, as a contrast between their two versions of the *Rubaiyat*'s third stanza shows.

And as the cock crew, those who stood before
The tavern, shouted 'Open now the door.
You know how little while we have to stay,
And once departed may return no more!'

(Edward Fitzgerald)

Loud crows the cock for his dawn drink, my Saki!
Here stand we in the vintner's row, my Saki!
Is this an hour for prayer? Silence, my Saki!
Defy old custom, Saki; drink your fill!

(Robert Graves)

a pedestrian repetitious plod of *Saki* after *Saki*, 'cup-bearer', literal but lumpish in contrast to the autumnal melancholy of the four lines by Fitzgerald.

Regrettably, Graves had been tricked. The so-called genuine *Rubaiyat* he had translated was a modern fake imposed on him by his 'collaborator, Ali-Shah, a forger'.[1]

The poetry of Fitzgerald has a lyrical assonance with the sudden emergence around AD 1100 of the lyricism of Guilhem of Poitiers, whose songs of love were in abrupt contrast to the popular *chansons de geste*, heroic epics that had been popular for almost five hundred years in Western Europe.

In his *Farai un Vers de Dreyt Nien* (A Song of Nothing), Guilhem wrote:

Que plus es blanca qu'evori
Per qu'ieu autra non auzori

She is whiter than ivory
And so I love no other

which was in gentle contrast to the lines of war from *chansons* such as:

. . . the din of slaughter in the great hall,
the spike-bossed shields in fierce men's hands,
skull-protecting helmets, all were shattered,

and the hall-floor thundered and resounded
with blows of death and cries of the dying . . .

    . . . . .

The dark raven hovered, waiting to feed . . .[2]
                           ('The Fight at Finnsburh', ll. 28–31, 35)

There were long centuries when fighting was almost part of life, with conflicts over family honour, feuds, revenge and invasions overseas for power, wealth and fame. Everywhere men fought. And it was fighting that they celebrated in their long halls, songs sung and performed by minstrels: stories of battles, blood and the bedlam of swords clashing on shields and stabbing through chain-mail. Not for them the gentle womanly words of troubadours. Their virtues were not those of devotion to a woman. It was manly courage, loyalty, death before cowardice that they praised. There was little trivial or frivolous in the poetry. Its heart was the valour of long-dead heroes, feats of audacity, stoicism, and frequently the fantastic myths of a vanished past.

These recitals were not an hour's entertainment after a gentlemanly meal. They were sung and acted to an already heavily drunken audience slouching in the firelight and shadows. One tale merged with another, interrupted by bellowed requests for another popular fable, the performance only ending when the listeners were drowsing, the story resuming next night with flash-backs to remind the audience of where the story had ended yesterday.

A small harp provided a musical background and the minstrel did not stand still. He raised a sword-arm, defended his body with an imagined shield, crouched, advanced, murmuring words, suddenly shouting in triumph as the survivors celebrated victory.

These *chansons de geste*, songs of brave exploits, were a medley of champions intermingled with horrors of man-eating ogres that stalked the sleeping halls for victims to eat. On any occasion men might be offered a choice of a battle – Brunanburh? Maldon? – or the flesh-crawling terror of Beowulf and Grendel.

Whatever the theme, it was presented in a poetical style that is almost forgotten today, no rhyme just alliteration, no beat or metre, just assonance. Each line was divided into two, and in it three words had to alliterate with the same letter. Instead of rhyme the final words had to contain similar but not identical vowel-sounds so that three lines could not end with 'fight, might, fright' but, rather, with, 'fighting, mighty, frightful'. It demanded skill to compose but it is alien to our ears. It is as different today as the fourteenth-century Langland's 'Piers Plowman' was from Chaucer's 'Canterbury Tales', two contemporary poems mentioned in the Introduction.

Differences in the methods of describing the same event were considerable.
The first is in 'modern' rhyming iambic lines:

```
^   /   ^   /   ^   /   ^   /   ^   /
```
We fought, we strove against the turbaned **hordes**,
```
^   /   ^   /   ^   /   ^   /   ^   /
```
We shattered shields, brought death beneath our **swords** . . .

whereas two lines of alliteration and assonance might read:

Fierce was the fight that day: against the foreign **host**,
sword against scimitar clashed: slashing to the **bone** . . .

For warrior societies, poems of famous battles, were always in demand.
Two –Brunanburh and Maldon – were reported in the *Anglo-Saxon
Chronicle* in slightly differing accounts.[3] On occasion those narratives were
transformed into high poetry by their anonymous singers. Victory at
Brunanburh was a triumph. Defeat at Maldon was a dirge for men who had
lost their leader and died to a man.

Brunanburh was fought in AD 927 because of an invasion by a coalition
of Irish Vikings and Scots led by Olaf (Anlaf) of Dublin. Alarmed at the
expansion of Saxon power northwards, a massive horde entered England
and fought against the Saxon king, Athelstan, grandson of Alfred the Great,
at Brunanburh, an unidentified site but possibly Brinsworth, a village near
Rotherham.[4]

The invaders were slaughtered and the victory was celebrated in one of
the finest *chansons*, which, centuries later, was translated by Alfred, Lord
Tennyson, the Victorian Poet Laureate.[5]

There are vivid lines in the Winchester or Parker (A) version of the *Anglo-
Saxon Chronicle*, whose composer clearly was not a prosaic scribe but a man
comfortable with the poetical conventions of the *chanson*, including such
characteristic understatements, *litotes*, as:

. . . *Myrce ne wyrndon*
heardes hondplegan hael . . .

The Mercians did not refuse
fierce fighting to any man   (ll. 24–5)

The poem is a shout of triumph.

. . . Thaer laeg secg maenig

. . . There lay many a warrior
of the men of the North, pierced by spears
flung over his wearied shield. And many a Scot,
exhausted by battle, lay lifeless.
All through the day the West Saxons in troops
pressed on in pursuit of the hostile peoples.
Fiercely, with swords sharpened on grindstone.
they cut down the fugitives as they fled.
Nor did the Mercians refuse hard fighting
to any of Olaf's warriors, who had invaded
our land across the tossing waters,
in the ships only to meet their doom
in this fight. Five young kings,
stretched lifeless by the swords,
lay on the field, likewise seven
of Olaf's earls, and a countless host
of seamen and Scots.   (ll. 17–32)[6]

It was a catastrophic defeat and it established Saxon supremacy over
most of England. But only for decades. The Battle of Maldon hardly half a
century later in 991 had a different and tragic ending.

That year invading Danes were marauding in southern England and
had already plundered in Kent and Suffolk. In Essex a strong raiding-party
landed their ships at Northey Island at the mouth of the River Blackwater
two miles east of Maldon. The islet was connected to the mainland by a
narrow causeway some 200 paces long that could only be used at low tide.
To attempt to wade across the river elsewhere was to risk a slow, sinking to
death in dark, unresisting ooze.

Saxons led by Byrhtnoth, ealdorman of Essex, benefactor of Ely abbey,
waited for the Danes. It was an uncertain force of a half-trained *fyrd*,
men obliged to fight when called by their lord, some nobles of uncertain
reliability, and Byrhtnoth's own thanes, followers sworn to attend and
protect their master at all times.

It was high tide and for an hour the two forces faced each other across
the river. Then, as the tide ebbed, the Danes advanced only to suffer as the
cramped causeway congested them and man after man was wounded or
killed by three Saxons guarding the crossing.

The *Chronicle* continued: 'Then did the hateful strangers turn to guile.'
The Danish leader asked permission for his men to across unhindered
and Byrhtnoth consented. The decision has been described as an act of

unnecessary chivalry or bravado but it is arguable that had the enemy been denied they would have sailed away to attack some less-protected place.

They reached the mainland and on an impulse of vanity or as an example to his hesitant men Byrhtnoth stepped out offering single combat. He killed but was soon killed himself and his head was triumphantly severed to be vaunted as a trophy of war. The *fyrd* disintegrated into men scurrying for safety. Despite their vows of loyalty several of the Saxon nobility rode away, amongst them Godric to whom Byrhtnoth had generously given many horses. The thanes remained, fighting, slowly overwhelmed but resisting and killing despite the numbers against them.

In the Winchester 'Chronicle' one of the doomed-by-choice Saxons, Byrthwold, shouted to his comrades that he would never leave the field alive, nor retreat one step now that his lord lay dead.

Hige sceal pe heardra: heorte pe cenre

Mind must be harder, spirit must be bolder,
And heart the stronger, as our might grows less.
Here lies our leader in the dust, the hero
cut down in battle. Ever must the cowards know shame
Who thought to sneak home from this battle.
I am old. But I will never leave.
I shall die beside the body of my lord,
And leave this life alongside my chief.   (ll. 312–19)

There were others. 'Aethelgar's son, Godric, also encouraged them all to the fray. Repeatedly he let fly a spear, a murderous javelin among the Vikings. So he advanced, foremost into that body of men. He hewed and struck until he dropped dead in the battle. He was not that Godric who fled from the fray.'[7]

The defeat at Maldon had bitter results for Saxon England. The fear of defeat and conquest by foreign invaders led to years of appeasement by payment of *Danegeld*, bribery that brought temporary relief and permanent demands for more. It was the first English land-tax, a charge of a shilling for every 120 acres, a fifth of a square mile, and was paid for over twenty years during the reign of Aethelred the Redeless or Unready, on one occasion giving over forty tons of solid silver.[8]

For Byrhtnoth there was a less wretched ending. At night when the fighting was over and the Danes had gone families came to gather the bodies of the dead. His was taken for burial over fifty tedious miles to the north along a neglected Roman road to the newly rebuilt Benedictine abbey, later Ely Cathedral, where his skeleton and those of six other Saxons was discovered, reburied in the choir and moved to Bishop West's chapel during restoration work in 1771. In place of his head mourners had left a roundel of wax.[9]

For the courageous thanes at Maldon it was probably better to die with one's lord than to continue an existence without him. Another *chanson*, a melancholy one entitled 'The Wanderer', concerned the miseries of a man who was forsaken of his guardian and benefactor.

> Where is the horse now, where has the champion gone?
> Where is the giver of treasure, and where the benches
> for feasting? Where are the pleasures of the hall?
> Alas for the shining chalice, the armoured warrior,
> the glory of the prince. That time is over,
> gone into night as though it had never been   (ll. 92–7)

He was alone with no hope of help. It was a fate that every man in the great hall would fear. As long as he had a lord he had food, drink, shelter, companionship and the prospect of riches from some successful skirmish.

And always in the hall there were meals with boisterous friends, plentiful strong mead, and there was entertainment, sometimes of heroes and their heroic deeds, sometimes of fearsomely inhuman things like that 'devil from Hell', the hideous Grendel, described in one of the greatest of all Saxon poems, 'Beowulf', as *Grim ond graedig gearo sona waes* (Grim and greedy, savage and unsparing). He was a cannibalistic monster who stalked the places where men slept. He ate them. He ripped out limbs, gulped blood from gushing sockets, sucked life from bodies.

Waking in the morning and seeing the bloodstained carnage, the survivors mourned, begged for their friends to return. Only the heroic Beowulf was calm. He was a man famous for his exploits, one of the bravest of all warriors, and he rebuked those who wept. Grief was for women.

> *Ne sorga, snotor guma!* . . .

> Sorrow not, you who were wise.
> It is better for a man to avenge his friend.   (ll. 1384–5)

Still thirsty for human blood and flesh, Grendel returned, smashing down the bolted door of the hall, laughing at the dormant feast before him.

> *Slaependne rinc* . . .

> . . . took a sleeping man, tore him,
> bit his locked bones, drank his blood,

swallowed, gulped. He ate everything,
hands, feet, all.   (ll. 740–3)

But, returning sated to his lair, Beowulf was waiting for him. They grappled
and the ogre was forced down, his arm was gripped, was wrenched from its
body, torn free, leaving the dying fiend to crawl into the night. As proof of
the exploit the hero hung the arm on the hall's gable.

It was all understated. There was no prolonged Hollywood duel up
winding staircases and along battlements. In fewer than 100 compressed
lines, Beowulf later searched for Grendel's mother, fought her, was almost
overcome, his chain-mail deflecting her mortal dagger just at the moment
when he found an enormous, ancient magic sword that cut into her neck,
slicing through vertebrae. 'She dropped in her track.' The hero cut off the
dead Grendel's head and returned to the hall.[10]

The impact on the imagination of these late night terrifying recitals was
far more shocking than the reaction of watching an adult horror film in
a cinema. There, images are imposed upon the viewer. One sees what was
given to the eye. A familiar film-star's face appears on a screen vaguely
distracting viewers with parts that she had played in the past. Not in a
chanson. There was no screen. There was no well-known celebrity of the
cinema.

There was no physical image. During a *chanson*'s performance each
man in the audience experienced only what came to his own imagination,
creating his own pictures, letting his own memories of what had scared
him in the past mingle with the terrors offered by the words and the music.
It was unique.

Every man evoked his own fears, and many of them drowsed uneasily
into sleep with semi-Christian, crossed fingers. If, during the restless night,
any man twitched into wakefulness it was to feel anxiously for both arms
and one or two legs.

What was remarkable about those songs of heroes and things that crept
in the darkness was not the bloodshed and the battles nor the unnatural
apparitions but the almost complete absence of women. Grendel's mother,
a 'swamp-thing from hell' and 'tarn-hag', hardly qualifies.[11] Real women
were either incidentals in a masculine saga or others who adopted a male
role, converting themselves into pseudo-men.

Females were remote figures in a backcloth but could be useful socially.
The 'Battle of Finnsburh' is an example. Girls were customarily given in
marriage as pledges of peace between feuding groups. Hildeburh of the
Danes was one and her story was interwoven casually in between the mighty
deeds of Beowulf's epic, providing a brief but welcome diversion from the
deep concentration demanded for the major episodes of his career.

There had been generations of antagonism between the Danes and the Frisians and to end it Hildeburh was married to Finn, their enemy's leader. Despite her brother's deep dislike of the match the wedding took place and sixty Danes visited Finn's hall to celebrate. They were treacherously attacked one night but a truce was hastily agreed and a long winter passed before fighting erupted once more in which Finn and many of his followers were killed. The Danes took Hildeburh home as a widow mourning for her husband, son and brother. She was just a poetical pawn in a game of men.[12]

In the majority of Anglo-Saxon poems women were almost unmentioned, a wife yearning for her absent husband, or an obsequious lady serving Beowulf with drink.

> Wealhtheow, queen of her lord, Hrothgar,
> stepped forward in the hall, to observe the courtesies,
> bejewelled, costumed, welcomed guests
> and, perfect lady, offered to her lord's protector
> the first brimming cup . . .   (ll. 325–9)

Otherwise women were given little more than walk-on parts or were implausibilities glorifying the victory of Christianity. One, 'Juliana', eulogised a saint.

She was a virgin who refused to marry a rich but pagan Roman governor of cities. For her obduracy she was persecuted by her father, flogged, tortured by the Roman, hanged by her hair, chained, boiled in oil, drearily debated with a devil and, finally, verbosely, beheaded. This compilation of unbelievable agonies drains belief as effectively as any third-rate 'B' movie and 'Juliana' is of such little merit that it is frequently omitted from anthologies.[13] It did little for women. Artistically, the poem of a near namesake, 'Judith', was far better.

In the early sixth century BC Holofernes, an Assyrian general of Nebuchadnezzar, was besieging the Palestinian town of Bethulia, perhaps today's Shechem near Nablus in Jordan. Water was cut off, cisterns were drying, and patrols prevented any relief force reaching the town. Its inhabitants were desperate.

The young and attractive widow, Judith, was still grieving for her husband, but she exchanged her robes of mourning for seductively glittering, provocative clothes. Then, with her maid, she went to the camp of the Assyrians to offer herself as an alluring gift to the general. He sent her to wait in his lavish tent.

Holofernes and his officers were celebrating the certain end of the siege.

> . . . *Da weard Holofernus*
> *goldwine gumina. on gytesalum*
> *hloh ond hlidde. hlynede ond dyenede*

> . . . Then flushed with wine
> in merry mood, the leader of his men,
> guffawed and roared, shouted, bellowed

and the laughter and the consumption of strong drink continued for hours until his men drooped into drunken unconsciousness. Holofernes remained wakeful.

> . . . *Het da nida geblonden*

> . . . Then, in sinful lust,
> he ordered the blessed maid to be made ready,
> laden with ornaments, adorned with rings,
> to provide pleasure in his bed . . .[14]

There was no pleasure. His drinking outdid desire. As self-indulgent as his followers, he slumped into alcoholic oblivion. Judith, unsullied, found his sword. One sharp blow sliced halfway through his neck. One more and his head fell to the floor. She gave it to her maidservant, who put it in a food bag. Passing the sleepily inattentive guards, they reached the town, where she presented the bloodstained object to her people, urging them to attack the camp. When the Assyrians learned their leader had been killed, they panicked and ran for their lives. 'Very few got home.'[15]

'Judith' is an exceptional poem, well written and based on the second book of the Apocrypha, one of some thirteen pre-Christian Biblical 'histories' included in the 1611 Authorised Version of the Bible but usually omitted from later Protestant editions of the thirty-nine books of the Old Testament.

Judith's *chanson*, may have been composed around AD 950 to honour an historical Saxon woman, Ethelfleda, 'Lady of the Mercians'. She was the eldest daughter of Alfred the Great, and, after the death of her husband, ruled as queen of east-central England for eight years. Sister of Edward the Elder, king of Wessex, the pair between them, with separate armies, defeated Danish force after force from 909 onwards, erecting fortresses in strategic situations, steadily advancing northwards.

Her own men overran a stronghold near Brecon in 916 capturing a king's wife. They stormed Derby in 917 and captured Leicester in AD 918. The distant but dispirited Danes of York submitted. Shortly afterwards on

12 June 918 the formidable queen died at Tamworth. Her statue, with her nephew Athelstan, stands on a tall stone pillar in the town's Castle Grounds. She was buried in Gloucester in the now-ruinous St Oswald's priory that she had founded.

The praiseworthy poem *Judith* may have been composed in Ethelfleda's honour. She has none of her own.

Although not gently feminine Judith, with her woman's guiles was an exception to the sexual machismo of Anglo-Saxon verse. There were no courteous songs of love in that corpus.

Any audience of warriors accustomed to the heroism of the *chansons de geste* would have laughed contemptuously at the words of Guilhem de Capestanh, a thirteenth-century troubadour from the Languedoc in south-western France who wrote:

Lo dous consire.domna.m fai dire

The gentle thought that tells me love,
my lady, bids me offer you these lines
thinking of your lovely, enthralling body.
I long to see you . . .

But the rough Saxons would have applauded the fate that came to this foppish fool who doted on Seremonda, lovely young wife of Sir Raymond de Castel-Roussillon. When her jealous husband learned of the affair, he had the singer killed, his heart cut out, baked and presented as a special dish for the faithless wife, Told what she had eaten she committed suicide. Or so the story goes.[16]

More to the liking of the halls, and later the castles, was the military drama of the best-known of all *chansons de geste*, the 'Song of Roland and the Tragic Battle of Roncesvalles'.

What exists today is fiction fashioned out of fact. The fantasy is that, on 15 August 778, the conquering army of Charlemagne was returning to France having defeated the Saracens and captured Spain. The army was huge and strung out for miles as it trotted, marched and waggoned its ponderous meander through the foothills of the westernmost Pyrenees. At the rear was a baggage train heavy with a ransom of heathen treasure paid by the subdued Moors. It was guarded by a rearguard commanded by Roland, Prefect of the marches of Brittany.

As the vehicles crawled through the cramped defile of Roncevaux at the foot of Altobiscar mountain, an avalanche of rocks, tree-trunks and missiles assailed the detachment, which, hampered by armour, was doomed. Despite valiant resistance, it was slaughtered to the last man, and the Basque mountain-dwellers who had ambushed them returned home with every valuable article. The plunder was never recovered. It is written that Charlemagne grieved for years over the disaster.

That is a summary of the story as it exists today in a form probably composed three hundred years after the genuine event.

A maker provides what his customers want. *The Song of Roland* contained every element that a gathering of fighting men could wish for: treasure; a perilous journey through enemy territory; an irresistible attack; heroic defence; defiant deaths of the leading men; and, for added flavour, treachery by one of Charlemagne's own followers.

The poem anticipated Hollywood by a thousand years in its complete disregard for history, preferring romance to reality. Local Basques were transformed into perfidious Saracen infidels. Charlemagne's 'conquest of Spain' never penetrated farther south than the River Ebro, taking less than one-twentieth of the vast peninsula. Even that was achieved only with the assistance of a local Muslim emir.

Spice was added to the make-believe by the insertion of a fictitious traitor, Ganelon, Roland's stepfather. He surreptitiously advised a Saracen leader to 'pay ransom' to Charlemagne as a gesture of lasting peace only to recapture it by ambushing the weakly guarded wagons.

The story was ingenious, worthy of a modern blockbuster, and that is what it became. It had so many intriguing plots and subplots that it demanded concentration. 'No one was going to sit down quietly and read this work to himself; it would be heard, it would be watched, probably in a busy baronial hall with servants and others coming and going, dogs suddenly squabbling, a messenger arriving, and now and then someone throwing fresh logs on the fire.'[17]

People in the *chanson* were not conventional puppets. They were realistic. Roland was brave, but he was over-proud of his reputation and he was also reckless. Oliver, his great companion, was wiser and more down to earth. Having noticed enemies appearing on the mountainsides, he urged Roland to blow his ivory hunting-horn, an 'oliphant', as a call for help to the distant Charlemagne.

Roland refused imperiously. It would be cowardly.

'A stupid thing to do!', Roland replied.
'I'd lose all my renown at home in France.'[18]

His sword, Durandal, forged of the finest steel, he wanted to see stained with the blood of those treacherous villains when they dared attack. They attacked. For hours the French fought, outnumbered, their heavy chain-mail and shields draining them of strength under the heat of the sun. One

by one they fell, but only when it was too late did the dying Roland raise
the horn to his mouth. The note reached through the hills and mountains
to the startled Charlemagne.

Renegade to the last, the slithery Ganelon argued that it was nothing
more than Roland showing off to his troops. Suddenly, sadly, realising that
the man was a traitor, Charlemagne had him arrested and departed with
his army in the hope of rescuing his trapped soldiers. But when the French
army reached Roncevalles they found nothing but death.

The corpses of Roland and Oliver were taken northwards to Blaye and
buried in a tomb of fine white stone in the chancel of St Romaine church.
Having survived Vauban's seventeenth-century refortification of the town,
when three hundred houses were torn down, the handsome sepulchre
was finally vandalised and destroyed during the iconoclastic French
Revolution.

There is also a poetic irony. Blaye was almost a full-stop in *The Song of
Roland*, but it was to be the twelfth-century castle of Jaufré Rudel, one of
the earliest troubadours, a good poet who was in love with a woman of
Tripoli whom he had never seen.

Death came to the treacherous Ganelon. He was deprived of armour,
shield, sword and knighthood and condemned to a shameful and agonising
execution.

> . . . Ganelon must die a dreadful death.
> Four great horses were led out, the traitor's hands and feet
> tied fast to them. Strong beasts they were,
> swift, straining at their bonds. Four servants held them.
>   Close to a stretch of water the fiery horses were freed,
> And this man was sent to hell. His sinews stretched
> and lengthened, his limbs were torn from his body.
> On the green meadow grass his bright blood ran.
>   Count Ganelon has died a felon's death.[19]

The Song of Roland was a superb story worthy of Hollywood except for an
essential. There was no lovely leading lady. Listeners had to be content with
the death of Aude, Oliver's sister and Roland's betrothed, who swooned and
died when she learned that her fiancé had been killed. 'The Frankish barons
mourned and wept for her.' It is unlikely that the audience did. The poem
preceded the Age of Chivalry by generations, and there were no love poems,
no lovers of ladies. In the thoughts of a dying warrior there were no sighs
for a lady. It was an epic about men composed for men and it was popular.

Military *chansons* were never common in the pleasure-loving south.
Love and laughter were preferred. A worthwhile exception was *La Chanson*

d'Antioche written by Gérald Béchade, a minor knight of 'Lastours castle, a man of fine spirit and adept in writing, who wrote a story of those battles in his native language', Occitan.

Long fragments, almost ninety of them, were discovered in a Madrid archive. They describe the protracted siege of Antioch during the First Crusade. The descriptions are vivid but despite the title of a recent book about the poem, *L'Aube des Troubadours*, 'dawn of the troubadours', Béchade was not the first of those singers. He was a poetical military historian writing in the 1130s, some decades before the first of them, Guilhem of Poitiers. His poem was as out of place and time in the Languedoc as Gibbon's *Decline and Fall of the Roman Empire* would have been amongst the Lake District poetry of Coleridge and Wordsworth.[20]

Chansons of heroism were favoured in the manly north. At the onset of the battle of Hastings in 1066 one was sung by Taillefer, knight, minstrel and good singer, he approached his leader, William of Normandy singing of Charlemagne and of Roland, of Oliver and of the many men who died at Roncevaux. He entreated to be allowed to strike the combat's first blow.

Permission granted, he advanced on the Saxons astonishing them by juggling two swords while on horseback, then killed two men before being surrounded and slain. That was in 1066. Five years later Guilhem of Poitiers was born. He was the first of the troubadours. With him came music and songs of love for women.

THREE

An Occitan Legend

THE BEGINNING OF THE TROUBADOURS

Once upon a time, many years ago, a penniless, downhearted troubadour, without lord or patron to support him, rode to the banks of the river Tarn that divided the lands of Languedoc from the kingdom of France to the north.

Ahead of him, across the water, were harsh courts, rough barons, uncouth manners. His southern accent would be mocked. So would his Occitanian words, the dialect of the *langue d'Oc*. Men would jeer at his southern ways. There would be drunkenness without decorum. But with the insults would come the rewards of riches and security.

Behind him was laughter, companionship – and the pleasure but poverty – of a homeland of merriment, sunlight song. He stared across the river for hours, edging forward, hesitating, twisting the horse's reins around his wrists. Hours passed.

As the evening darkened he turned to the south.

FOUR

GUILHEM OF POITIERS

Qu'ieu mi nom «maistre certa
My name is 'Lord of Love', bed's troubadour.
A woman after my night of teaching Cupid's ways
Next day implores, entreats for more.
Nothing before had set her so ablaze,.
An ecstasy undreamt. My gift's so rare
If up for sale, a fortune it would raise
In any female market, anywhere.
       (Guilhem, Count of Poitiers, Poem VI, *Ben vuelh*, ll. 36–42)

Guilhem of Poitiers and the Poetry of Sex, 1080–1127

He lived an adventurous and often an unedifyng life, and seems to have been a jovial sensualist caring little what kind of reputation he might obtain in the eyes of the world about him.

(Chaytor, 1912, 41)

Guilhem, 7th Count of Poitiers, 9th Duke of Aquitaine, born in 1071, was the largest landowner in France. He possessed a third of the country, three times more than the French king (Fig. 2). He was also a fine poet and musician.[1]

We are fortunate enough to know a great deal about William, the ninth Duke of Aquitaine and seventh Count of Poitou, the earliest known troubadour. His character, as described by the chroniclers of the period, accords perfectly with the role of the first known secular poet of the modern world. He was vigorous, brash, amorous and proud – thus possessing the characteristics needed to dispel the mists of anonymity that shroud much of earlier medieval poetry.[2]

A medieval biographer wrote a *vida*, 'life', that was copied into one of his songbooks as the *Los coms de Peitieus . . .* 'Le comte de Poitiers'.

The Count of Poitiers was one of the greatest courtiers in the world, and one of the greatest tricksters of women, a good chevalier in arms and grand in his handling of women. And he knew how to compose well and to sing, and he went for a long time through the world to deceive the women. And he had a son who took for wife the Duchess of Normandy from whom he had a daughter.[3] The daughter, 'alia-Aénor', became the famous Eleanor of Aquitaine, who, divorced from the under-sexed king of France, married the man who became Henry II of England.[4]

Guilhem was an innovator. One of his poems, VII, begins with a line that, for troubadours after him, was the equivalent of today's 'Once upon a time . . .'. It celebrated the coming of spring.

Pus vezem de novelh florir . . .
Now we see the first flowers appearing . . .[5]

With variations, that celebration of new birth and life would appear in countless numbers of songs. The sharpest break with *chansons de geste* came, however, with 'unmanly' sentiments about a woman in Guilhem's tenth poem, another celebration of spring: *Ab la dolchor del temps novel* (In the sweetness of the new season). Its fourth verse began:

Enquer me membra . . .

I still remember that morning
When we ended our long resistance.
She gave me a splendid present,
her love and the ring that she wore . . .

One can almost hear the scornful guffaws in the mead-halls and baronial courts. But the derision would have turned to delight when the men heard the last line:

C'ajas mas manz sotz so mantel . . .
That I can put my hands beneath her skirt.

Were that permitted it was an invitation to intimacy. In the Middle Ages well-born married couples 'slept naked, and before rising put on linen undergarments, drawers for the lord, a long chemise for the lady. After washing in a basin of cold water they donned outer garments.'
As for other noble women, the clothes and jewels of Guilhem's lady proclaimed her high status. With her hair braided in a net of silken thread and her face framed in a wide linen band from ear to ear passing under her chin, she wore a long gown of fine wool. Under the gown was a close-fitting kirtle, and, inside it, in colder weather, a smock, similar but of less expensive and plainer material. Underneath the smock she wore nothing to protect her modesty.[6] The poem is typical of his poetry, a mixture of sincere tenderness, love and straightforward carnality.
Guilhem came from a rich and powerful family. His father, Gui-Geoffroi, was well read and owned a large library, which was rare in those subliterate times. Seven years before Guilhem was born he had joined the King of Aragon to attack the prosperous *alcazar* or palace and city of Barbastro near Lérida in northern Spain. As was customary in any conflict between Christians and Muslims, the town was destroyed and almost all its inhabitants slaughtered. Among the survivors were some 'wonderful Moorish women-singers'.[7]

The enforced captivity of some of these survivors in Poitiers, and their songs, that not only spoke of love but also manifested unusual respect for women – attitudes almost incomprehensible to the warlords of northern France – may have influenced Guilhem in his career as a poet.

It is a question that has stimulated controversy. It is arguable that of his eleven songs the majority – IV, V, VI, VII, VIII and XI – do have a Moorish construction. So do numbers IX and X with minor variations. Only the early poems, I, II and III, are akin to *chansons*. 'All the poems of Guilhem which we possess agree very closely in their form with the verse structures employed in current Hispano-Moorish poetry.'[8]

There has been almost vehement disagreement with this, mainly from non-European sources, suggesting alternative origins in classical Roman poets such as Ovid and Martial. They are unconvincing. Sincere expressions of love between men and women are few in the works of those cynical observers. The verse structures used by the count, however, do have persuasive origins in church music. A merging of several sources for the 'new' poetry is probable.

Nicknamed 'The Younger' as a son, Guilhem was known, not entirely unjustly, as a successful seducer and a not so successful soldier, or equally succinctly by a not-unbiased cleric, Geoffroi le Gros, as 'the enemy of all chastity and all feminine virtue'.[9]

Inheriting what was almost an empire when his father died on 25 September 1186, eight years later for premeditated dynastic reasons he married Philippa, young widow of the king of Aragon and daughter of Count William of Toulouse. Through her inheritance the new duke claimed that great city and its lands. Like many of his territorial ambitions, it brought him problems but little satisfaction.

As a great nobleman he led his own life, indulgent and hedonistic, with a persistent demand for pleasure and women. Two lines from Poem VII, *Pus vezem . . .*, said so:

Per tal n'ai meyns de bon saber . . .

If my satisfaction is less than other men's
it's because I desire what I cannot have.

Not great poetry but honest about himself.

Outside his amorous private life, wars for territory continued both in France and in more distant regions. Local conflicts over land developed between France and England. The over-running of the Holy Land and the capture of Jerusalem by Seljuk Turks resulted in a protracted series of crusades that disrupted European societies.

Like many great barons, Guilhem was a vassal of King Louis I, 'The Fat', but like many of his contemporaries he frequently opposed the monarch to prevent the French kingdom encroaching on his own lands. For this reason Guilhem occasionally sided with the English in their claim to Normandy.

England was in confusion. There was no custom of primogeniture and on the death of William I, the Conqueror, the throne did not pass to his eldest son, Robert, but, by the dying king's will, went to the third son, William II, known as 'Rufus' from his florid complexion and reddish hair. The second son, Richard, had been killed in a hunting accident. The fourth, Henry Curthose, was bought off with a gift of 10,000 pounds-weight of silver.[10] Fraternal unrest was guaranteed by the allocation of Normandy to Robert. It upset two kings, William Rufus and Louis the Fat.

In 1090 William Rufus, partnered by Guilhem and others, invaded France to recover from Robert what he asserted was the property of England: Normandy. There was little resistance. Local barons had been easily bribed.

In desperation, Robert appealed to the French king, a monarch who possessed little but Paris and some neighbouring castles and estates. Always lazy, Louis accepted bribes to help the prince against the English, but, 'inactive, and belching from his daily surfeit, came hiccupping, though replete, to the war', took the money, and cynically 'unbuckled his armour, and went back to his gourmandising'.[11]

It was stalemate. A treaty the following year between the pair of royal brothers brought Robert's allegiance on the agreement that at the death of one the other would inherit all the lands, England, Normandy and other territorial scraps.

Such local skirmishes and personal quarrels were no more than incidentals to the Christian world. Of major importance had been the loss in 1072 of the Holy City, Jerusalem, to hostile unbelievers. Seljuk Turks had taken it from the caliphs of Cairo. Since 969 the Egyptians had governed the city but had respected that centre of their second prophet, Jesus. Followers of Christ had not been persecuted. That changed.

In what is now Asia Minor the Seljuk Turks rebelled against the tyranny of their overlords, the Holy Roman emperors of Constantinople. In 1071 they were strong enough to defeat an emperor at the battle of Manzikert. Then, free to invade Anatolia, they captured Jerusalem the following year.

It remained theirs for twenty years, but Turkish power weakened through internal struggles for dominance. It was a dynastic disintegration accelerated by the murder of a Muslim leader, Janah-al-Dawla, by a fanatical religious sect known as the Assassins.[12] The waning of Turkish dominance encouraged the idea of a crusade to overcome them and regain Jerusalem.

Wars between Christians and Muslim unbelievers had already been fought for centuries, especially in Spain, but there the enemy had been Moors from the western Mediterranean. Jerusalem, far to the east, had been unmolested. Now that had changed, and in 1095 the Pope, Urban II, proclaimed a crusade against different Muslim infidels, Seljuk Turks, who were soon joined by the warlike Saracen nomads of the Syrian and Arabian deserts.

By 1095 Robert, titular duke of Normandy and enemy of his younger brother, William Rufus, tiring of the futile bickering, was eager to join that crusade, and to finance his expedition he mortgaged Normandy to his unloved brother.

Guilhem, Duke of Aquitaine, also announced his enthusiasm, but when the new Count of Saint-Gilles, Raymond IV, left France for the crusade and abandoned Toulouse to the protection of the Church and his young son, Bertran, the acquisitive duke marched into the county and took control of the city.

There was a problem. He had to pay for his crusading. Despite his enormous landholding, he had little available cash for the ruinous expense of equipping a private army. Any hope that William Rufus would lend him the money in return for past services and a mortgage on Aquitaine ended near sunset on 2 August 1100.

It was said that Rufus had gone hunting in the New Forest and had wounded a stag. A nearby companion, Sir Walter Tyrrell, seeing another, took aim and fired, only for his arrow to kill Rufus. 'The king William was shot with an arrow in hunting by a man of his.'[13] The knight fled in panic to France and was sheltered in the Benedictine abbey of Saint-Germain-des-Prés, Paris, by Abbot Suger, a powerful cleric later to be the enemy of the philosopher, Abelard, a man whose own poetry was to bring joy to a woman and disgrace to himself (Appendix 2).

Whether the death of Rufus was an assassination, an accident, a royal sacrifice to the Devil, or intentional murder by William's younger brother, who immediately became King Henry II, was uncertain at the time and impossible to resolve today. Contemporary reports told differing stories: that Tyrrell was an expert marksman; that he had not been near the king; that he had been involved in a plot; that he was innocent but falsely implicated.[14]

Whatever the truth, the death left Guilhem as 7th Count of Poitiers and 9th Duke of Aquitaine without adequate finances for his ambitious private army. Characteristically impractical and impetuous, he sold the entire county of Toulouse back to Bertran of Saint-Gilles and never regained it.

Ezra Pound, the twentieth-century American 'modernist' poet, who lived for many years in Italy and Provence, was well versed in troubadour songs and often quoted them. He knew of Guilhem's financial irresponsibility.

. . . Guillaume sold out his ground rents
(Seventh of Poitiers, Ninth of Aquitain).

(Pound, Canto VI, ll. 3–4)[15]

But the money was obtained and he started to assemble his knights and their footmen.

The crusades began with fervour but quickly collapsed into a tragic fiasco. A rabble-rousing preacher, Peter the Hermit, bare-footed, unwashed and unwholesome, amassed a disorganised rabble of disaffected peasants and knights without a lord and led them towards the Holy Land. At Nicosia they were routed and massacred by the Turks, who 'led away young girls whose face and form was pleasing in their eyes, and beardlesss youths of comely countenance'.[16] Peter abandoned his Peoples' Crusade and joined the Pope's at Constantinople, only to desert during the prolonged siege of Antioch.

It had been the appeal for aid to the Pope by Alexis Comnenus, Byzantine emperor of Constantinople, that was the catalyst. Its call for help and protection caused the formation of three separate armies to march on Jerusalem. From Lorraine, Godfrey of Bouillon and his brother, Baldwin, led one. Raymond IV of Toulouse led a second from Provence. Bohemond commanded the third, travelling from Normandy by land and sea. With him was Tancred, his nephew, who was to become one of the most eminent of all the crusaders.

The realities of the ambitious enterprise of the late twelfth century were underestimated. The logistics were appalling: roads were poor; the countries to be crossed were difficult with rivers, ravines, marshes, hills, passes, mountains; there were hostile natives; and there was hardly a port except for Constantinople.

That city was reached only after a debilitating, sometimes starving trek of 1,500 miles. Then the Bosphorus had to be crossed, one part of the strait so narrow that a dog barking on one side could be heard on the other. But currents were unpredictable, ships were few and unreliable. And across the water the way to Jerusalem was a further 800 miles through enemy lands, a journey of heat, privation, sieges and battles. Most crusaders never reached the Holy City.

It is necessary to describe the hardships because many troubadours chose to go on a crusade. Jaufré Rudel of Blaye, a probable forebear of Savaric de Mauléon's companion, went on the Second. Pons de Capduelh died on the Third. Gaucelm Faidit was on the Fourth, accepting the fighting but dreading the sea.

Raimon de Vaqueiras was on the same crusade and present at the Christian city of Constantinople during the three days of ransacking and rapine by crusaders in April 1204, disgracing their own religion. Simon de Montfort, the commander of the destructive Albigensian Crusade in the Languedoc only five years later, refused to take part in the sacrilege. Sordello, another troubadour, may have accompanied Louis IX on the Seventh Crusade. There were also other crusading troubadours, including, of course, Guilhem at the, by then unnecessary, end of the First.

Crusading armies were accretions of leaders, knights, squires, followers, wagons and servants, supplies, vast hosts that straggled across Europe, columns of lords with their private armies stretching for miles, untidy crowds of horsemen, clerics, foot soldiers, crossbowmen, archers, servants, carpenters, endless trails of riders and footmen intermingling with carts of food, wine and weapons. The lines were so long that it took a day to walk from the front to the rear in a choking, swirl of coughing dust, and a stench of sweating clothes and horses, an odour growing staler and thicker the farther back a person was.

Not all were crusaders. There were hangers-on, beggars, thieves and prostitutes, the customary baggage of a military expedition. In 1191, a hundred years after the First Crusade, and when the crusaders were besieging the city of Acre a Saracen noble and historian, Imad ed-Din Zengi, described those camp-followers.

Three hundred lovely Frankish women, he wrote, had arrived by ship, young and beautiful, assembled from beyond the sea and offering their sinful bodies as physical rewards for God's spiritual crusaders. They were 'licentious harlots' with beautiful bottoms and 'fleshy thighs that swayed like saplings', 'like drunken adolescents, making love and selling themselves for gold, bold and ardent, loving and passionate, pink-faced and unblushing, black-eyed', with their own tents in which 'they dedicated as a holy offering what they kept between their thighs . . . their posturing bodies as territories for forbidden acts were willingly spread out on the carpet of amorous sport'. On occasion, even Saracens took surreptitious advantage of their compensations.[17]

Lubricious they were, envious the historian may have been, but the women did provide pleasure and consolation during the tedious, irksome and sluggish march towards Constantinople.

At the dust-free head of the column were the great lords and their squires, the lords on their horses. There were horses everywhere. Even a poor knight had a palfrey for everyday riding and a heavier, short-legged warhorse. A rich nobleman had a stable full of mounts. There were horses for his mounted men-at-arms, mules and hackneys as baggage animals to carry weapons, armour, tents and food. Above all there was his powerful destrier, a warhorse whose cost was prohibitive. An ordinary horse cost four times the expense of a strong, healthy bull. A destrier's price was five times that of a horse.

Trotting, trudging, creaking wheels rolling, moving at an ox-plod pace, crossing and recrossing twisting rivers, an arsenal of wagons lumbered on with their freight of weapons, dismantled siege-towers, scaling-ladders, battering-rams, monstrous slings and catapults of trebuchets and mangonels. The three separate armies did not so much advance as crawl down old, worn, weathered Roman roads. It was dirty and tiring. Progress was no more than 8 miles a day.

In France there were civilian counterparts to the military expeditions. Persecutions not only of Muslims but of Jews were commonplace. Some were so intense and remorseless that whole villages were emptied of their inhabitants.

Overseas – *Outremer*, as the crusaders called it – the armies pressed deeply into Turkish lands, and by 1097 the crusaders had captured the cities of Iconium and Nicea. In 1098 they took the walled city of Antioch, 300 miles north of Jerusalem, after a siege that had endured for nine months. Five thousand of seven thousand horses perished of disease and starvation. So many men died that their corpses could not be buried, and there was an outbreak of plague. Women perished in their scores. But finally, on 3 June, the city was taken. Just over a year later the weakened crusader army captured Jerusalem after a brief but bitter month's siege. A recent eclipse of the moon had been interpreted as God's sign that there would soon be an eclipse of Muslim crescent.[18]

It was 15 July 1099. There were ferocious resistance and ferocious reprisals. It became a pogrom. Forty thousand of the population were put to the sword. Mosques and synagogues were burned down. Godfrey of Bouillon refused the title of king and became the 'Defender of the Holy Sepulchre'. It was the foundation of the Latin kingdom of Jerusalem. When Godfrey died a year later, he was succeeded by his brother, Baldwin.

Two thousand miles to the west in France some women of good birth were achieving importance. Their status changed – for the better. No longer merely amenable chattels, subservient to their husbands, in the absence of their lords many wives assumed command of affairs. With men absent for months, sometimes years, many never returning, wherever wives could rely on the loyalty of stewards and servants they took charge of the running of estates, the collection of dues, the dispensing of local justice. For the first time, from childhood to marriage, they had independence.

Even though many were young and impressionable, aware of temptation, and the enticing lures of seduction by men around them, the women, some of them still girls, also had the responsibility of maintaining their good name. Only self-respect guarded them.

A titbit of common error can be dismissed. 'Chastity belts are surrounded by myths and folklore, the most common of which is that they were first used by crusading knights on their wives.' But in the early thirteenth century there was no device to enforce pure living. The belts were not mentioned until 1405, when Konrad Keyeser von Eichstätt referred to them in his *Bellefortis*, a manual about contemporary military technology: '*Est florentinarum* . . .' (These are hard iron breeches of Florentine women which are closed at the front).[19]

There is an unexpected explanation for their use in Italy. It is probable that such devices, often of precious inlaid and engraved silver, were willingly accepted by wives as gifts to pledge their fidelity to departing husbands. Three centuries earlier it was the woman herself who remained the only guardian of her body and honour.

Not all women stayed at home. Some went on crusades. Eleanor of Aquitaine accompanied her husband, Louis VII, on the Second Crusade. During it other chain-mailed women were seen riding mounted in the ranks of the knights and men at arms, not on palfreys but on fine warhorses, 'boldly sitting their saddles astride after the manner of men . . . dressed in armour just like men', with pennant-decorated lances. Another woman, Margaret of Beverley, having accomplished her long and sometimes dangerous pilgrimage from England to Jerusalem in 1187, joined in the fighting when the Holy City was attacked by Saracens, putting on a metal breastplate and using a cauldron as a helmet.[20]

At the siege of Acre in 1191 'three Frankish women fought from horseback and were recognised as women only when captured and stripped of their armour'. At the same siege a woman archer in a sleeveless, green cloak killed many Muslims before she herself was killed. Her bow was given to Saladin, 'who was greatly astonished.[21] After the conflict the screams of women in agony shrieked piercingly above the groans and shouting of wounded men.

Despite the obvious perils, at least one noblewoman joined Guilhem on his own semi-private crusade. The Dowager Margravine Ida of Austria, famous as a great beauty in her youth, joined him. She did not return. Christian historians such as William of Malmesbury and Albert of Aix say nothing about her. It is probable that she was killed just a few months later on the disorganised, badly directed expedition

It was not until the spring of 1101 that Guilhem was ready to leave for the by then irrelevant sequel to the First Crusade. Had he been as attentive to martial enterprises as he was to be in extramarital exploits, things might have gone better for his expedition. But his was a light-hearted jaunt that concluded in disaster.

The richly apparelled force straggled through Bulgaria and reached Constantinople by June. The emperor entertained them. No news had reached the city of the misfortunes suffered by the three earlier armies. So Guilhem's army left, crossed the Bosphorus and entered the friendly countryside of Nicomedia. It was the final pleasure of a carefree excursion.

As they tramped southwards there was no food, no friendly natives, no welcoming cities, just abandoned villages and scorched earth. By early September they were starving, desperate of thirst, suffering from the unceasing heat. They staggered and limped over 400 miles of empty land from Constantinople to the walls of Heraclea and the fresh waters of the River Tarsus. It gave them no comfort.

> [Turks], aware that the army was suffering from hunger and thirst, as they had been wandering about the marshes and desolate places for several days, encountered them with three hundred thousand archers. Never was there conflict more disastrous to the Franks, as it was impossible for flight to save the coward or courage to rescue the bold from danger for the battle was fought in a confined situation, and nothing could prevent the effects of clouds of arrows on men who were crowded together. More than a hundred thousand were slain, and all the booty carried off.[22]

Even disregarding the preposterously exaggerated numbers, it was a catastrophe. Somehow Guilhem and very few others survived, and in desperation struggled to the crusaders' city of Antioch, where they were welcomed by its ruler, Tancred. It may be, however, that the lady Margravine had been less fortunate, not slain and free from living degradation but captured and taken to 'a distant seraglio where she gave birth to an earthly Messiah as various Arabic legends had it'.[23]

Guilhem was more fortunate. He was free, and he was royally entertained by his host. Tancred, a knight praised as 'of distinguished piety' by William of Malmesbury, was already famous for his heroism at the dangerous sieges of Nicea, Tarsus, Antioch and Jerusalem. He enhanced his reputation by establishing the domain of Galilee, becoming its prince before being appointed regent of Antioch. In 1106 he was to besiege and capture an Assassin base near Aleppo.[24] His exploits were extolled in the sixteenth-century epic *Jerusalem Liberated*, by the Italian poet Tasso. To his destitute and temporarily impoverished guest he was a generous host. The entertainment was lavish and probably, on occasion, of questionable taste.

Antioch, a prosperous Syrian port and powerful citadel at the eastern end of the Mediterranean, was famous for its splendour and luxury and, for centuries, had also been notorious for its opulent depravity. Every pleasure was available, as an early Latin poem suggested:

Copa Surisca

Dancing girl of Syria, her hair caught up in a fillet,
very subtle in swaying those quivering flanks of hers
in time to the castanet's rattle. Half-drunk in the smoky tavern
she dances, lascivious, wanton, clashing the rhythm . . .[25]

It may have been the kind of music and verse that appealed to the burgeoning poetical mind of Guilhem, Count of Poitiers. It is written that at Antioch he composed and recited a mock epic about the ambush and his fictitious capture by the Saracens, reciting the mock miseries of his imprisonment 'in rhythmic verses and funny measures'. The cleric William of Malmesbury added: 'Moreover, he rendered his absurdities so pleasant by a show of wit; exciting the loud laughter of his hearers.'[26] Their response may have been the ideal spur to encourage a novice entertainer. It is a minor literary misfortune that, if this early venture ever existed, it has not survived.

Leaving Antioch, Guilhem and his companions reached their goal of Jerusalem by Easter 1002, and by October, daringly returning by sea, were back in Poitou and the semi-empire of Aquitaine that his wife, Philippa, had zealously supervised on his behalf.

He was free to pursue his real enthusiasms, poetry and women. They were blatantly expressed in what were probably two of his earliest poems, I and III of the order in which Alfred Jeanroy arranged the eleven. His standard edition is still available: 'Its only disadvantage is that the more ribald (and hence amusing) passages are left untranslated.'[27] It was true of poems I, III and V. The remaining eight were published in plain French.

There is little information of how the songs were performed. The one unhelpful morsel of Guilhem's music that survives is little guide. 'But in a fourteenth-century play, the *Jeu de Sainte-Agnes*, there is a text that is to be sung, according to the stage directions, *in sonu del comte de Peytieu*, 'to the melody of the Count of Poitiers.' The melody given there is incomplete; but enough of it survives to allow us to see that it would fit the poem *Pos de chanter m'es pres talentz*.[28]

On Duisit's compact disc the eleven poems are loudly declaimed against a background of slow, low-pitched raspings from an early form of violin, the *vièle*. For Guilhem the bow may have been played by an accompanist, a jongleur or minstrel. Duisit thought so. (For his compact discs see Appendix 1.)

'As an eleventh century prince's education did not generally include the learning of a musical instrument, I thought it would be wise to have a jongleur,'[29] who may have been the Daurostre of poem VII or even the Monet of V.

Many of these minstrels were accomplished and versatile players of: the *vièle*, the *gigue*, the *rebeck* and other instruments, of which there are many images in church carvings and illustrated manuscripts. The sadness is their silence. Without any contemporary notated score one can only imagine the music that they played. But, as the poet, John Keats, comforted:

'Heard melodies are sweet, but those unheard
are sweeter.'[30]

Guilhem may have exercised discretion in his repertoire, offering socially acceptable verses to audiences of women, and of men and women, changing to bluer versions for gatherings of men only.

Poem IX:

Mout jauzens me prec en amar
Full of joy I abandon myself to love

was one of the former, pleasant, complimentary but inoffensive, almost deferential in its 'lord, in reality a lady' . . . as though the woman was his master, demanding of his loyalty and subservience. Its fourth verse expressed his humility.

Totz jois li deu humiliar

All other joys bow down to it
And all other riches obey
My lord (and lady) – for her beautiful bearing
And her beautiful charming looks;
A man would live a hundred years
Who had held the joy of her love.

But Poems I, III and V were very different, and it is sad in a sardonic way, to find how coy some commentators have been about the vocabulary and the thrust of the three songs.

As Brian Stock remarked in his attractive translations of some medieval Latin lyrics, 'the erotic was a normal aspect of the love experience in the Middle Ages. The suppression of the erotic in medieval poetry, is a distinctly modern prejudice', and to demonstrate this he provided an example of a poem from the Ripoll Collection of the tenth to the thirteenth centuries, *Sol ramium fervens* 'At noon . . .' –

Cuius crus tenerum tenui, quod non negat ipsa,
in super et coxas, sponte sua tetigi;
nec vetuit niveas post me tractare nimis fuerat.
Venimus ad lectum, connectimur insimul ambo;
cetera, que licuit sumere, non piguit.

I held her tender thighs – she could not refuse –
And above, with her consent, I caressed her middle.
Afterwards she did not forbid me
To touch her snowy breasts.
To caress them was a pleasure too sweet to bear.
We went to bed; at once we two were one.[31]

– which was direct without crudity and without prudish evasions.

Sadly, the recent censorship was not confined to Jeanroy in 1927. It occurred even more recently in 1970 with Wilhelm, whose renderings – sometimes expurgated or sanitised through either omissions or non-translations such as 'And I f—d them this many times' – were dolefully reminiscent of Thomas Bowdler's *The Family Shakespeare* of 1818, in whose ten volumes 'those words and expressions are omitted which cannot with propriety be read aloud in a family'.

Transforming such forthright poems into versions that would edify elderly maiden aunts in bath-chairs did the poet no justice. Better to excise them altogether and admit that only genteel verses have been included.

To the contrary, poem I, *Companhon farai un vers qu'we convinen . . .* 'Companions, I'll compose a fitting verse . . .' is an example of what Guilhem intended and how it can be misrepresented.

It concerned two horses, both metaphorical. One was wild, untameable, the other docile and lovely, coming from Confolen ('Confolens' today). The fourth verse was allusive but grossly explicit for attentive listeners.

S'ill pogues adomesjar a mon talen

If I could only tame them to my will
I would never want to put my equipment
In any other place, for I would be
Better mounted than any man alive.[32]

Wilhelm parodied it in Wild West fashion, almost 'ride 'em, cowboy!'. Topsfield never quoted it. Yet few of Guilhem's amused audience would have missed the *double entendre* of stallions converted into mares, and horses metamorphosed into women. Another, very minor troubadour, Jean de la Tournelle, made the same joke, complaining that a rich man had stolen the horse that 'I used to ride day and night'.[33]

There was also a pun hidden in the first line of verse 6: *L'autre fo noiritz sa jus part Confolen . . .* 'The other came nearby from Confolen . . .'.

The choice of the town is unlikely to have been accidental. Today it is an attractive medieval city with a ruined castle, its name coming from the confluence of the two rivers, Vienne and Goire. It lies south of Poitiers and south-west of Niort, a nearby town in which Guilhem proposed to set up a brothel.

Confolen did end with the 'en' that rhymed with the two succeeding lines, 'escen' and 'argen', but there were many other ordinary words that could have been used. Nor did the other horse, the unmanageable one, have a place of origin.

Aware of the poet's allusive and anatomically aware imagery, his listeners probably chuckled lustily at 'Confolen' as they picked up the concealed and amusingly indelicate meaning of the place name, just as schoolboys snigger at 'Cockermouth', 'Titfield' and 'Bumble Hole'.

The place-name, Confolen, contains two scholarly puns that academic and pedantic evasions decipher as *vagina–scrotum* from the Latin. As will be seen shortly, Poem III needed no pun for 'con'.

Classic literature was just one of several sources from which this early troubadour derived his inspiration. They are many and different: the *chansons de geste*; Moorish attitudes towards women; church music; earlier French poems of love; and ancient Roman poets.

The *chansons* were traditional entertainments, acted and sung musical recitals that celebrated manly heroism. They were established types of performance that transformed smoothly into those of Guilhem despite the contents being so different. So, also, was his language, no longer French but a hybrid patois of French and Occitan, coming as he did from Poitiers on the border between northern France and the southern Languedoc.[34]

Native military epics were seldom composed in the south. Northern ones were known, often performed by jongleurs or minstrels at wedding feasts. But, by choice, gentler forms of poetry were preferred there, perhaps because of influences from Spain.

In the Languedoc 'we find a number of petty courts, living in a rich and happy obscurity in a country comparatively free from the ravages of war under which northern France suffered until late in the ninth century, and open to Spanish and Arab influence through connexions with the courts of Barcelona and Aragon, living, moreover, in a climate softer and warmer than that of northern France'.[35]

Through his father's library as well as the wonderful, captive singers from Barbastro and his own stay at Antioch years later, Guilhem was firmly acquainted with Moorish music and Moorish attitudes towards women.

Church music also affected his poetical style. As one example, he wrote his horse poem, No. I, in triplets, a succession of three-line rhyming verses.

> The triplet form is an exact imitation of the *conductus*, strophic compositions in Latin which had been developed at the monastery of St Martial, an important musical centre in Guilhem's own dominions. The *conductus* were more elaborate than the older hymnody for one or more voices. A man like Guilhem would delight in taking over a religious form and turning it to bawdy uses.[36]

The *conductus* was a form of Gregorian chant that combined rhythmical verse with music and 'it was the Roman model which was the basis of many melodies used by the troubadours of Provence and the trouvères of northern France'. Unfortunately for Guilhem, there is only one tune of his in existence. It is in a fourteenth-century manuscript and much too meagre to give any impression of his music.[37]

Despite a widespread belief to the contrary, there also existed native poems of romance that he would have known. There is a very attractive one in Latin of the tenth century from the MSS of Salzburg, Canterbury and Limoges. It is the oldest of all known medieval love songs. It has been set to three different melodies. Paradoxically, it is well known today, because the Elizabethan playwright, poet and genius Christopher Marlowe paraphrased and improved its first line:

> *Iam dulcis amica, venito . . .*
> Come sweetheart come . . .

into

> Come live with me and be my love.
>   (H. Waddell, *Medieval Latin Lyrics*, 4th edn, 1933, 144–7)

Classically educated, and translator of the Roman poets Ovid and Lucan, Marlowe took the medieval verse and turned its pleasantness into charm, as a comparison between its translated ninth verse with Marlowe's third shows:

Ibi sunt sedilia strata . . .

Here there be couches spread,
tapestry tented,
flowers for thee to tread,
green herbs sweet scented . . .

and Marlowe:

And I will make thee beds of roses,
and a thousand fragrant posies,
a cap of flowers and a kirtle
embroidered all with leaves of myrtle.[38]

A lesser poet than Marlowe, Guilhem may also have known the Latin poem of which the ninth verse reads:

Iam nix glaciesque liquescit . . .

Now the snow's melting,
out the leaves start,

to be compared with Guilhem's Poem VII:

Pus vezem de novelh florir

Now we see the meadows and orchards
flowering and verdant once more . . .

a format followed, often tediously, by many later, unadventurous troubadours.

To the *chansons*, Spain, the church and older poems, there was one more, very important form of inspiration that was used by Guilhem, particularly in his coarser works. It was Rome. Of the few classical poets whose works were available in the twelfth century, he enjoyed the cynicism and outspokenness of Ovid and, particularly, Martial. An even more direct poet, Catullus, remained unknown for over three centuries.[39]

Of all those poets, including Ovid and Horace, it was Martial's *Epigrams* that were quoted most frequently. He was plagiarised and imitated. And it was that poet most liked by celibate churchmen for his irony and, even more, for his coarse wit.

Despite the iconoclastic barbarism of the early Christian years in Europe, libraries with ancient manuscripts occasionally survived in the great monasteries. The illiterate iconoclasm of the Dark Ages destroyed much, but in the twelfth century a revival of learning discovered Martial and his quotations, even his vicious turns of phrase.

A few pagan poets like Martial survived because Christianity and sexual abstinence were their unlikely saviours. Privileged brethren, having renounced sexual intercourse, could, like closet-pornographers, alleviate their bodily desires by reading bawdy literature in the privacy of monastic cells, the *Epigrams* among them.

They were enjoyed by scholars and high churchmen like John of Salisbury. Educated monks travelled freely in Britain, Ireland and France, often exploring the miraculously preserved manuscripts of antiquity. A late contemporary of Guilhem, John met the monk and scholar Peter Abelard, lover of Héloïse, in Paris. In 1170 in Canterbury Cathedral he witnessed the murder of Thomas à Becket. In 1176 he became Bishop of Chartres. He also read Martial and Ovid. It was not always high learning that appealed to him,[40] but also eroticism, like these epigrams of Martial.

> *Galla prostibilis . . .*

> We're told that Galla's services as a whore
> cost two gold coins. Throw in two more
> and you'll get some extras as an encore.

and

> *pedicare negas: dabat hoc Cornelia Graccho,*
> *Julia Pompeio, Porcia, Brute, tibi; . . .*
> *pocula Iuno fuit pro Ganymede Iovi . . .*

> 'No sodomy!' cried my wife. Yet Cornelia agreed
> to become her spouse's Ganymede.
> Portia and Julia too, when husbands so decreed.
> Even the goddess Juno bent to Jove's foul need.[41]

And it was through Martial that 'Con-folen' can be understood. *No m'azauta cons gardatz*, wrote Guilhem in Poem III, 'I abominate protected cunts'. 'Cons' is derived from the Latin *cunnus*, a word never found in school dictionaries and only defined with anatomical primness in less censorious publications as 'the female pudenda'. 'Genitals' would be more forthright.

'Folen' was quite possibly a French/Occitanian adaptation of Latin *folliculus* or *follis* meaning the scrotum, so that a conjunction of 'con-folen' would translate in the vernacular as 'cunt-bag', filthily funny to Guilhem's appreciative audience.[42]

Topsfield rendered 'cons' as 'a married woman who was guarded'. Horace was less reticent, using the word to mean a wife engaged in adultery. Martial was unashamedly explicit, *cunt*. He used it over thirty times. In his *Epigrams* alone there are many examples, none complimentary, 'hoary', 'licked', 'washed privately', 'aged', 'bony'.

Catullus, a poet unknown to Guilhem, used it: *meientis mulae cunnus* . . . 'a grin as wide as a mule's cunt pissing in a heat-wave'. The word occurs frequently in the graffiti scrawled on the walls of Pompeii and Herculaneum, particularly in the vicinity of brothels.[43] Guilhem had no scruples about using the term in his Poem III.

Companho tant ai agut d'avols conres . . .

Comrades, of many cunts I've been denied,
and I must sing about my injured pride,
but I don't want the mishaps gossiped far and wide.

even though he was broadcasting them himself – if the deprivations were not just imaginary jests. What, in fact, he was doing was making a hypocritical protest against false modesty that obstructed his desires:

No m'azauta cons gardatz
I don't care for a guarded cunt;

Qui anc premiers gardt cun
why not lay a curse on those who first guarded cunts?;

Con cals es sa leis
because here is the law of the cunt;

and

. . . e cons en cries

Cunts flourish with use just like nurtured
woodlands, cut one tree, three more grow.
It is wrong to cry 'damaged goods' when
there has been only benefit.

Guilhem was not complaining about non-existent chastity belts. Entirely selfishly, he protested against the unnecessarily obstructive irritants of over-protective husbands, sterile church morality, misplaced marital fidelity, silly maidens with fears of losing their virginity.

Orz es ca hom planh la tala quant negumdan la I a pres
'It is wrong to deplore a loss when there has been nothing but gain'.

Autocratic, arrogant, he could tolerate nothing that hindered his desires. He led an uninhibited life. Even when excommunicated as an adulterer for the second time by the Catholic Church, he refused to give up his current mistress, the famously beautiful Viscountess of Châtellerault, and installed her in one of his many households.

Stories about his behaviour were recorded by William of Malmesbury, an early twelfth-century Benedictine monk. A dispassionate historian of the Saxon and Norman kings of England, he was one of the more reliable medieval chroniclers. In his preference for using original sources – documents, visual evidence and anecdotal material – he was one of the pioneers of the historical method. Much that he wrote has been confirmed by later research. Although a churchman and therefore indignant about profanity, he quite faithfully described the count's character:

At that time lived William earl of Poictiers; a giddy unsettled kind of man; who after he returned from Jerusalem, wallowed as completely in the stye of vice, as though he had believed that all things were governed by chance, and not by Providence. Moreover, he rendered his absurdities pleasant by a show of wit; exciting the loud laughter of his hearers.

Finally, erecting, near a castle called Niort, certain buildings after the form of a little monastery, he used to talk idly about placing therein an abbey of prostitutes, naming several of the most abandoned courtesans, one as abbess, another as prioress; and declaring that he would fill up the rest of the offices in like manner.

Repudiating his lawful consort, he carried off the wife of a certain viscount [his mistress, Dangereuse, wife of Aimery. Guilhem nicknamed her 'Maubergeonne' as a caustic pun on the name of his castle's new and 'unpenetrable' keep], of whom he was so desperately enamoured, that he placed on his shield the figure of this woman; affirming, that he was desirous of bearing her in battle, in the same manner as she bore him at another time. Being reproved and excommunicated for this by Girard, bishop of

Angoulême, and ordered to renounce this illicit amour, 'You shall curl with a comb', said he, the hair that has forsaken your forehead, ere I repudiate the viscountess', thus taunting a man, whose scanty hair required no comb. Nor did lie less when Peter bishop of Poictou, a man of noted sanctity, rebuked him still more freely; and, when contumacious, began to excommunicate him publicly: for becoming furious, he seized the prelate by the hair, and flourishing his drawn sword, – 'You shall die this instant', said he, 'unless you give me absolution'.

The bishop, then, counterfeiting alarm, and asking leave to speak, boldly completed the remainder of the form of excommunication; suspending the earl so entirely from all Christian intercourse, that he should neither dare to associate nor speak with any one, unless he speedily recanted. Thus fulfilling his duty, as it appeared to him, and thirsting for the honour of martyrdom, stretched out his neck, saying, 'Strike, strike'.

But William, becoming somewhat softened, regained his usual pleasantry, and said, 'Certainly I hate you so cordially, that I will not dignify you by the effects of my anger, nor shall you ever enter heaven by the agency of my hand.'

After a short time, however, tainted by the infectious insinuations of this abandoned woman, he drove the rebuker of his incest into banishment; who there, making a happy end, manifested to the world, by great and frequent miracles, how gloriously he survives in heaven.

On hearing this, the earl abstained not from his inconsiderate speeches, openly declaring, that he was sorry he had not dispatched him before; that, so, his pure soul might chiefly have to thank him, through whose violence he had acquired eternal happiness.[44]

One can almost imagine a benign smile on the face of William of Malmesbury as he recorded Guilhem's un-Christian laughter. Perhaps the unfortunate Bishop of Poitiers was not of the Benedictine order.

William would not have smiled, however, if ever he read Poem V, *Farai un vers pos mi soneilh*, the most explicitly immoral of the count's repertoire. Known as the 'Story of the Red Cat', it had fifteen verses with an additional apocryphal but satisfyingly vengeful ending. If ever it had a forerunner it is lost. It certainly had a successor.

Two hundred years after its composition, the Italian writer Giovanni Boccaccio included an adaptation of it in his *Decameron*. Its theme was identical. A dumb man was the ideal provider of illicit sex to frustrated women.

A young, good-looking labourer, Masetto, pretended to be both deaf and dumb in order to become a gardener in a convent of nine nuns and an abbess. Unafraid of any scandalous revelations from a man who was speechless, the nuns used him continually and exhaustingly. Despairingly he went to the abbess, 'Madam', he groaned, 'they say that whereas a single cock is quite sufficient for ten hens, ten men are hard put to satisfy one woman'.[45] Despite the rather unfortunate translated choice of adjective, 'hard', it was a medieval belief that women were lustily insatiable. It is also interesting that there was no fear of a dumb man writing about his experiences. Or people reading them. For centuries literacy remained an unknown art for the majority.

In its direct language Guilhem's poem was barrack-room humour, but it was skilfully stylised, fifteen verses with a demanding rhyme scheme of A, A, A, B, A. B, the lines following a simple iambic beat. It also had profanity.

Another word was added to the vocabulary of Occitanian crudity, 'fotens', in the first line of verse 15, *Tant las fotei* . . . It derived from the Latin *futuo*, 'sexual intercourse' in polite translation but 'fucking' in Guilhem. Martial used it in his *Epigrams*:

   quod futuit Glaphyrum Antoninus
   'because Antony fucks Glaphyra'

Catullus used it in one of his scurrilous poems in a phrase that would have delighted Guilhem: *novem continuas fututione* ('nine uninterrupted fuckings'), although the count was to brag that he had done twenty times better.[46]

Here the complete poem is given in English by a variety of translators, of whom only Lindsay has attempted to follow the original format.

What must be appreciated is that its performance would not have been that of a child reciting poetry at a parents' evening. For those listening to Guilhem there would have been not only spoken words but significant pauses, whispers, gestures, eyebrows raised, lips licked. And music.

A well-trained minstrel was a one-man band, conversant with many instruments, and every event in the poem was enhanced: a pipe lilting like a woman's voice, twangs and ripples of a harp for the movements of clothes, trumpets at a climax, the suggestive dragging of a bow across the strings of a vièle. Enthusiastically it was also accompanied by the stamping feet of applause.

Poem V began with the drum plodding like horses' hooves.

1 *Farai un vers pos mi soneilh . . .*

I shall compose a song while I sleep,
Riding along in the sunshine.
There are ladies who are troublemakers,
And I can say which ones
Those who abuse
A knight's love.

2 *Domna fai gran pechat mortal.*

A lady commits a great and deadly sin
If she does not love the loyal knight
But becomes infatuated with a monk or cleric:
She is insane
And deserves to be burned
With a poker!

3 *In Alvernhe part Lemozi*

In Auvergne, past Limousin,
I was travelling alone in silence;
I met the wife of Sir Garin
And that of Sir Bernard.
They greeted me simply
By St Leonard.[47]

4 *La una.m diz en son latin:*

One of them said to me in her local speech,
'May God keep you, my lord pilgrim. By my
troth, you seem to me to have a very fine
character, for we see too many foolish (and
immoral) people travelling about the world'.[48]

5 *Ar auziretz qu'ai respondut . . .*

Now you shall hear my answer:
I said neither 'boo' nor 'bah'
Nor spoke of this or that;
My only words were,
'Barbariol, babariol,
barbarian'.

6 *So ditz Agnes a Ermesson . . .*

And then Agnes said to Ermesson
'We've found what we've been looking for,
By God; let's take him home with us,
He's mute all right,
And he'll never tell a soul
About the things we do'.[49]

7 *La una.m pres sotz sos mantel*

One of them took me under her cloak [nudity]
And this was just fine with me;
They led me to their 'hearth' [*fornelh* was an 'oven'. meaning sexual
    organ]
And the 'fire' [*foc* = vagina] was good,
And I warmed myself willingly
At the big coals ['good flesh'].[50]

8 *A manjar mi deron capos*

They gave me capons to eat, and I tell you
There were more than two of these;
And there was no cook there or scullion,
But only we three, and the bread was white
And the wine was good
And the pepper thick.[51]

There are double meanings in the 'bread' and the 'white' and the 'thick
pepper'. The hidden alternatives were not for polite society.

9 *Sor aquest hom es enginhos*

'Sister, I think he's a sly one;
Dropped his speech just for our account;
Let's bring out that big red tom-cat
Right this minute.
That'll loose his tongue in a hurry
If he's fooling.'

10 *Agnes anet per l'enujos*

Lady Agnes went out for the beast;
It was big and red and had long moustaches.
The minute I saw him come in,
I was scared;
I almost lost all of my courage
And my nerve.

11 *Quant aguem begut e manjat*

After we ate and we had some drinks
I shucked off my clothes as they asked,
And they brought up that cat behind me –
That evil thing!
And the one dragged him along my shank
Down to the heels.[52]

12 *Per la coa de mantenen*

They pulled his tail. The villain cat
Dug in his claws and tore and spat,
A hundred gashes laid me flat
Immediately.
But for my acting they would soon
Have ended me.

13 *Sor diz Anges a Ermesson*

Said Agnes after that, 'You hear!
He's dumb: that certainly is clear.
Come now, let's take our bath, my dear,
And then our pleasure.'
There, in that stew, eight days and more,
I lay at leisure.

14 *Tant las fotei com auziretz*

I fucked them,[53] I precisely state,
A hundred times, plus eighty-eight.
I thought I'd split my loins, the rate
Became excessive.

To tell the after-pains I find
No words expressive.[54]

15 *Ges no'us sai dir lo malaveg*

To tell the after-pains I find
No words expressive.[55]

A 16th verse was added as a medieval 'punch-line'.

16 *Monet, tu m'iras al mati*

Monet, you'll travel for me in the morning
You'll take my *vers* in the saddlebag
Directly to the wife of lord Garin
And to that of lord Bernard
And tell them, for the love of me,
To kill that cat![56]

Men tumbled from their benches in uncontrollable laughter at the climax.
Even the disapproving Ordericus Vitalis, Anglo-Norman historian and
Benedictine monk, was honest enough to write: 'he was daring, gallant,
and full of mirth, outdoing even the strolling players in the gaiety of his
entertainments.'

It is for this poem and its companions, I and III, that Guilhem is usually
remembered, a versifier of amusing but unrepeatable smut. Yet he was more:
an innovator of the celebration of spring and the world's reawakening. He
also wrote many lines of loveliness and sincerity, these from the third verse
of Poem X, *Ab la dolchor . . .*

La nostr' amor vai enaissi

Our love is like
the hawthorn branch
which, at night, trembles
beneath rain and ice
until day comes and the sun spreads
through the boughs and green leaves.[57]

He was the first of the troubadours, and those lines became a poetical
template for his poetical successors. He had no known predecessors. Nor
was there a contemporary except for the ephemeral and unworthy 'school'

of his noble friend Ebles II of Ventadorn, whose court was some 100 miles south-east of Poitiers, overlooking the drearily stunted oaks on the moors of Corrèze. Froissart called the viscount's fortress 'the strongest castle in the world'. Today it is a ruin.

A troubadour, Cercamon, dedicated a *planh*, 'lament', to Ebles on the death of Guilhem's son in 1147. Another troubadour of that period, Marcabru, wanted nothing to do with that nobleman. "I'll never be a singer in his school' because the viscount's court extolled the improper conquest of women even more blatantly than Guilhem. Troubadours at his castle seemed to be carrying on 'the lewder side of Guilhem IX with rejection of the courtly code'. No poem of that school survives.[58]

The first quarter of the twelfth century was uneasy but not widely calamitous. Battles were fought. Great men died. A famous woman was born. And there were troubadours. Some were of noble birth, others were impoverished bastards abandoned on doorsteps. But each of them sang the joys of courtly and courteous love, often in castle halls to ladies whose lord was often absent on some minor feud or raid. In the Holy Land, *Outre-mer*, 'across the sea', matters were quiet if not at peace. In France the Anglo-French conflict over Normandy continued. In 1119, almost by chance, the opposing armies converged at Brémule in the Vexin near Noyon.

For once Louis VI, 'The Fat', acted impulsively. His reproachful mentor, the ubiquitous Abbé Suger, wrote: 'King Louis and his men thought it unworthy to plan carefully for battle and rushed against the foe in a bold but careless attack.' The two armies were small, the fighting was brief, but the French defeat left Normandy firmly under the control of Henry I, King of England.[59]

Three years later Eleanor of Aquitaine was born, perhaps in the palace of Poitiers, or of Bordeaux, or in the nearby castle of Bélin. In 1136 the lords of Aquitaine swore allegiance to her on her fourteenth birthday. Some years later her dalliance with the attractive troubadour, Bernart of Ventadorn, was one of the royal scandals of the early Middle Ages.[60]

Earlier, far away in Persia, the world lost a poet, one not as proficient as Guilhem nor as gifted as Bernart but far better known than either of them. Fifteen hundred miles east of Jerusalem and twice that distance from Poitiers, a contemporary of Guilhem, the Sufi philosopher Omar Khayyam, died in Naishapur in Persia. He is acclaimed throughout the world for his *Rubaiyat* and its cynical fatalism of 'eat, drink and be merry for tomorrow we die', but, ironically, it was not Khayyam's verses but Edward Fitzgerald's wondrous – and inaccurate – paraphrase of 1869 that has delighted and enthralled readers.[61] Even more ironically, like Thomas Bowdler's 'family' Shakespeare, Fitzgerald's *Rubaiyat* was also purified. Objecting to the frequent references to alcoholic drink, a later translator of the *Rubaiyat* in 1883, E.H. Winfield, decided to 'exclude from this translation a number of quatrains in praise of wine, and exhortations to live for the day, which occur in the manuscript with the most wearisome frequency'.[62] No one reads Winfield today.

The treble irony is that in the beginning no one read Fitzgerald either. Anonymously published in a plain brown paper wrapper in 1859 and priced at five shillings, his first edition, a 'transmogrification' of Omar Khayyam, was ignored. Only two years later it was being sold on secondhand stalls for a penny. Today a first edition is worth several thousand pounds.[63] Khayyam's death occurred in 1131, four or five years later than that of Guilhem of Poitiers in 1126/7. He was buried a few miles outside Naishapur (see Appendix 2).

Guilhem, 9th Duke of Aquitaine and 7th Count of Poitiers, was interred with rich ceremony in Poitier's Montierneuf church, the 'new monastery', that his father had endowed only some thirty years earlier. It was consecrated by Pope Urban II in 1096. Of its four steeples, two were wrecked and a third damaged by Calvinists in the sixteenth century. The church is in the north of Poitiers, near the aptly named Musicians' Quarter with its charming streets of medieval houses. Ecclesiastical history claims that Guilhem rests undisturbed in a sealed chapel beneath the pavement.

Even though born in Poitiers, closer to Paris than to Toulouse, Guilhem was Occitanian in heart, and his language had far more of the Languedoc than of France in it. Poem IV expressed his preference

Qu'anc non ac Norman ai Frances
For I have had neither Norman nor Frenchman in my house.

The same poem provided a strange anticipation of what was almost immediately to follow him. From lines in Poem IV's verses 6 and 7 Guilhem was seemingly in love with a woman that he had never seen:

Anc no la vi e am la for

Never have I seen her but I love her greatly,
She has never done me right or wrong . . .

No sai lo luec ves on s'esta

I know not the place where she lives
Whether it is in the hills or in the plain . . .

　·　·　·　·　·
And it saddens me that she remains here
When I am leaving.

Just a few years before Guilhem died, an even finer singer of lyrical poetry, Jaufré Rudel of Blaye, was already composing songs. He also loved an unseen woman, someone 2,000 miles away, unattainable overseas.

Guilhem, Duke of Aquitaine and Count of Poitiers, brought the music of the south to his homeland, blended it with church rhythms and the coarseness of Martial. Innovator, pursuer of women, lover of mirth and melody, he was the man that began the great tradition of romantic poetry in Western Europe.

And Poictiers, you know, Guillaume Poictiers
Had brought the song up out of Spain
With the singers and viels . . .

Ezra Pound, Canto VIII
(lines near the end of its very many unnumbered lines)

FIVE

Jaufré Rudel

No sap chantar qui so non di
He can't sing who has no melody
> (Jaufré Rudel of Blaye, Poem VI, 1)

Nuihls hom no.y. s meravilh de m[1]

No man should be astonished at my theme
that I love an unseen lady although we
may never meet. For this is joy to me
to think of her as someone in a dream.
No other joy's so strong in my esteem,
Though uncertain what good it can be.
> (Jaufré Rudel, Poem VI, 2)

Jaufré Rudel and Two Loves: Near and Afar, to AD 1150

During the Middle Ages, Rudel's love for a lady unknown to him save by report, was not looked upon as ridiculous or even odd, and . . . it never occurred to any one to doubt the truth of the beautiful story.

(Barbara Smythe, 1929, 12)

The nobleman Jaufré Rudel was born during an exciting and contrasting half century between 1100 and 1150. A second crusade was called in 1147 after the Muslims had captured Edessa, a city in a convenient buffer state above the northern border of the Christian kingdom of Jerusalem.

In the preceding years there had been affairs of love as well as war. Jaufré Rudel himself had two loves, one whose castle was many miles from his own, another who lived even more distant, miles across the sea at Tripoli.

A higher-born woman, Eleanor of Aquitaine, would be rushed past Tripoli by her husband, Louis VII, following her suspected earlier dalliance with her host and uncle.

Jaufré Rudel may also have suffered for love. Prince or Viscount of Blaye, he was born at the beginning of the twelfth century, and was probably an earlier kinsman of the Jaufré Rudel who accompanied Savaric de Mauléon on their frustrated wooing of that virginal vamp Guilhelma.

The first Rudel became lord of Blaye as a young man some time after 1126. His date of birth is unknown. Except for the most illustrious of persons, no scribe bothered with anniversaries. Even the year of the death of that powerful Duke of Aquitaine. Guilhelm, is uncertain, probably 1126 but maybe 1127. One can only guess that the new lord of Blaye was in his very early twenties.

Blaye, a port on the river Garonne, had a long and important history. Henry II of England witnessed the marriage of his son, Richard, later the Lionheart, to the daughter of the King of Aragon at Blaye in 1160.

Earlier, Rudel's father had rashly defied Guilhelm, Duke of Aquitaine, who, troubadour or not, was imperative as an overlord and retaliated by having the town's walls and keep dismantled. It was that hastily rebuilt fortress that Jaufré Rudel inherited.

It was in Blaye's St Romaine church that the heroes of Roncesvalles, Roland and Oliver, were buried in their elaborate tomb. Almost all the town was destroyed by the military engineer Sébastien Vauban in 1683, when he remodelled it as a citadel to become one of a ring of fortifications that cordoned France. The tomb was destroyed during the French Revolution. Little remains of Rudel's Blaye.

He was born in a brutal age. Fathers had complete control of their family. They could kill wives or sons without condemnation. Theft by night meant death. Any captured murderer was buried alive below the corpse of his victim. It was an age of decisive retribution, whether domestic, political or ecclesiastical.

Jaufré Rudel was one of the earliest and most accomplished of troubadours, and he wrote beautifully:

Qan lo rius de la fontana . . .

When the fountain's stream runs clear
and the wild rose appears,
And the nightingale begins to sing,
Making his song soft and gentle,
It is seemly I should make
My words and music just as lovely.   (Poem II)

Despite the calm words, Rudel was to experience the effects of family retribution when one of his affairs brought retaliation from the woman's relatives.

In 1137 Eleanor of Aquitaine, granddaughter of Guilhem, was married to the 16-year-old Prince Louis, who was almost morbidly pious and who within a week became King Louis VII.

Celebrations after the wedding in Bordeaux were lavish. Luxurious varieties of food were served, fine wines were poured and there were constant entertainments. Being so close to Blaye, and being a nobleman, Jaufré Rudel was probably among the crowds of guests. There would also have been professional troubadours, possibly including Cercamon and Marcabru. The problem with such singers and their jokes was that what was amusing to southern ears was offensive filth to the grimmer minds of the north.

Marcabru's misogynistic melodies about unfaithful married women – *putas ardens* (flaming whores) he termed them, 'Lady Goodandexcited', 'those cunts that are nymphomaniacs in bed' – might have seemed appropriate at a wedding banquet to the carefree people of Aquitaine but not to the priggish prelates of Paris.[2]

Had Eleanor been observed to laugh by any of those scowling bishops they would have concluded that for its future queen France had acquired a woman no better than a harlot from the alleyways of Babylon. It was not a good beginning.

The year 1137 was also a critical one for the crusades, for France and for England. It was the year in which Saladin, formidable and brilliant Muslim opponent of the crusaders, was born. It was the year when Matilda, daughter of Henry I of England, married Geoffrey Plantagenet, Count of Anjou.

King Henry had made Matilda his heiress after the tragic death of his son when *The White Ship* in which the prince was sailing crashed drunkenly into rocks outside Barfleur in 1120. Henry I died in 1135, but Matilda was denied the throne by Stephen of Blois, grandson of William the Conqueror, the first Norman king of England, and the ensuing civil war almost ruined England. It was only when Stephen died in 1154 that Matilda's son became Henry II. He had married the divorced Eleanor of Aquitaine two years earlier.[3]

Important though they were, it is unlikely that these political disruptions disturbed the poetical life of Jaufré Rudel. But they were the beginnings of a struggle between France and England that would decide the history of the troubadours, just as the determination of the Catholic Church to eradicate the blasphemous heresy of the Cathars would cause its end in France.

Little is known of Jaufré Rudel's private life. When he began composing is conjectural, although it is thought the decade before 1147 was a flourishing one for him. Six, perhaps seven, of his poems survive, four with melodies, a very high proportion.[4] (For his compact discs see Appendix 1.)

Admired troubadour though he was, there is more of romance than reality in stories about him. The so-called biographies, the medieval *vidas*, of troubadours were interesting but frequently untrustworthy. Ida Furnell remarked on the contradiction when writing about Rudel 'The following is one of the most beautiful of the Lives, but also, it is to be feared, one of the least authentic; it has in it all the extravagance and the delicate unearthliness that is the essence of the ideal Provençal chivalry.'[5] It was a strange 'Life'.

Jaufres Rudel de Blaia so fo molts gentils hom, princes de Blaia . . .

Jaufré Rudel of Blaye was a right noble prince of Blaye, and it chanced that though he had not seen, he loved the Countess of Tripoli for her excellence and virtue, of which the pilgrims coming from Antioch spread abroad the tidings.

And he made of her fair songs, with fine melodies but with poor words, till he longed so greatly to see her, that he took the Cross and embarked upon the sea to gain sight of her.[6]

The 'Life' was based more on hearsay than fact and was probably written by Uc de Saint-Circ some fifty years after Rudel's death. 'Poor words' did not mean clumsily chosen but the use of simple and direct language. Yet some critics have performed intellectual contortions over the poems to create non-existent complexities, turning the unseen lady into a confusion of real-remote-imagined-mysterious unlikelihoods.

The Italian Petrarch thought so highly of the troubadour that Jaufré Rudel became one of only fifteen to be included in the poet's *Triofoni d'Amore.*

Rudel was a romantic lyricist and, possibly, also an escapist. Of all the troubadours his poems were the most elusive with surfaces as calm as a quiet sea but covering depths that swirled with powerful currents.[7]

His love for the unseen Countess of Tripoli was stated in his *vida* as a fact, one so astonishing that it was remembered long after his death. Rudel himself, *in Quan lo rius de la fontana,* apparently referred to her in the second stanza.

> *Amors de terra loingdana . . .*
> *Per vos totz lo cors mi dol*

> Oh love of a distant land,
> for you my whole body aches   (Poem II, stanza 2)

Nothing is certain, not even the identity of the seemingly incontestable 'Countess of Tripoli'. His 'Distant Love' may have been a genuine countess, Odierna, the unhappy wife of Count Raymond II of Tripoli, an obsessively possessive husband who kept her almost imprisoned against the world around her.

By 1152 the marriage was so bad that Odierna's eldest sister, Mélisande, Queen of Jerusalem, came to Tripoli to arrange a marital truce, and it was agreed that Odierna should go to Jerusalem for a break. Raymond II accompanied them for a short distance. But perhaps, being the Christian warlord of Tripoli, he became the prey of assassins who ambushed him outside the gate of his town and slew him. Odierna became regent and oversaw the upbringing of her young son, Raymond III.

She had three sisters, Mélisande, married to Fulke V of Jerusalem; Alice, wife of Bohemond II, Prince of Antioch; and Yvette, Abbess of Saint-Lazare. None was ever Countess of Tripoli.

No alternatives are known. Odierna's daughter, also a Mélisande, beautiful and good, had an unjustly questionable legitimacy because of her parents' quarrels and was jilted by her intended husband, the elderly widowed ruler of Constantinople. Already ill, she died in 1161, not yet 20 years of age. Her mother, Odierna, Countess of Tripoli, was still alive.[8]

In their anxiety to identify the elusive woman adored by Jaufré Rudel some editors have even disembodied the lady, transforming her into a metaphor for the crusaders' goal of the city of Jerusalem or the Holy Land itself. Other scholars thought she was the most worshipped of all women, the Virgin Mary. More imaginative but less probable suggestions have been the idyllic but legendary Helen of Troy, even the living Eleanor of Aquitaine.

As a final frustration, Rudel's 'distant love' may have been no one, just an imaginary personification of a perfect woman, never to be known, platonically to be adored from afar.

There is one other possibility, puzzlingly unmentioned elsewhere. It may be that Odierna, weary of her enforced semi-imprisonment and, like her sisters, by nature headstrong and full of gaiety, heard rumours of an unknown and remote admirer. The disenchanted wife and beautiful countess, learning also that the intriguing stranger intended to visit Tripoli, may have considered the pleasures of a discreet flirtation. It is possible.

Rudel lived at the beginning of the great time of the troubadours. It became a world of music. It was a time when rich courts and shabby backstreet taverns were learning the loveliness of song.

There had been minstrels for generations, entertainers who went from town to town with their repertoire of well-known songs and stories. Also known as *jongleurs*, 'jugglers', the word reveals their variety as performers, singing, dancing, and playing instruments. They went everywhere where there was patronage: Toulouse, Castile, Barcelona, Normandy, even England. Some were well born, which explains their easy manners in courts. Some were *jongleurs* with bad reputations, 'base, treacherous, debauched, drunken, lying bar-proppers of taverns'.

William Langland, the contemporary of Chaucer, knew of them:

And somme chosen chaffare. They cheuen the bettere,
As it semeth to owre sygt . that such menne thriveth;
And somme murthes to make as mystralles conneth,
And geten gold with here glee . giltles I leve.
Ac iapers & iangeleres . Judas chylderen,
Feynen hem fantasies. And foles hem maketh,
And han here witte at wille . to worche, zif they sholde
(*The Vision of Piers Plowman*, Prologue, 33–6)

which has been translated as:

Then there were the professional entertainers, some of whom, I think, are harmless minstrels, making an honest living by their music; but others, babblers and vulgar jesters, are true Judas' children. They invent fantastic stories about themselves, and pose as half-wits, and yet they show wits enough whenever it suits them, and could easily work for a living if they had to!

Among such rogues were 'goliards'. They were performers with a difference. They were tonsured clerks who had forsaken their calling for the more amusing, more perilous existence as wandering minstrels. 'Ribald clerics', the Church condemned them, 'ruffians', spendthrift vagrants, with their frequently indecent repertoire of songs in Latin, French and German. They became so numerous that they established a bogus order of their own with a bogus Golias as their Grand Master. They sang, they begged, they drank.

A few prospered. William the Conqueror gave one *3 vils and 5 carucates* in Gloucestershire three – parishes and five plots of land, each large enough to need eight oxen to plough yearly. Most goliards, however, lived for the day, or, more longingly, for the night, singing where they could, eating and drinking wherever there was chance. Chance brought a German goliard to Orléans:

Were div werlt alle min . . .

Were the world's great lands all mine
From the seas unto the Rhine,
I'd forgo their wealth and charms
If England's queen could be in my arms.

In song 10 of his musical adaptation of the *Carmina Burana*, Carl Orff set the verse to music: a tribute both to the goliard's skill as a poet and to the attraction of the glimpsed Eleanor of Aquitaine, King Henry II's wife.

The greatest of the goliards, known as the Arch Poet, is anonymous. Despite his fame and the delicacy of his verse, the patrons he entertained and the probability that he was German, he has no name. Among his works is what Helen Waddell described as 'the world's greatest drinking song', his *Confession*, with its twelfth verse:

. . . In taberna mori,
Ut sint vina proxima
Morientis ori . . .

When the hour of Death comes by
Let me in the tavern die
With a jar of wine close by.

Fitzgerald's Omar Khayyam would have understood (see Appendix 2).[9]

It was from that itinerant rabble of the pedestrian and the inspired that the troubadours developed. They were similar but better. They were musicians who wrote their own words, composed their own melodies, some as a soloist, some with a minstrel as an accompanist. Among the pioneers who followed Guilhelm of Poitiers were Jaufré Rudel, Marcabru and Cercamon.

Cercamon was one of the first troubadours, but, in contrast to Guilhelm, Rudel and Marcabru, he was mediocre. He was accorded only the briefest biographies by his medieval chronicler.

Cercamos si fo uns joglars de Gascoigna . . .

He was a singer from Gascony. He wrote pastorels in the old style. He went all over the place and for his travels he was nicknamed cherche-monde, 'search the world'.

Little more is known. He wrote *pastorelas*, pretty poems in which a nobleman and poet, passing by a lovely shepherdess, stopped and offered her his love. After modest hesitation she accepted. None of those poems has survived, and we have only five of his other compositions, not one with a tune. One rather self-conscious poem is quite well known.

Plas es lo vers, vauc l'afinan

The poem is plain and I have refined it,
Removing all vile, false and misused words.
It has been so improved
that it has only the most polished language
and it will be improved still farther
if it is sung and performed with artistry.[10]

Such men were the precursors of a Golden Age of courtly music. Many of their verses survive, but of their music there are only whispers. Instruments are known, the stringed harp, psaltery, lyre, harp, trumpet, cornet, pipe, flute, the cornemuse or early bagpipe, the orgue (organ), the percussive tambourine, cymbal and drum. Modern renditions have been recorded, but there are inescapable problems.

Of more than 2,500 poems, fewer than 300 have surviving melodies. What does exist in manuscript is so simplified that it is unknown whether or how it was orchestrated, how many instruments were involved, how many instrumentalists, how many singers, at what speed, what pauses

were needed to allow the player to draw breath. It is a loss but it is not a
vacuum. The troubadours lived and they brought art and loveliness to the
Languedoc.

Jaufré Rudel was a far better poet than Cercamon. In one of his songs
spring was celebrated in the manner that Guilhelm of Poitiers had
innovated.

Lan qan li jorn son lonc e mai

When days grow long again in May
I hear birds singing far away.
That pleasure passes even as I stray,
thinking of a love unknown, never to hold.
In solitude I mourn, live empty hours
When songs of birds nor hawthorn flowers
Can bring more cheer than winter's lifeless cold.   (Poem V, stanza 1)

It seems, however, that there had been a time before that ethereal wraith
when Rudel was enraptured by another woman, also distant but this time
real. She lived a long way from Blaye.

Luenh es lo castells e la tors . . .
Far is the castle and the tower   (Poem III, stanza 3)

In an age when nobles visited other courts and were welcomed, his
nameless love may have required two, three, even more days journeying for
him. As for every anxious lover, the ride seemed endless. In his Poem I he
feared he would never reach her.

Quant lo rosignols el fuoillos
D'aquest' amor son tan cochos . . .

When the nightingale amongst the leaves . . .
With eager heart I ride to meet
My lady before my heart should break.
I gallop forward. She does retreat,
My horse goes backward, hooves seem to brake,
So slow our plod the snails overtake.
Unless she halts I ride in vain.
I'll never reach her. Miles seem years.   (I, stanza 2)[11]

But he did reach her, imagining, hoping, longing for her favours.

A! com son sei dit amoros

Ah! How loving are her words,
How sweet and pleasing what she does.
Never, anywhere, was there born
Anyone with such loveliness.
She would be good to me
If she made me a gift of her love.
She has a fine, firm, fair body
With not one blemish.
And her love is pure and good for me.   (Poem I, stanza 4)

But there was the inevitable problem.

Far is the castle and the tower
Where she sleeps – her husband too.

These were centuries when young girls were domestic commodities to
be traded in marriage for monetary gain, to end a feud, to settle a debt,
for protection. Unwanted, unmarried teenage girls were despatched to
nunneries, not always to their liking. 'This nunnery confines me', wailed
one in a long *motet*.[12]

Je suis jolïete . . .

I am a merry
Gracious, charming
Young girl,
Not yet fifteen.
My little breasts are swelling
With time.
I should be learning
About love and turning my mind
To its delightful
Ways;
But I have been put in prison

Honnis soit de Diu qui me fist nonnerie!
May God curse the one who made me a nun!

Also there were unhappy marriages, sometimes affairs. Illicit love
demanded care. Methods of contraception were ineffective and pregnancy

could be dangerous. Few dark-headed husbands looked complacently at babies with ginger hair.

Guiraut de Bornelh, a later troubadour than Rudel, and a better one, knew the problem:

> *E si.s n,apercep lo gilos?*
> 'What if her husband catches me?'

> *Adonc n'obraretz plus ginhos.*
> 'There's no danger if you both are careful.'[13]

And sometimes even innocent flirtation brought physical punishment. A *trouvère* (a title given to both male and female troubadours in northern France) composed a ballad about an unhappy young wife, the 'Chanson de Malmarié'.

> *Por coi me bait mes maris?*
> Why does my husband beat me?

> *Laissette!*
> Poor blameless girl!

> *Je ne li de rienz meffis*

> I've done him no wrong,
> said nothing against him
> just embraced my lover,
> all alone
> Why does my husband beat me?
> Poor blameless girl!

> *Et s'il ne mi lait dureir*

> And if he won't let me be,
> to lead a good life,
> I'll have him proclaimed a cuckold.
> without a doubt.
> Why does my husband beat me?
> Poor blameless girl!

> *Or sai bienque je ferai*

I know exactly what to do,
how I'll get my revenge:
I'll lie in bed with my lover –
Naked!.
Why does my husband beat me?
Poor blameless girl![14]

For Rudel the existence of a husband and of a brother suspicious of the poet's hopes meant a secret meeting place was needed near the castle, somewhere where he and 'his' woman could meet in privacy. They arranged a place for what Press termed 'a low, furtive, adulterous and humiliating type of love',[15] although that is not how the two would have thought it.

According to Rudel there was no fulfilment. Instead, one night she came to him, not for love but to warn him of danger.

Mas tart mi vi a tart mi ditz

But late she came and late she told me
'Dear friend, rough and angry people
are in such a passion that it will be long
before we can enjoy each other'   (Poem III, stanza 6)

The message came too late.

Mielhs mi fora jazer vestitz

It would have been better being clothed
than lying naked under a sheet.
And I can tell you, without reservation,
about the night when I was badly assaulted.
I will always recall my humiliation
when they went away laughing,
leaving me in tears – harsh memories!   (Poem IV, stanza 6)

What Rudel had suffered is uncertain. Whether it left him, as earlier it had Abelard, scholar and seducer of Héloïse (see Appendix 3), an emasculated eunuch 'we shall probably never know, but it is tempting to answer in the affirmative, for this would do much to explain the haunting melancholy of his verse'.[16]

There was worse for Rudel. After shame came frustration and resentment.

Que tot can lo fraire.m desditz

What the brother has denied me
I know the sister enjoys elsewhere.   (Poem IV, stanza 7)

Jaufré Rudel, troubadour and abased lover, was transformed into a visionary. Remote adoration of a hearsay woman a world away from France was greatly to be preferred, and considerably safer, than the worship of a bodily woman, sister of a vindictive and over-protective brother.

Qu.ie.m temp per ris e per manen

And let it be known
That I am now rich and blessed
Because I am rid of my mad burden.   (Poem IV, stanza 8)

Matters overseas encouraged him. In 1144 the fortified city of Edessa, one of four Christian fortified citadels acting as northern bulwarks against an infidel drive towards Jerusalem, was overrun by the Muslims, who prised open the gateway to the south. Antioch would be next. From there it was hardly 300 miles to the Holy City. In alarm, the new Pope, Eugenius III, proclaimed the Second Crusade. Jaufré Rudel vowed to join it, both in dedication to the cause and in the hope that he might at last meet his distant love. .

The troubadour wrote what is often considered to be his finest work, Poem V, the spelling of whose first line varies, *Lanquan le jorn son lonc en may* 'When days are growing long in May . . .' to which there is an existing, very haunting melody.

'That strain again! It had a dying fall:
O! it came o'er my ear like the sweet sound
That breathes upon a bank of violets'.
                    (Shakespeare, *Twelfth Night*, I. 1. 4–6)

It is a strange poem and a clever one. Its seven stanzas are full of ambiguities and contradictions but its structure is as rigid as a block of concrete. Thoughts swing from secular to religious, from physical to spiritual, but everything is held together by the repetition of *loing* (far distance), as an identical rhyme at the end of lines 2 and 4 in each verse. *Loing* is also placed close to *amor* in a 'mysterious linking of love and distance that dominates the poem'.[17]

A further voluntary imposition by the poet was to have the end of the seventh line rhyme with the seventh line in all the other stanzas.

Lanquan le jorn son lonc en may . . .

When days are growing long in May
I like the lilting songs of birds from afar,
For as in distress I wander away
I am reminded of a love from afar;
And drift sadly through mournful hours,
When neither song nor bright hawthorn flowers
Pleases me more than winter's frozen snow.

Never shall I enjoy love, only despair,
If I do not enjoy this love from afar.
No nobler lady do I know, nor fair,
Anywhere near or far.
Her name is so worthy, true and fine
That to the very Saracens' kingdom, were she mine,
I would, for her, a willing captive go.

Frustrated I'll depart, both sad and gay
In hope of seeing this love afar,
When I'll be there to see her no man can say
For our lands are very far:
There are many ports and passes, roads between.
I am not a prophet, the outcome's unforeseen.
It must be as it pleases God so.

When I find her, indeed, joy will come to me
For the love of God, the love from afar
And if by fortune, I should chance to be
Near her, although I am far.
Our harmonious conversations will resound
With her gentle words when my love is found.
Farewell to sorrow, no more woe.

I hold indeed that lord to be great
Through whom I shall see the love from afar:
Except that one thing remains my fate.
I have two sorrows – because she is so far.
And, Ah! Would that I were a pilgrim that

My staff, my cloak my cockleshelled hat
Might in her lovely eyes reflected glow.

God who made all that lives and dies
And guaranteed this love from afar,
Give me strength. I have a heart that cries
That soon I may see that love from afar.
If in some nearby place she were in my sight
Then, whether chamber or garden, it might
To me forever into a splendrous palace grow.

He speaks truth who accuses me of greed
And desirous of love from afar,
For no joy pleases me more than that I need,
The enjoyment of love from afar;
But what I want is also what I hate,
For thus did a godfather decree my fate –
That I should love but no love know.

What I want is also what I hate,
Cursed be that godfather who should state
That none to me would her love show.   (Poem V)

Rudel was not isolated in his idiosyncrasy. Other poets of his times loved
women they had not seen. In his fourth poem, *Farai un vers* 'a poem about
absolutely nothing', Guilhem of Poitiers proclaimed:

Amigu'ai ieu, no sai qui s'es
I have a loved one, I don't know who she is

Qu'anc non la vi
For I've never seen her . . .

Raimbaut d'Orange, also known as Raimon d'Aurenga, wrote that he
had an idyllic love for the renowned Countess of Urgell near Toulouse.
They never met, but when, years later, she became a nun, she is supposed
to have to have said that 'if he had come she would have granted him
his pleasure and permitted him to touch her bare leg with the back of
his hand' (*tocado la camba nuda*)[8] – meaningless until it is remembered that
women wore nothing beneath their skirt.
    Another, Bernart-Arnaut d'Armagnac, heard stories of the attractive
but never seen by him Lady Lombarde of Toulouse. He went to her and

'il demeure avec elle en grande intimité, la requite d'amour et fut son ami intime'[19] – an intimacy that had the happiest ending of these detached romances.

Rudel had loved real women but spurned them after his mishap, preferring the safety of his imaginary ideal. He joined the Second Crusade, in the hope of visiting Tripoli. There were two ways of reaching the Holy Land, overland or by sea (see Fig. 3). He chose to sail. Louis VII, King of France, preferred the land.

The obsessively religious Louis neurotically vowed to expiate his unintended massacre at Vitry-sur-Marne in 1143, where attackers setting fire to thatched cottages caused flames to reach the church in which panicking villagers had sheltered. Over a thousand were burned alive in a town known for years afterwards as Vitry-le-Brûlé. 'King Louis, moved by pity, is said to have wept, and some hold that on this account he undertook his pilgrimage to Jerusalem.'[20]

Ignoring Urban II's earlier edict following the debacle of Peter the Hermit's 'crusade' that no women, elderly persons or children should ever again go on such an expedition, Louis took his wife with him. 'She had . . . so bewitched the young man's affections by the beauty of her of her person . . . he felt himself . . . so strongly attached to his young bride, he resolved not to leave her behind.'[21]

Eleanor likened herself to Panthesilia, Queen of the Amazons at the siege of Troy, and she and her women attendants 'dressed in cherry red boots and white tunics, with the crimson cross splashed across their breasts, galloped on white horses over the hillside at Vézelay brandishing swords and spurring the faint-hearted to heed the call of the Almighty'.[22]

Unfortunately for that full-blooded and high-spirited young woman, her husband had sworn a vow of total chastity for the duration of the crusade.

Even in France he was said to abstain from intercourse throughout Lent, from Ash Wednesday from the first day of Easter to Holy Sunday, and at Advent, the four Sundays preceding Christmas, all saints' Feast Days, the vigils of major festivals, the week before Pentecost, Whit Sunday, and often Wednesdays, Fridays, and Saturdays throughout the year. Unsurprisingly, the royal couple had no children.

Eleanor bitterly remembered such self-inflicted denial. 'I thought I had married a king and found I had married a monk.'[23]

The crusading army left on the feast day of St Denis, patron saint of France. The 'crusade' was a farce, badly arranged, a disastrous campaign with two leaders, Conrad III of Germany and Louis, on separate routes, with no plan of campaign and chain of command. Their armies never met.

After three tedious months Louis reached Constantinople, whose inhabitants remembered the rapacity of earlier crusaders and would not admit him. Baskets of food were lowered from the walls in return for advance payment. By trickery, the departure of the French was delayed until it was too late. On 26 October, at Dorylaeum, nine-tenths of the German army were slaughtered by the Turks.

Louis defiantly continued towards the Holy Land. Choosing the shorter, more dangerous coastal road and ignoring orders always to camp on high ground, the French pitched their tents in a more congenial valley. It was muttered that it was Eleanor's decision. That night the encampment was bloodily overrun by Seljuk Turks.

The survivors trudged 40 agonisingly foodless miles towards the coast. There, Louis and his entourage, starving, paid for ships to cross the strait. The soldiers were left to continue an endless, often lethal march. Their king wept.[24]

For the king, his wife and his entourage life became better. On 19 March 1148, Raymond, lord of Antioch, grandson of Guilhem of Poitiers, and uncle to Eleanor, rode 10 miles to greet them at the port. He was tall, handsome, courageous and unfailingly courteous. After the coarse and uncouth manners of the French court, he was a delight to Eleanor, a woman more of Poitiers than of Paris.

She was comfortable at Antioch. It was a fine city with eastern manners of decency and cleanliness. The dour French were appalled at its decadence. Its inhabitants

> dressed like Saracens in silken turbans and flowing *burnous*, their ladies' faces painted against the sun. To a visitor from the primitive west the luxury of their villas seemed sinful; outside there were courtyards, rooftop gardens and fountains and wells with water piped from mighty aqueducts; inside there were mosaic floors, carpets on to which sit, tableware of gold, silver and faience, coffers inlaid with ivory and sandalwood, sunken baths and beds with sheets . . . Obviously the queen enjoyed it all.

There was even the additional pleasure of hearing the *langue d'Oc* spoken, as many of the officials came from the south of France.[25]

The friendship and ease between Eleanor and Raymond created jealous eyes. Raymond wanted crusaders to attack Edessa against the great war leader, Nur al-Din, emir of Aleppo, before he could attack Antioch. Louis doubted the honesty of the southerner and refused to help him, even though the recapture of Edessa had been the entire purpose of the crusade. The single-mindedly religious king was obsessed with a determination to reach Jerusalem.

The days passed. Raymond and Eleanor talked and laughed together, often away from the company. In the background there was a different kind of talk. Suspecting minds searched for signs of scandalous infidelity, and, like the silken adhesions of spiders, doubts became enmeshed in minds. Chroniclers, almost all of them churchmen, none of them in Antioch, many writing years later, formed opinions.

The abbot, Suger, was discreet in his advice to Louis. 'Concerning the Queen, your wife, I suggest you conceal the uneasiness she is causing you, until after you have returned to your kingdom when you can decide dispassionately about that and other matters.'

Others differed. To John of Salisbury: 'The attentions paid by the prince to the queen, and his constant, indeed almost continuous, conversation with her, aroused the distrustful king's suspicions. These were greatly strengthened when the queen wished to remain behind' - as she did later following her ill-treatment from Louis.

Richard of Devizes was ambivalent: 'Many know what I would none of us know. This same queen, during the time of her first husband, was at Jerusalem [Antioch]. Let no one say any more about it; I too know it well. Keep silent!'

Thirty years after Antioch William of Tyre was less equivocal. 'Her conduct before and after this time showed her to be, as we have said, far from circumspect. Contrary to her royal dignity, she disregarded her marriage vows and was unfaithful to her husband.'

There were other suspicions in clerical minds. 'Scandal spoke of liaisons with her uncle, Count Raymond of Tripoli, and with Henry's father, Geoffrey of Anjou,' Henry being her second husband, the later Henry II, king of England.

The moralising troubadour Cercamon accepted the rumours about the queen. 'She has no worth from this time on . . . better for her never to have been born rather than to have committed the fault which will be talked about as far away as Poitou.'

The better troubadour Marcabru also referred to the matter, although more obliquely. He was well known for his moralising satires and attacks. 'And much was his name noised about in the world, and much was he feared because of his tongue. For so slanderous was he that, at the last, he was done to death by the chatelains of Guyenne of whom he had spoken much ill.'[26]

He had heard of the scandal. In a late poem of about 1149 he wrote:

Lo vers e.l son vouill enviar
A.N Jaufre Rudel outra mer

I wish to send this poem and the melody
To Sir Jaufré Rudel, over the sea;
And I would that the Frenchmen heard it
So as to gladden their hearts,
For God can grant them this;
Wherever sin is, may there be mercy.[27]

The 'sin' among the French was presumably the sins of their shamed queen and the busy tattling about her disgraceful indiscretions. News of such scandal had obviously travelled quickly, even across sea and land.

Whether Eleanor was an adulteress has been disputed for centuries. According to William of Tyre, Raymond was 'no glutton, no drunkard, no womaniser'. Conversely, Eleanor was described by the anti-feminist Bernard of Clairvaux as 'one of those daughters of Belial who put on airs, walk with heads high, and with mincing steps, got up and adorned like a temple'.[28]

As Raymond and she were uncle and niece, a sexual relationship would have been religious incest, and fear of Hell's-fire may have discouraged any carefree concupiscence.

It has been observed: 'In the face of all the reliable contemporary evidence, it is puzzling to find that most of Eleanor's modern biographers do not accept that she had an adulterous affair with Raymond.'[29] Yet clerical guesswork about ancient rumours does not constitute certainty. If a verdict has to be decided, it would be the ambivalent Scottish 'Not Proven', one that condemns more than it acquits.

Guesswork became belief. Louis acted. On the advice of his spiteful eunuch Thierry Galeran, whom the queen hated and mocked, one night 'she was snatched and forced to leave for Jerusalem'. It was a shameful abduction. 'His departure was so ignominious, and there was no concealing the fact that the Queen was in disgrace.'[30]

The party hustled southwards under claustrophobic security, passed Margab, avoided Tripoli and on May 1148 reached Jerusalem. Louis was elated, but the disorganised crusade had not only failed militarily but had disgraced itself. Henry of Huntingdon decried the so-called crusaders who had 'abandoned themselves to open fornication and to adulteries hateful to God, and to robbery and every sort of wickedness'.[31]

The humiliated, proud and unforgiving Eleanor demanded a divorce, insisting that the king and she had never been lawfully wedded, as they were related in the fourth and fifth degrees. It had been known at the time of their 'marriage'. Abbé Bernard agreed. In 1143 consanguinity in France had been condemned by Louis himself when objecting to some intended but inconveniently powerful dynastic unions.[32]

Divorce would be doubly shameful to the king, who would lose not only a wife but also her entire territories. When her betrothal had been suggested, Eleanor's father, William X of Poitiers, son of Guilhem, had insisted that Aquitaine should not become a royal possession on her marriage. If divorced, Louis would lose it and with it two-thirds of his lands in France. Despite the king's feeble protests, his queen obtained a divorce on 21 March 1152.[33] Two months later she married Henry Plantagenet, Duke of Normandy, who became King Henry II of England in 1154.

There was a tragic climax to the Antioch affair. On 29 June 1149 Nur al-Din ambushed Raymond at the battle of Inab, killed him, beheaded his corpse and sent the skull in a silver casket to the Caliph of Baghdad, where it was mockingly displayed on the city's gate.[34]

Unlike Louis VII, stumbling his ill-chosen and disastrous way across the unwelcoming lands of Europe, Jaufré Rudel chose to travel by sea.

Reaching the Holy Land from western Europe in the mid-twelfth century was not easy either by land or by water. Even avoiding the unnecessary risks of the Atlantic and the Bay of Biscay, there were 400 miles of France to cross before reaching the harbour of Port-de-Bouc west of Marseilles. There would not be a closer place to reach the Mediterranean until Louis IX had a canal dug at Aigues-Mortes, *aquae mortuis*, 'dead waters', for his journey on the Seventh Crusade a hundred years later. And that shortened the overland distance only by 40 miles.

But in 1147, in the cheerful company of his cousin and lord, Guilhem IV Taillefer of Angoulême, who took his wife and child with him, and Rudel's friends Alphonse Jourdain, Count of Toulouse, Bertrand, bastard of Toulouse, and Hugh VII of Lusignan, Jaufré Rudel, crusader and hopeful lover, set sail.

There were no luxury liners. There were just clumsy, cramped and damp galleys with only the unreliable compass of a magnet-shaped needle bobbling in a bowl of water as a guide to direction. Experienced captains preferred to stay close to the visible coastline.

Rudel's mission inspired later poets. In 1903 'perhaps the greatest tribute to Jaufré's supposed *Liebestod* came from Edmond Rostand whose play, *The Far-Off Princess*, 'La Princesse Lointaine', made the imaginary lady of Rudel's dreams a dramatic vehicle for the chief actress of the day, Sarah Bernhardt'.

The Victorian poets Browning and Swinburne heard of Rudel and his longing for the woman he loved but had never seen. Robert Browning wrote three laboured verses 'To the Lady of Tripoli', ending:

In vain this Rudel, he not looking here
But to the East – the East! Go, say this,
   Pilgrim dear!

Algernon Swinburne was more lyrical and more direct, composing a
'masterpiece in lyric':

There lived a singer in France of old
By the tideless dolorous midland sea.
In a land of sand, ruin and gold
There shone one woman, and none but she,
And finding life for her love's sake fail,
Being fain to see her, he bade set sail,
Touched land, and saw her as life grew cold,
And praised God, seeing; and so died he.
Died, praising God for his gift and grace:
For she bowed down to him weeping, and said,
'Live', and her tears were shed on his face . . .[35]

The reality was less dramatic. Even the tideless Mediterranean was
unpleasant. In unavoidably crowded conditions, although the vessel hugged
the shoreline, a central berth was preferable advised an experienced pilgrim,
'as nyghe the myddes of the shippe as ye may, for there is leest rollynge or
tomblynge to kepe your brayne and stomache in temper . . .'.[36] (see Fig. 3).
   From the beginning to its very welcome end the voyage was unpleasant,
and sometimes dangerous. They suffered seasickness, storms, shipwreck,
fear of pirates and death or slavery. No passenger rested easily. Nor did time
pass quickly. From Marseilles to Acre, a distance of some 2,000 miles, even
with good winds the journey could easily take a month or more.[37]
   A later, widely travelled troubadour, Gaucelm Faidit of Uzerche, who
went on two crusades, wrote of the discomforts of sea travel. He was an
accomplished poet and composer but a poor singer, 'worse than any living
man'. He wandered from court to court, lost all his money at dice and was
an obese glutton who married a beautiful prostitute, Guillaumette Monga,
who gradually became as fat as himself. Among his works is a fine *planh*, a
lament for the death of Richard Coeur de Lion:

Lo rics valens Richartz, reis del Engles
Es mortz

The noble, valiant Richard, King of England
Is dead! – Ah God! What a loss . . .[38]

From his travels he remembered the horrors of the sea: *del gran golf de mar* (the great basin of the sea).

> *Qu'era non dopti mar ni ven*
> *Garbi, maistre ni ponen*
> *Ni ma naus no.m balanza.*
> *Ni no.m fai mais doptansa*
> *Galea ni corsier corren.*

> I no longer fear the sea, nor the winds
> from west and south, nor the mistral.
> My ship no longer rolls,
> Nor I do dread attack from an enemy
> galley nor pursuit by a corsair.[39]

Rudel and his companions suffered all the discomforts, and, even when Acre was reached on 13 April 1148, their problems had not ended. The shore was some distance off and to reach it passengers had to jump hazardously from the high side of the galley into a waiting boat. In rough seas, a misjudged leap could end in the swirling waters. Many pilgrims drowned.[40]

As with so many ambitious Christian ventures in the Holy Land, there were more disasters than triumphs. Once on land the eager crusaders all failed. Within weeks Alphonse Jourdain, count of Toulouse, had died at Caesarea. Poison by Raymond II of Tripoli, husband of Odierna, was suspected, because the newly arrived count had an unwelcome legitimate claim to the lordship of Tripoli.

Hugh of Lusignan died in battle after the disastrous siege of Damascus. Bertrand of Toulouse was captured in 1149 and imprisoned. It was not until 1161, twelve years later, very ill, that he returned to France.[41]

Of Jaufré Rudel nothing is written after he left France in 1147. What is known is that one of his relations was Lord of Blaye in 1167. A continuation of his *vida* stated:

> *E per voluntat de lieis vezer, el se crozet e mes se en mar, per anar lieis vezer: ll. 4–9.*

> And for the sake of seeing her he took the Cross and set out to sea.
> And on the voyage a grievous illness fell upon him, so that those who
> were in the ship, with him thought he was dead, but they brought
> him to Tripoli and carried him to an inn, thinking him dead. And it
> was made known to the Countess, and she came to him, and took

him in her arms, and he knew she was the Countess, and recovered consciousness, and praised God and thanked Him, for letting him live to see her. And so he died in the lady's arms. And she had him honourably buried in the Church of the Templars, and on that she became a nun, through the grief that she felt by reason of his death.[42]

Had the 'Countess' been Odierna, she could not have taken the veil if Rudel died in 1148. Her husband, Raymond II, was still alive, being killed by assassins only four years later in 1152. Religious law forbade wives who were not widows from becoming nuns. On her husband's death, moreover, Odierna became responsible for the upbringing of their son, Raymond III. She was not a nun.

If it was Uc de Saint-Circ who was responsible for the *vida*, he would not have written it much earlier than fifty years after Rudel's supposed death. By that time all that Uc learned would be from versions of the six poems, some memories of any surviving contemporaries of the poet, and unreliable anecdotes. In such a collection there would be more conjecture than fact.

It is known that in 1134 the Knights Templar established a house for pilgrims in Tripoli and 'it is reasonable to assume that pilgrims returning from Antioch brought news of Tripoli'.[43]

Not a fact is that the news contained anything about the countess or that Rudel heard of it, although that is likely because his companion, Alphonse Jourdain, born in the Holy Land, had strong claims to the territories of Tripoli.

There are facts to be found in the six poems. All of them mention a distant woman, although 'distant' could mean 'aloof' rather than far-off.

There are also oblique references to the Holy Land: 'Bethlehem'; 'Jewess'; 'Saracen'. It can also be inferred that, with his three friends, he did embark on the Second Crusade. Stanza 5 of Poem I observes that 'he who remains here full of delight, and does not follow God into Bethlehem, I do not know how he may ever have prowess'.

A very significant fact, however, is that nowhere, anywhere, in any of the thirty-four variants of the six poems is there a single mention of Tripoli. Also a fact is that Tripoli was almost 100 miles north of Acre. If Rudel did go there, he went alone. His friends went southwards towards Jerusalem.

Perhaps, after all, the legend is true and he did die at sea during that arduous voyage towards Acre, probably in 1147.

The Italian poet Petrarch, Francesco Petrarch, knew the story:

Giaufré Rudel, ch'usò la vela e'l remo
a cercar la sua morte . . .

And tuneful Rudel, who in moonstruck mood
O'er ocean by a flying image led,
In the fantastic chase his canvas spread;
And where he thought his amorous vows to breathe,
From Cupid's bow received the shaft of death

(Trionfo d'Amore, Book, Part 4, ll. 52–3)

And that is the way his story must end, not with a fact but with a whisper.

SIX

Cathars and Catholics:
Confrontations, Mid-Twelfth Century

The Languedoc was a land of sun and song. There had always been sun, but now there was song, sung and played in the luxurious courts of the nobility, in the halls of lesser fortresses, in the claustrophobic *donjons* of minor knights. Such petty keeps were squashed, perched on hillocks. In purpose they were like early versions of peel towers on the Scottish borders, fortified dwellings sturdy enough to repel outlaws and an occasional raid by their neighbours. These walled retreats were everywhere in the Languedoc, often only 3 or 4 miles apart.[1] Whether court, castle or cramped fort, the places attracted troubadours.

It was a land of sun and song. It was also a land of contradictions. It was a land of courtly romance that blended, sometimes uncomfortably, as a land of the Cathar faith. Perhaps stronger among women than men, more popular in the countryside than in the cities, those blurred distinctions did not obscure the fact that, to the Catholic Church, the Languedoc was a land of the heresy of Catharism.

Disgust of the physical was fundamental to Cathars. To them the Catholic Eucharist, the belief in transubstantiation, in which the body of Christ could be transferred to believers, was an illusion. Anything material was evil. The pure spirit of Christ could never have been flesh and blood. Coming from God into the world of man, he had merely adapted a human body. Because he was spirit, he could not have been bodily crucified for our sins nor eaten the Last Supper. With no fleshly body, he could not have been resurrected. With no crucifixion, the crucifix and the cross were no more than superstitious baubles. There was no Trinity of God the Father, Son and Holy Ghost.[2]

To Cathars, sin had no redemption. In a corrupt world of physical things, sin was unavoidable. Only the last rite of the Cathar *consolamentum*, administered by a Good Man, could save a soul. The Catholic Mass was a contradiction. So were Heaven, Earth and Hell. The Earth itself was Hell.

Preachers of Catharism, known to their followers as Good Men, the *Parfaits,* lived in extreme poverty, abstaining from meat, fasting three times a week, co-habiting with no woman. Their possessions were meagre.

To believers, the *credentes,* they explained that God's eldest son, Satan, had rebelled and created the material world of man. God had given humans a soul, but Satan tempted their weak wills with evil pleasures and turned them into his slaves. Such a belief in dualism, the conflict between Good and Evil, was centuries old. To save the fallen souls of men and women, God's second son, Jesus Christ, had come to earth in an apparent body and redeemed men and women.

Ironically, 'Cathar', from the Greek *katharos,* 'pure', was a word never used by Cathars. It was a sneer at the self-appointed 'pure ones' made by Catholic priests, who jeered that the word came from 'cat', in whose form Satan appeared. The heretics kissed its filthy backside. Accusations of devil worship, blasphemy, sodomy and sexual perversion were made against Cathars. They burned Christian crosses, destroyed altars and churches, fouled them by turning them into brothels.[3] In contrast, the obvious honesty and self-imposed austerity of the Good Men appealed to huge numbers of men and women in the Languedoc already disenchanted with the greed, idleness and self indulgence of many Catholic priests.

In the summer of 1145, alarmed at the decline in influence of his Church in south-eastern France, Pope Eugenius III appointed the finest preacher of the time, Bernard of Clairvaux, founder of the Cistercian Order, together with two abbots, to go to Languedoc on a mission of reform to return heretics to the true faith. Bernard had been preceded by Alberic, Bishop of Ostia, but he had been a failure. At Albi he had been greeted by a mocking carnival, townsmen coming to meet him riding asses, and beating kettle drums in derision. When he celebrated Mass in the church, expecting every inhabitant in the congregation to be there, hardly thirty came. Bernard replaced him.

Bernard was later to become a saint, but tolerance and gentleness were not his most commendable characteristics. Only six years earlier he had been raging in Paris against the Cistercian monk, Abelard, whose teaching that there were no universal truths, only individual ones, was unorthodox and grossly heretical to the Church. Calling him 'a thorough hypocrite, having nothing of the monk about him but the name and the habit', whose words stank, Bernard was almost hysterical in his denunciations. He reacted similarly to Cathar ideology.

His mission of reform was partly successful in Toulouse, where his eloquence persuaded many to return to Catholicism, and he was triumphant in Albi, where a papal legate had been humiliated a few years earlier, but Bernard's addresses and sermons brought crowds from their homes and filled churches, whose bells rang and pealed in joy.

Bernard achieved some satisfaction in the cities. He failed completely in the conservative countryside. When he began his words of denunciation at Verfeil, deep in the Aveyron region far east of Toulouse, the congregation walked out of the church. When he attempted to speak outside, mounted knights clanged and clashed on their armour. Inside their locked homes, villagers beat loudly on their doors. Nothing but the din could be heard. Furious, the abbot kicked the dust. It was to be an omen. All would be dust. 'May God wither you, Verfeil', he cursed, grimly making a pun of the name, *verte feuille*, 'green leaf'. The Languedoc was, he realised, 'a land of many heretics'.[4] It was the first general threat. Until that time individuals had been caught, examined, punished. Now a whole population was endangered.

A mission of two brief months with too few missionaries to accomplish a general conversion was little more than a venture into the impossible. Bernard knew it. An over-optimistic correspondent assured him that 'the wolves have been tracked down'. To the contrary, they roved in packs. There were Cathars everywhere, increasing daily. The Pope's hoped-for reform was blocked by an imperturbable heresy.

A Council of Tours denounced Catharism. It continued. Apprehensive because there were so many suspected Cathars in the countryside around Albi, the Catholic Church decided to challenge and accuse the leaders of the heretics in a 'debate' at the nearby small town of Lombers, organised by Giraud, Bishop of Albi. It was after this that 'Albigensian' became applied to all Cathars, even though the majority lived far from Albi, including the villagers of Montaillou 80 hilly miles to the south. Many years later a military crusade was ungeographically named after Albi and the city became the title of a book, *Historia Albigensis*, of 1212–18 by the monk Pierre des Vaux-de-Cernay.

The Lombers' confrontation was a nervous, half-hearted affair. With many opponents all around them, Catholic clergy were unlikely to condemn anyone to death. Even so, the meeting attracted an astonishing audience of five bishops, seven abbots and Constance, wife of Raymond V, Count of Toulouse, and sister of the king of France. The chairman was the seemingly impartial Raymond-Trencavel, Viscount of Béziers and Carcassonne. Appearing before this illustrious assembly was a group calling themselves, not Cathars, a word hardly known at that time, but Good Men. A man, Oliver, was their leader.

Caution was essential for the Cathars. Condemnation meant death by burning. In O'Shea's sardonic words: 'Everybody . . . on that day knew that there was dry wood in the vicinity.'[5] Despite this, the Good Men were confident enough to reject much of the Old Testament as fables, deplore the baptism of infants, and state that the swearing of oaths was a sin. In a less apprehensive court it would have been sufficient for them to be condemned of heresy.

Instead of retreating or pleading innocence, they accused the self-satisfied bishops and abbots of being mercenaries, hypocrites, seducers, 'false prophets and wolves in the midst of the Lord's flock' and 'lovers of this world's honours and goods'. They were anathematised, excommunicated from the Church and deprived of its protection.

They almost shrugged. In a Cathar countryside with many supporters, including noblemen and knights, Catholic words of condemnation were no more than a tumble of pebbles on a distant hillside. They had already rejected the strongest Catholic beliefs, so that the condemnation meant little. Their accusers lacked courage. The Good Men were released, and across the Languedoc the Cathar religion was unaffected. For decades it remained so.[6]

Finally, in March 1206, a despairing Pope Innocent III sent Dominic Guzman, later St Dominic, the founder of the Cistercian Order, to the Languedoc to preach to the unfaithful, speaking to them not as an overbearing, aristocratic prelate but as a simple preacher coming to the villages in humble clothes and addressing his listeners in ordinary words. Even he would fail.

It could be asked how many troubadours were also Cathars, but the answer is unknown. What is certain is that, in the early years of the thirteenth century, some southern singers were writing bitter verses against French invaders from the north and against the self-indulgent Catholic clergy. There was sharp resentment that conquering French barons were occupying the castles of dispossessed local knights, the *faidits*, 'exiled ones'. Even more loathed and despised were monks of the Dominican Order, who had become not only heartless, near-sadistic Inquisitors, but insulting, swaggering bullies in the cities.

Guilhelm Montanhagol of Provence, writing around the mid-thirteenth century, began one *canso* criticising the Inquisition:

Ar se son fait enquererdor . . .

Now the clergy are made Inquisitors
And make judgements just as they please . . .

before a shiver of panic persuaded him to be less outspoken:

I have nothing against the Inquisition
To the contrary, I praise it because
It seeks out error.[7]

Earlier that century another troubadour, Guilhelm Figueira of Toulouse, had a firmer backbone: In a *sirventes* of twenty-three outspoken stanzas he itemised the many faults of the 'holy' brothers: avarice, gluttony, cruelty, lust and rape.

Roma trichairitz cobeitatz vos engame . . .

Treacherous Rome! your greed is clear,
Because, down to their skin and flesh,
Your shear and steal the wool
From the very sheep that are your flock.[8]

Most outspoken of all the troubadours was Peire Cardenal, who was writing for much of the thirteenth century. He hated the inhumane greed of the monks:

Tartarassa ni voutor . . .

By their nature buzzards and vultures know
Where some decaying carcase smells.
Even more quickly, monks and friars go
To where a rich but dying man dwells.
Promising Heaven they empty his purse,
And hypocritically follow his penniless hearse.[9]

But theirs was a rage against the misdoings and arrogance of the Catholic Church. It was not the criticism of Catholic doctrine that a true Cathar would have made. If any troubadour had been a Cathar, it is likely that he would have come from one of the many country districts where that faith was deepest, such as the Montagne Noire, the Minervois or the Cabardès with its hamlets and villages in the hills.

Miraval-Cabardès was one, a huddle of a few farms, a small church and an almost equally small *donjon* in which the troubadour Raimon de Miraval had a quarter share. If there were troubadours who were Cathars, they would probably have been someone like that, keeping their beliefs but practising their art as he did in splendid courts like Raymond VI's at Toulouse.

In the mid-twelfth century it was a centre of luxury and delight. Troubadours such as Arnaut de Marueil and Bernart de Ventadorn knew it.

There is one final and considerable irony. Few troubadours may have been Cathars. But one trobairitz, Gormonda, had been a believer who became a Catholic nun in Montpellier. The conversion would cause her anguish.[10]

SEVEN

Bernart de Ventadorn and Others

Ja nus hons pris ne dira sa reson . . .

No prisoner will ever speak truthfully of his mind
Until he sighs that for freedom he pined.
Then, words for a hopeful song he might find.
I have many friends but help is slow, confined.
Shame will be theirs if no ransom is consigned
And I remain in prison two winters more.[1]

(Richard, Coeur de Lion, King of England,
captive in Dürrenstein castle, Austria, 1192–3)

The Glory of the Troubadours, Late Twelfth Century

Peire Vidal per paor d'aquest fait . . .

Peire Vidal, afraid for the folly he had committed, embarked on a ship and went to Genoa. And he stayed there till he could go overseas with King Richard . . .

(Boutière and Schutz, Vida, no. LVII, p. 366)

From the middle of the twelfth century onwards there was a confusion of troubadours all over the south of France. Two of them, Arnaut de Mareuil and Bernart de Ventadorn, reveal the many contrasts between that teeming medley of singers.

With a developing liking for the new 'music of love', troubadours and their minstrels went everywhere where there was patronage: in the Languedoc, in Provence, even farther (Fig. 1). Each palace, court or castle became an overnight *caravanserai* where a player could arrive, entertain, be entertained and depart like a passing prince. The age was an intermittent cavalcade of song.

Troubadours were the celebrants of Western Europe's first lyrical verse.In his Victorian paraphrase of Omar Khayyam's *Rubaiyat*, by a chronological coincidence composed in the same decades as those wandering troubadours, Edward Fitzgerald transformed such a passing-place into a day-or-two rendezvous for poets:

> Think, in this batter'd *caravanserai*
> Whose doorways are alternate night and day,
> How sultan after sultan with his pomp
> Abode his hour or two and went his way.

(Fitzgerald, quatrain 16)

Robert Graves, better poet, lesser translator, lost the music.[2]

The drift of troubadours was widespread, from Ventadorn in the west to Die in the east, from Ventadorn in the north to Miraval and Carcassonne in the south, a peripatetic musical box of 3,000 square miles (Map 5). In it were great cities, Valence, Cahors, Montpellier, Toulouse. The roads were poor, sometimes dangerous, the distances arduously long, but at their ends were courts and rewards. The hardships were severe. The compensations could be considerable.

Among the conventional singers of courtly romance there were several unusual troubadours: one who preferred the pleasures of war to the delights of women; a king in captivity, an undercover agent from Picardy.

Of more musical importance are two others. The little-known Arnaut de Mareuil, almost ignored in anthologies, composed enticing love songs that he claimed, somewhat evasively, were letters written by other admirers of his secretly adored Lady. And across the same years, perhaps the finest of all the troubadours, Bernart de Ventadorn, was serenading, his words and music bringing enjoyment to many great ladies, including the greatest of all of them, Eleanor of Aquitaine, Queen of England. That was the good time.

The bad time was one of religious and political disruption. Some forty years after the death of Jaufré Rudel on his way to the Holy Land there was a Third Crusade. In 1177 Saladin, Sultan of Egypt and Syria, defeated an occupying Christian army at Hattin, and then rapidly went on to capture citadel after fortified citadel, including the Holy City of Jerusalem. Only the crusaders' port of Tyre remained untaken.

The fading century was a period of unrest. In Greenland the volcano of Hekla erupted in 1167, its poisonously choking fumes affecting wide landscapes of Europe. Six years later there was a widespread epidemic of plague. The following year in June a meteorite collided with the moon. Monks in England observed it. 'A flaming torch sprang up . . . from the crescent moon, spewing out, over a considerable distance, fire, hot coals and sparks.' Then, in 1177, the sea 'broke through the dykes of Holland . . . drowning almost all the cattle, as well as a multitude of men: the rest were with difficulty saved by climbing trees, or getting on the tops of houses'. To the superstitious medieval mind these were omens of worse disasters to come.

There were social antagonisms. The crusades had fermented latent hostility against non-Christians. 'No Jews or Saracens shall be permitted to have Christian servants in their houses, either under the pretence of educating their children, or as slaves . . . Moreover, let those be excommunicated who presume to live with them.'[3]

Everywhere there was tension. In the Languedoc, followers of the Cathar faith were ubiquitous, yet thousands of their neighbours attended Catholic masses. It was a peaceful, almost unconsidered coexistence. Only the hierarchy of the Catholic Church was obsessed with the determination to cleanse the Christian world of the ungodly 'Albigensian' cancer.

In politics, England and France continued hostilities. Henry II had become King of England, but only two years later, in 1154, his brother, Geoffrey, arbitrarily seized the lands of Anjou and Maine. Seeing advantage in supporting that usurper against the English, Louis VII 'the Young' of France offered military aid.

Worse, in 1173 Henry's sons, Henry Plantagenet and Richard, rebelled against him, encouraged by their badly treated mother, Eleanor, perhaps resenting her husband's flaunted adultery with the lovely Rosamund Clifford (Appendix Four).

Henry II captured his defiant wife. The chronicler Gerald of Wales recorded that in 1174 Henry 'imprisoned Queen Eleanor his wife as a punishment for the destruction of their marriage' despite the king's persistent infidelity, having maintained Rosamund Clifford as his mistress for years. Taken back to England, Eleanor was imprisoned in the grimly bleak Old Sarum castle near Salisbury. She remained in captivity for fifteen years until her husband's death.[4]

Henry and Richard, with French encouragement, continued to struggle against a father who favoured his youngest son, John, at their expense. The fraternal 'alliance' intended to invade England, but the plan collapsed in 1183 with the death from fever of Henry's second son, the 'Young King', Henry Plantagenet.

The minor nobleman and troubadour Bertran de Born, who sang not only of love but, much more intensely, of his love of battle, was acquainted with the English royal family. He wrote of his sorrow that the prince had died.

Si tuit li dol e.lh plor e.lh marrimen
Contra la mort del jove rei engles

If all the world's distress, suffering, pain and misery were bundled together it would be as nothing
compared with the death of the young English king'.[5]

Exhausted by the disloyalty of his family and an unending threat from Scotland, Henry II died in 1189. Because of the death of his elder brother Henry six years earlier, Richard became King Richard I of England. In the same year he joined the Third Crusade to recapture the Holy City.

It was led by three great rulers. Richard, Philippe-Auguste II of France and Frederick Barbarossa, the Holy Roman Emperor. The imposing triple alliance was not fortunate. After a sequence of inconclusive sieges and conflicts, Philippe-Auguste, always a reluctant crusader, pretending illness but in reality having quarrelled with Richard, sulkily returned to France. On his own way home, Frederick 'Red Beard' drowned in the river Saleph in Anatolia.

The most determined and successful of the three, Richard, now nicknamed 'Coeur de Lion' from his courage and prowess, also embarked on the long and treacherous voyage to England. Almost predictably shipwrecked in bad weather near Dubrovnik and deciding to avoid an unsafe journey through the unreliable territories of Philippe-Auguste Richard chose a seemingly safer passage through Austria. It was not. He was captured by Leopold, Duke of Austria, a man he had humiliated at Acre, and imprisoned in Dürrenstein castle on the north bank of the Danube in Bohemia, two days' hard riding west of Vienna and 8,000 hostile miles from London.[6]

His mother, Eleanor of Aquitaine, nominal ruler of England in his absence, was desperate to have him released. Having already appealed unsuccessfully to Pope Célestine III for his intervention she sent a second, even more intemperate letter, raging against papal inactivity. It was written on her behalf by the erudite cleric Peter of Blois. Her words seethe.

> The kings of the earth have set themselves and all the rulers have agreed to set themselves against my son, the Lord's Anointed. One tortures him in chains, another destroys his lands with a cruel enmity, or to use a common phrase, 'One shears, another plunders, one holds the foot, another skins it'. The supreme Pontiff sees all this, yet keeps the sword of Peter sheathed, and thus gives the sinner added boldness, his silence being presumed to indicate consent.
>
> Eleanor, by the wrath of God, queen of England.[7]

But Célestine was powerless and Richard remained imprisoned in Dürrenstein. It was in that fortress, while an extortionate ransom was being negotiated, that the surreptitious search of a troubadour grew into a romantic legend.

Charles Dickens told the story.

> There is an old tune yet known . . . by which this King is said to have been discovered in his captivity. BLONDEL, a favourite Minstrel of King Richard. as the story relates, faithfully seeking his Royal master, went singing it outside the gloomy walls of many foreign fortresses and prisons; until he heard it echoed from within a dungeon, and knew the voice, and cried out in ecstacy, 'O Richard, O my King'. You may believe it if you like; it would be easy to believe worse things. Richard was himself a Minstrel and a Poet.[8]

Dickens was right. It is a good story, popular, with occasional truths in it. Richard the warrior was also well known as a composer of pleasant tunes. Blondel also wrote lyrics and music. He did know the king.

But these few certainties were no more than threads in an elaborated tapestry. Over the years variations fashioned a legend that contained constant contradictions: Blondel searched Germany rather than Austria, always singing the private song that Richard and he had written together, finally hearing the King's voice from the window of a dungeon. Further embellishments added jailors' daughters, daring escapes, a disguised Blondel, until the dramatic climax of discovering Richard when he heard that familiar voice singing the second verse of their secret melody.[9]

Most of it is fiction. Yet beneath that swirling sea of speculation there is a bedrock of fact. Blondel existed, even though he was a talented composer rather than a mere minstrel. Richard, King of England, was imprisoned in the castle at Dürrenstein. These were realities. Everything else is embroidery. Even that personal song may never have existed. It was searched for, one was suggested, accepted, dissected, and rejected.[10]

In his *Hydriotaphia* or 'Urn Burial' of 1658 Sir Thomas Browne wrote: 'What song the *Syrens* sang . . . is not beyond all conjecture.' It was not. More than two thousand years before Browne, the Greek poet Homer had provided a version in his *Odyssey*. There is none for Blondel and Richard.[11]

Even the simplest examination of the legend of Blondel's exploit shows its unlikelihood. The account is a fantasy, not recorded until a hundred years after the event. It is an attractive fairy story, a fable unhindered by facts. The popular version of the discovery is unlikely. There were hundreds of castles in Austria and Bohemia. For a wandering minstrel to visit them, sing, wait for a voice to reply would have taken days at each, standing frustrated by the high towers separated from him by wide, deep moats. Richard could even have been in a dungeon and inaudible. There is a much more plausible explanation for the reality.

Blondel was a nobleman. His Christian name was Jean. There were hundreds of thousands of Jeans in the Western world, just as there are many Franks. But in the same way that there was only one Sinatra, there was only one singer known as Blondel. It was a surname. He was Jean Blondel, first lord of Nesle, a town in the far north of France, not far from Amiens in Picardy. He was a *trouvère*, writing in medieval French rather than in the Occitan of a *troubadour* from the Languedoc, 400 miles and four great rivers to the south.

Blondel was a good poet and composer. No fewer than twenty-four of his songs have survived, all with his original music, proving his popularity.[12] Being well born and an attractive singer, he would have been doubly welcome at the tables of courts and castles, where he could sit at feasts, drinking the good wine, chatting, listening to gossip, waiting for the casual, unconsidered hint of where his king's prison might be. The mission was not haphazard but planned – and successful. News of the discovery reached England.[13]

That news also brought the expected fear that an enormous ransom had to be paid. The Holy Roman Emperor, the youthful, diminutive and unpleasant Henry VI, had 'bought' Richard from Leopold and was demanding 100,000 silver marks, 50 galleys and the use of 200 armoured knights and their retinue for a year for his intended invasion of Sicily and southern Italy. England was almost ruined by the extortion, but the terms were accepted, and early in 1194 Richard Coeur de Lion was released.

It had been a financial disaster. All clerics, abbots, priests, earls and barons paid a quarter of their year's income. Pigs were slaughtered, Cistercian sheep were shorn, church gold and silver were given, but the avaricious Henry VI was paid. 'Forewarnings of this calamity had appeared in unusual seasons – inundations of rivers, awful storms of thunder and rain three or four times in each month, with dreadful lightning throughout the whole year; all of which caused a scantiness in the crops of fruit and corn.'[14] But troubadours rejoiced. The versatile, madcap Peire Vidal jeered at the ambitions of the conceited emperor. Richard would confront him in Sicily and Italy:

E si.m creira Richartz, reis dels Engles . . .

And if Richard, England's king, believes it
In a short time the strength of Palermo
And Reggio will be taken by him
Because he paid for them with his ransom . . .

Another troubadour, Bertran de Born, almost shouted his delight at the king's release:

Ar ve la coindeta sazos . . .

Now is the joyous season
When our ships come to land
With our incomparable king, no one braver.
We shall see a cascade of gold and silver

The instant celebrations were the prelude to a mournful outcome. Of the four participants in Richard's captivity, only Blondel may have seen the beginning of the thirteenth century. Even that is questionable.

There is no agreement about the *trouvère*'s death, 'who was born *circa* 1150 and died some time between 1197 and 1200'. He lived in the 'second half of the twelfth century'. 'He is generally believed to have lived until 1220, but it is really only tradition that says so.'[15] Earlier may be closer to history.

There is no disagreement about the others. Leopold V of Austria fell from his horse and broke his leg. It became gangrenous, and after days of pain, when no doctor dared amputate the limb, he desperately had a servant with a hammer hack it off with an axe he held himself. It was too late. He died on 31 December 1194.

Henry VI, emperor and king, son of Barbarossa, conquered Sicily in 1194. In 1197, preparing to join a crusade, he fell ill in Sicily, perhaps with malaria, and died in Messina on 28 September. He was 31 years old.

In 1199 Richard I was besieging the French castle of Châlus in the Limousin. On 26 March he was struck by the bolt of a crossbowman, 'one Peter Basilii, with a poisoned weapon'. The bolt was not poisoned but neither was it sterile, and, unattended, the wound became septic. Within a few days 'this warlike man gave up his spirit'.[16] He was buried at Fontevrault.

Troubadours grieved at the death of their valiant monarch. One of them, Gaucelm Faidit, composed a fine lament, a *planh*, for Richard's death.

Fortz chausa es que tot lo major dan . . .

'Tis a terrible thing that the greatest pain
And the greatest sorrow, alas, that I have ever had

Lo rics valens Richartz . . .

Great Lord and God who offers pardon
Thou who art God and Man and Life indeed,
Grant him that pardon that his sins do need,
His faults and failings Thy mercy overlook.
Remember that for Thee the Cross he took.

Faidit was widely travelled. Although dreading the dangers of sea voyages, he had gone on two crusades, one led by Richard himself. Despite his fears, he returned safely to England.

He was a talented poet and a composer of good music but by reputation a very poor singer, tuneless, always out of key. He was also self-indulgent, fond of food, becoming very fat. He fell in love with an attractive and educated harlot and married her.[17]

A fellow troubadour, the nameless Monk of Montaudon, lightheartedly mocked him in one of the nineteen verses in which the Monk gently lampooned other colleagues.

E.l cinques es Gauselms Faidtiz

And the fifth is Gaucelm Faidit
The maker of music who made a good trade
From lover into husband of a lady, no maid,
Enjoying for nothing what other men had paid.
Good were his songs, good music he made
But where others sang Gaucelm just brayed.
Jeered at if from his Uzerche homeland he strayed

The Monk satirised others of his contemporaries: Peirol from the Auvergne, the complex Arnaut Daniel, the hare-brained Peire Vidal, even himself, who had drifted irreligiously from his Church.

Perhaps the most pitiful of those laughing targets was the ninth, 'Arnaut de Maruelh'.

E.l noves, Arnaut de Maruelh . . .

Whenever I see him he's deep in his woes.
His lady's uncaring whether he comes or goes.
He's heartbroken at her heartless pose.
His eyes weep for pity, he's always morose,
And whenever he sings the water just flows.

It was not exaggeration. There are over twenty tearful pleas for help in his songs. As a troubadour he is surprisingly ignored, seldom quoted in either anthologies or books about troubadours. The indifference is only partly explicable by some collections of troubadour poems being cannibalised copies of predecessors. It is true that his lines are gossamer in contrast to the sinew of others, but they possess a delicacy appealing to sensitive ears. In his own times he was much appreciated. No fewer than twenty-six of his 'Songs' exist, six with music, preceded by five 'Letters', the *Saluts d'Amour*. They form a single cycle composed for Azalais

Marueil was tall and handsome, with a good figure and a melodious voice, so it is understandable that a young woman would find him an acceptable entertainer. But he is mentioned so seldom that his surname itself is debatable.

Even in those days of go-as-you-please spelling there is little agreement about what to call him. There are no fewer than eight variations of his name in ancient records, ranging alphabetically from Mareuil to Marvoil. In his *vida* he is Maroill. Akehurst and Davis suggest following the Hill-Bergin form of 'Marueill' even though that occurs in only one other source.[18] To accept their advice would also mean exchanging 'Guilhem of Poitiers' to 'Guillem de Peitieus', an archaic form long out of fashion.

Of the two most popular spellings from ancient documents, 'Mareuil' and 'Maruelh', the first is chosen here for two reasons, the first because it is the one accepted by the poet's two critical editors, Bec and Johnston, and, secondly, because it is also the modern name of the place in which he was born, Vieux-Mareuil, a village with a Romanesque church a few miles west of Nontron halfway between Périgueux and Angoulême in the Dordogne.

To complete the inconsistencies, the troubadour's first name is usually given as the accepted 'Arnaut', but one of his two editors, Pierre Bec, calls him 'Arnaud'. This can be considered an aberration.

Born of a poor family Arnaut de Mareuil had sufficient talent to become a proficient musician, so accomplished that the great Dante admired him, and Petrarch termed him a Tibullus. In an anonymous Italian poem, 'Hero and Leander', he was acclaimed the best of the Provençal singers. He was flourishing around 1180. Instead of choosing the customary itinerant existence, going from court to court, he stayed in one place, emotionally attached to an unattainable lady. It was his tragedy. His *vida*[19] says:

Arnautz de Meruoill si fo l'evesquat de Peiregors, d'un castel qui a nom Meruoill . . .

[He] was from Perigord diocese, villager of a castle called Mareuil. And he was a clerk of low rank who, as he could not earn much as a scribe, took to a vagrant life, being very skilled in singing and writing verse. And he loved the Countess of Burlatz, daughter of the valiant Count Raymond, and wife of the Viscount of Béziers, called Taillefer'.

Having read something in Ford Maddox Brown's *Provence*, Robert Briffault elaborated on the *vida*. 'In the castle of Burlatz, not far from Castelnaudary, where all the inmates were massacred, the Countess Constance, wife of Raymond Bérenger and sister of the king of France, and Adelaide, Viscountess of Taillefer, held what bears all the appearance of a Court of Love.'[20]

Most of this was wrong. Burlatz was not near Castelnaudary. It was 36 miles away. There was no Albigensian massacre of Cathars there. Geographically, the nearest town to Burlats, today's spelling, was Castres, five pleasant countryside miles to the north-east. Nor was there a garrisoned castle at Burlats that staged judicial Courts of Love. But, like butterflies attracted to buddleias, troubadours were drawn there by the expectation of welcome, hospitality and appreciation.

Briffault's description did have murmurs of truth. Constance, daughter of the French king, Louis VI, was the disillusioned wife of Raymond V, Count of Toulouse, the most powerful noble in the Languedoc and a harsh husband. She left him in 1165. They had a daughter, not the modern-day 'Adelaide' but originally the Occitanian 'Azalais'. As a girl she was married to Roger II Trencavel, Viscount of Béziers and Carcassonne, who died in 1194 leaving her as a temptingly available and wealthy widow. Their son, Raymond-Roger, born in 1181, was callously left to die in his own dungeons at Carcassonne by Simon de Montfort's crusaders in 1209, breaking their promise of a safe conduct. Effectively, Carcassonne became one of the first cities lost to the troubadours, being garrisoned by uncouth knights from northern France.

Long before that treachery, Constance and Azalais used the 'castle' at Burlats as a quiet retreat for leisure and enjoyment. Azalais was sometimes known as the 'countess of Burlats' because she had been born in the comfortable house. It still stands, a twelfth-century half-timbered building in a square close to the church and facing the river. It is called the Pavillon d'Adelaide. On the wall is a notice board:

> Adélaide's pavilion forms part of a twelfth century castle built by the lords of Trencavel, Béziers and Carcassonne, the vassals of the Counts of Toulouse. The building is a simple example of civil Romanesque art. The lower level has no windows and was probably used as a cellar. The ground floor which had access to the grounds was probably used to defend the castle given its many narrow openings or arrow-slots. The upper level was used for living purposes. Constance of France, the daughter of Louis VI, defected from her husband, Count Raymond V of Toulouse, and fled to Burlats. Her daughter, Adélaide, the violet-eyed princess, lived in the castle and held a 'love-court', a cultured meeting-place for Occitan poets.

Arnaut de Mareuil was one of them, but to him Burlats was not a casual *caravanserai*, one court of many on the troubadour circuit, to be visited for a few pleasurable and lucrative days. It was a residence. He had become besotted by the charms, loveliness and courtesy of Azalais, Viscountess of Béziers, and could not leave her. Indulgently, she encouraged his attentions. He serenaded her. But being of low birth he was unable to declare his desire. His *vida* said:

E si fasia cansos . . .

He loved her greatly and sang her praises in beautiful songs but dared not admit that they were his. He pretended that other men had written them.

Those 'anonymous' epistles were his five Letters, the *Saluts d'Amour*, I–V.[21] They were extravagant expressions of ardour from an unknown admirer, two more than 200 lines in length, all flattering, some comparing the medieval courteous, virtuous love with a catalogue of famous lovers from long ago: Hero and Leander, Paris and Helen, Pyramus and Thisbe, and they all praised Azalais in the lightest of compliments like delicate caresses, the most seemly of intimacies.

Doma, genser qe no sai dir. . .

Lady, more gentle than I can hope to sing,
For whose love, often, I weep and sigh,
This from your most sincere and loyal friend
You have to know and understand
That silently, secretly, I send you this letter
Filled with love and admiration
But which will never have health or any virtue
If it is not to your sensitive liking.

(*Salut d'Amour*, no. I)

The succession of spurious 'Letters' intrigued and delighted the impressionable Azalais. She wondered who this unknown suitor could be, one who declared that their unspoken romance was as deep and sincere as those of Tristran and Isolde, that she was as beautiful as the legendary Cleopatra. He praised her goodness, her loveliness, her courage, her truth, and he languished in the cause of a love that gave him no joy, only sadness. He longed to see her gentle smile again. He despaired.

The captivated Azalais begged Arnaut to tell her who this phantom admirer was. She longed, almost pined for one who could write such tenderly emotional words. And, because Mareuil felt as strongly towards her as she towards her fictitious suitor, he nervously admitted that it was he, Arnaut de Mareuil, humble troubadour but passionate man, who had composed the letters. His *vida* continued: *Anz disia c'autre qu'el las fasia . . .* (He pretended that other men had written them. After some time, however, so deep was his love, that he was forced to write an admission).

La grans beutatz e.l fis ensemhamens . . .
The great beauty, the fine manners . . .

('Song 1', stanza 1)

Qu'ieu vos am tan, domna, celadamens . . .

For I loved you, my Lady, so secretly
that only Love and I knew it, not even you,
so extreme was the fear which prevented me
from telling you; Now I am terrified that you
will be angry and insulted, my great Lady,
because of this love. But as I dared say nothing to you
when we were alone, at least I could tell you in my songs.

('Song 1', stanza 3)

His *vida* went on:

E la comtessa no.l esquiva, anz entendet sos precs . . .

The Countess did not rebuff him but listened to his reasons and
gave him many favours. She provided fine clothing and equipment,
honoured him, offered him the most proper of pleasures and spoke
to him so encouragingly that he became bold enough to write more
directly about his love. He stayed at her court and was honoured
there above all others. He loved her openly and wrote many beautiful
songs of love to her. In return she sometimes praised him highly. Yet
on other occasions she treated him very badly.

The effect of a troubadour's performance should not be underestimated.
He was serenading a woman. However decorous the words, gentle the
melody, he was singing directly to her. Every one of his movements,
gestures, glances, was towards her. It was making love with music. It would
not be surprising if, on occasion, infrequently, with discretion, there was an
unexpected but passionate reward.

Over long years of experience in the art of seduction it became customary
for ardent troubadours to approach their target in a stealthy campaign of
almost Ovidean cynicism. It had four stages. At first the singer was just
an aspirant, a *fegnedor*, worshipping the woman, with muted words of an
accepted convention about the effect that she had on him. If those songs
were liked by her then the singer became a suppliant, *precedor,* gathering
bravery to declare his love. Arnaut de Mareuil had at last attained that
level. From there, if there were smiles and kind words, he would be an

accepted suitor, an *entendedor.* That was a stage that could endure for a long time, waiting, waiting for the final approval. Sometimes, quite frequently, it never came. Occasionally, it did. Man and woman joined in bed. With that culmination, the long-awaited physical intercourse, the successful seducer was a *drut*, 'a lover' who had achieved his intention.[22]

Arnaut de Mareuil, *entendor,* waited for the last encouragement. It was at that point that his *vida* ended, but a *razo*, a kind of appendix, had been added.

> E.l reis N'Anfos, qu'entendia en la contessa . . .

And the King Alphonso who also courted the lady saw the affection between the two and became so jealous that he accused her of being over-fond of the troubadour. The great nobleman of royal birth complained for so long and so vehemently that resignedly she sent for Arnaut and forbade him ever to sing to her again about his love.[23] She was implacable.

Powerless, Arnaut was heartbroken and so distracted that despairingly he left Burlats and went to the court of William of Montpellier, his true friend and lord. He stayed with him for a long time, always deeply upset and filled with sadness. In his final 'Song 25', he wrote:

> Mout eron doutz miei cossir . . .

Very sad were my thoughts, and with no bitterness
When, suddenly, the lovely lady of comely body
Gentle, honest, kindly mannered, told me
To abandon my love, which I could not do,
And because she did not want to keep me,
That it was useless to implore her compassion,
I lost every joy that I had known, all gone,
Everything gone with her.[24]

It is said that Arnaut de Mareuil died young.

Azalais married Alphonse II of Aragon, but gained nothing. Her Spanish lover died only two years later in 1196 and even during that short time was unfaithful. He also cheated his trusting wife of property. Contemporary stories stated that 'he robbed her . . . of two cities and a hundred castles'.[25] Azalais did not outlive him for long, and was herself dead by 1200.

It may not have been only the resentful interference of Alphonse that caused Azalais to reject her troubadour. It was unlikely to have been through lack of opportunity. 'The crowded castles of the aristocracy gave noble women little privacy, and in the constant flow of guests and strangers apparently no one would think twice if a man was deft enough to catch some time alone with the lady of the castle.'[26]

It was not the fear of being discovered. It was the chasm between a high-born viscountess and a peasant, however endearing he was with his music. An affair would enhance his status. It would besmirch hers. There could be not a whisper that there had been over-familiarity. Another fine lady wrote of the void between high and low:

Na donzela, no m'en podetz rependre . . .

Maiden, I can't understand your reasoning.
I gave him my love with on the understanding
That he'd be mine to give away or sell
And that he'd always be at my command.
But he has wronged me so grievously
That he can have neither excuse nor defence.
I do no wrong if I deprive him of my love.
Never for him could I debase my honour.[27]

It may have been such a social distinction that deprived Arnaut de Mareuil of his deepest desire. It was a medieval division that applied even between men and women of the nobility. It was the woman who had to be obeyed, she the *Domna*, her man ordained by the laws of courtly love to be an obedient servant in all matters.

Maria, Viscountess of Ventadorn, daughter of Raimon II, Vviscount of Turenne, and wife of Ebles V, expressed this forcibly to Gui d'Ussel, the man she loved, even though he himself was noble. He was a man but she was a lady, a *Domna*. His social status was less than hers, being no more than a lord of many castles. In the third verse of the *tenson* or debate between them she stressed the difference and the manner in which he should conduct himself:

Gui, tot so don es cobeitas . . .

Guy, the lover must always humbly ask
As favours, not rights, what his heart desires,
And the lady should command or grant
Within her firm limits of propriety;
And the lover should do her bidding
As towards a friend and Lady equally,

And she should honour her lover
As a friend – but never as an overlord.[28]

It was an entrenched attitude of society that protected many women from
disgrace and contempt.

In his *L'iverna vai e.l temps s'azina* . . . (the winter passes and the weather
grows warmer . . .) Marcabru, the moralistic troubadour, condemned
women who demeaned themselves by their debased misdeeds:

Domna no sap d'amor fina . . .

A lady who makes love with a household menial
Knows nothing of true love. She couples unnaturally
Like a greyhound bitch with a mongrel. Ai!

He distinguished sharply between *amor*, 'pure, decent love', and *ama*, 'filthy
desire':

Amars vai et ataïna . . .

Bad love encourages self-deceit
When a young man yearns for cunt
His longing collapses into unclean lust . . .[29]

Despite Marcabru's condemnation, there were many occasions when
passion overpowered prudence.

In addition to accepted social morals, there was also a proprietary
guardianship exercised by husbands suspicious of a rival. Through
it an earlier Viscountess de Ventadorn, the wife of viscount
Ebles III, was humiliated by her indignant husband. The affair involved
the young troubadour, Bernart de Ventadorn, whose patron was that
husband.

The boy had been born in the castle of Ventadorn but not to the noble
family. There are garbled accounts of his upbringing. His *vida* said that
he was of humble origins, the son of a serf tending the furnace of the
oven that baked the household bread. The 'biography' was written by
Uc de Saint-Circ who obtained the information from Viscount Ebles V de
Ventadorn early in the thirteenth century when much had been forgotten,
perhaps deliberately so.[30]

Earlier snippets, probably more accurate, came from Peire d'Alvernhe
in his satire about fellow singers. He had met Bernart at the castle of
Puivert.

E.lh tertz Bernartz de Ventedorn . . .

And the third is Bernart de Ventadorn
Who is not as tall as Bornelh.
His father was a penniless serf
But a good handler of a laburnum bow,
And his mother heated the castle oven,
Collecting brushwood for it.

Bernart's beginnings had been unpromising, but he was doubly fortunate. By genetic chance he was intelligent, healthy and gifted. He also happened to be born in a castle long famous for its patronage of troubadours. His overlord was the son of Ebles II, *Ebolus cantator*, 'the singer', a contemporary and friend of his lord, Count Guilhem of Poitiers. Ebles created a 'school' of poets whose amoral sentiments were severely disliked by Marcabru because of their advocacy of pleasure without consideration for the consequences – *amar* rather than *amor.*

Jamais no farai plevins . . .

I will never make an oath on behalf of
The lascivious writings of Sir Ebles
For he supports unworthy and silly beliefs
In utter contradiction of reason.[31]

Ebles II was the lord of a great castle near Limoges in the bleak Corrèze region of Limousin. Today it is a ruin. Some of its towers still rise above the rocky Luzège gorge, at the tip of a narrow spur above river valleys and a sterile countryside. The castle was abandoned in the sixteenth century when the viscounts went to Ussel to escape its feudal plumbing.

It had formidable defences, impregnable except for treason. The historian Froissart called it the strongest castle in the whole world, and one of its dukes boasted to Louis XIV: 'All the straw in the kingdom would not be enough to fill the moats of Ventadour.'

In disuse it mouldered and decayed for centuries. Its restructuring has only recently begun. But on a pedestal in the lane by the workmen's gate is a glass plaque displaying poems by both Bernart and the much later Marie de Ventadorn. With them is a caption: 'These stones saw them live. In these lines they live again.'[32]

Ebles III, son of Ebles II, continued the tradition of being the liberal patron to entertainers. To his castle came jugglers and acrobats and strongmen, but it was the troubadour and his musicians who were most gladly welcomed. In his childhood Bernart was enthralled by their performances and he learned from the players.

He listened, asked questions, and, as he had a pleasantly musical voice, he was encouraged. Minstrels showed him how to play instruments, to blow the flute and the trumpet, strum the guitar, pluck the harp, use the bow for the vièle and the rebec, tap the percussion drums and tabors rhythmically. Troubadours told him how to write verse and compose music. Over the years of his adolescence he became a proficient troubadour himself, almost a genius with words. Eventually he played and sang in Ventadorn's court. His playing, his voice, his magical words enchanted people. And one in particular. The *vida* wrote:

> The viscount had a young wife who was well born and full of spirit. She took a liking to Bernart and his songs and she fell in love with him and he with her. He wrote songs and poems for her, telling her how he loved her and her merits.

Which of Ebles's two wives it was, Marguerite de Turenne or Alais de Montpellier, is unknown. Whichever one she was, from what was remembered it is clear that Bernart's words sang to her heart:

Als non sai que dire . . .

> I cannot say anything
> Except this: that I am obsessed, beyond sense,
> To love and to desire
> No other lady save for the loveliest in the world . . .

Lonc temps duret lor amors anz que.l vescons . . .

> Their love continued for a long time before the Viscount or anyone noticed it but when the Viscount did he was enraged. His wife was imprisoned. He dismissed Bernart, evicting him from his lands.

Ezra Pound wrote about the marital drama in Canto VI:

> My Lady of Ventadour
> Is shut by Eblis in
> And will not hawk nor hunt
>   Nor get her free in the air
> Nor watch fish rise in bait
> Nor the glare-winged flies alight in the creek's edge
> Save in my absence, Madame . . .[33]

Bernart de Ventadorn was forbidden ever to return to Ebles's domains. Worse, the viscount ordered his wife to pronounce the eviction to Bernart personally. She did so harshly, dismissing him almost with a shrug. Bewildered, hurt and angry, the troubadour looked at her for the last time.

Be m'an perdut lai enves Ventadorn . . .

Down there, around Ventadorn, all my friends
Are lost to me, for my lady does not love me
So, it is right I must never return there . . .

To him it was a disaster, and yet his expulsion was a triviality of life in contrast to the fate of another troubadour who had dallied with a nobleman's wife. Guilhem de Cabestanh was a knight from a village near Roussillon whose lord was Raimon de Castel-Roussillon, rich, powerful and vindictive. He was married to a woman called Seremonda .

It is said that she did not resist Cabestanh's advances. When her husband learned that she had been seduced, he met the troubadour out hawking, had him killed, beheaded, and his heart cut out. He had it roasted in a pie seasoned with pepper and gave it to his wife as an enticing dish.

She ate it. Asked whether it was enjoyable, she replied that the taste had been exceptionally good. Raimon then jeeringly told her that it was her lover's heart and to prove that he was dead displayed his severed head. She threw herself from the castle's window.[34] Ezra Pound turned the suicide into poetry in Canto IV.

And she went toward the window, and cast her down
All the while, the while, the swallows crying:
    Ityn!
 'It is Cabestan's heart in the dish,'
 'It is Cabestan's heart in the dish?'
 'No other taste shall change this.'
And she went toward the window,
   The slim white stone bar
Making a double arch;
Firm even fingers held to the firm pale stone;
Swung for a moment,
And the wind out of Rhodez
Caught in the full of her sleeve,
the swallows crying:
    'Tis, 'Tis, Ytis'.[35]

It is a good story but it is a fairy story. Others were not. A knight, Gautier des Fontaines, imprudently fell in love with the wife of the Count of Flanders. She did not resist. The insulted count had him beheaded. Elsewhere, the *trouvère*, the Châtelain de Coucy, died at sea on his way to the Fourth Crusade. By his request his heart was sent back to France for the woman he loved. Her resentful husband threw it away.

A legendary minstrel from Brittany also lost his heart – in reality, not figuratively. And even farther back in time there is a ninth-century version of the fable as distant as India. The reality was that Seremonda outlived her husband and remarried. Cabestanh continued to sing – wholeheartedly – for many years.

Leaving Ventadorn, Bernart, an exile, wept at his fate:

Et es be dreihz que ja mais lai no torn . . .

And so it is right that I never return there

.   .   .   .   .
She shows me a gloomy, angry face
Because I loved her. I am resigned to it,
She is resentful, complains for no reason.

Unaccustomed to searching for patronage, Bernard may have drifted for years before arriving at the court of Eleanor, Queen of England. Throughout that tedious period he brooded about the woman he had loved. Peire, probably Peire d'Alvernhe the cheerful lampoonist of fellow singers, shared a *tenson* with him, 'Amics, Bernartz de Ventadorn', about the affair. The poem's attribution to Bernart has been questioned, but his name is in it, its sentiments are relevant to his plight and it is probably authentic.

Peire wrote:

Amics Bernartz de Ventadorn . . .

Friend Bernart de Ventadorn
How can you possibly stop singing . . .

And in the sixth verse his companion explained why there was no song in his heart.

Peire, mout ai lo cor dolen . . .

Peire, my heart fills with grief
When I remember one false lady

Who killed me, I know not why
Except that I loved her faithfully . . .

But eventually, around 1154, he came to Eleanor's glittering court. His *vida* described the change in his fortunes.

Et el s'en parti e si s.en anet a la duchesa de Normandia . . .

Then his heartless lady sent for him and commanded to leave the lands of her husband. And he left, and went to the Duchess of Normandy, who was young and of great nobility, with a great liking for virtue, honour and songs that complimented and praised her. She was very pleased with Bernart's singing. She received him and made him welcome. He stayed at her court for a very long time. He fell in love with her and she with him and he wrote her many songs.[36]

Eleanor was one of the most powerful women of her time: in her youth the Duchess of Aquitaine, since her marriage to Henry II in 1152 she had been Queen of England. She was given the title of Duchess of Normandy in 1154 when Henry was crowned king. Instead, ever inventive and ever inaccurate, Jean de Nostradamus had her marry 'Richard, roi d'Angleterre', who was her son.[37]

It was not illicit incest. It was bad history. Richard was not born until 1157.

Eleanor was a king's wife with unusual liberty to enjoy herself. She had marital freedom. Henry, only 21 years old at his coronation, had troubles everywhere: in England, in Scotland, in Anjou and Maine, and against the kingdom of France. The vicious civil war between Stephen and Matilda had left England in chaos. By 1152 there were plundering soldiers to be suppressed, unpaid mercenaries to be evicted or killed, rebellious barons to be left impotent by the demolition of their fortresses. Malcolm IV, King of Scotland, was forced to abandon the northern counties his troops had occupied. In Anjou and Maine, Geoffrey, Henry's brother, had to be pacified by diplomatic bribery. Above all, there was the never-ending struggle, sometime warfare, against Louis VII, the French king. Henry was energetic and tireless. For six ceaseless years of conflict he fought to establish stability in his kingdom, until in 1161 he achieved peace. During those long years Eleanor was able to relax in France, indulging in the luxuries of pleasure.

At that time, rather than at Poitiers, her court was probably at Angers, a city dominated by its stupendous castle, which resembled a Krak of the crusaders miraculously transferred from the Holy Land to Western Europe, its pepperpot-roofed towers rising above attractively banded walls of alternating courses of dark schist and pale sandstone. To an impressed and astonished onlooker they looked like slices of layer cake prepared by a giantess.

Three centuries later another poet, vagabond and genius, François Villon, visited it and its gardens on the ramparts when the stronghold was the court of the poet-nobleman René, Duke of Anjou and Lorraine.[38] In the middle of the twelfth century it was the coruscating court of Eleanor of Aquitaine and Normandy.

She dazzled and impressed. She was lovely, described as *perpulchra*, 'more than beautiful'. She was literate. She was well read, 'wise, of great virtue', so learned that the Anglo-Norman poet Robert Wace of Jersey dedicated his *Brut* of 1155 to her, a French version of Geoffrey of Monmouth's British *Historia Regum Britanniae*. Wace's was the first work to mention the Round Table, and the exploits and challenging encounters of its knights were very much admired and liked. 'It has been argued that Eleanor was the model for Wace's portrayal of Guinevere, presumably because he felt that the subject matter would both meet with her approval and reflect her interests and concerns.'[39]

It was an age when legendary stories of illicit love between a queen and a man of lower rank enthralled listeners: Guinevere, King Arthur's wife, with his nephew Mordred; Iseult, wife of King Mark of Cornwall, with his nephew Tristran. The lovers fascinated because of their disregard for the conventions of courtly love. The lovers could be envied, pitied, but never admired or emulated – to public knowledge. Eleanor may have enjoyed the romances. She would not consider joining them. Her court provided enjoyment enough.

Local descriptions of the time described those courts as centres of liberality at the very boundaries of taste and extravagance. The courtiers dressed fantastically. They dressed in rich, rare materials whose colours daily matched their moods.

The chronicler Geoffrey de Vigeois, a moralising monk – from northern France, of course – who had deplored Guilhem de Poitiers for 'his excessive love of women', also wrote disapprovingly of Eleanor's court and its lordly inhabitants What he said about the luxuries of Poitiers would have been as true of Angers a few years earlier. 'They flaunt slashed cloaks and flowing sleeves like hermits. Young men grow their hair long and wear shoes with pointed toes.' A censorious viewer could mistake ladies for serpents because of their incredibly long, trailing trains. It was a carefree society of young people, spontaneous, free and natural. Gifts of rich handkerchiefs were casually exchanged, circlets of gold or silver, brooches, looking-glasses, purses, girdles, combs, sleeves, gloves, rings, caskets, whatever lady needed for her toilet or her dressing table.[40] Strangely, Vigeois was the only historian to mention Bernart of Ventadorn.

Not unexpectedly, music was a very important part of life at the court. Many kinds of instruments have been mentioned, the lyre, flute, tambourine, harp, drums, usually accompanied by the 'sweet songs'. They were sung to the light of flambeaux burning in their brackets on the walls, the flames brightening the tables and benches on the flag-stoned floor, smoke rising sootily to the ceilings. Servants fetched delicacies of food and drink, musicians playing in the background, courtiers dancing, some singing familiar tunes, the silks and the satins mingling in one of a thousand nights of aesthetic indulgence. It was into those courts of enjoyment that the new arrival, Bernart de Ventadorn, was welcomed. Already with a reputation of high poetry and pleasing music, he was expected to bring even more delight to Eleanor's gathering.

There was a trap. By the middle of the twelfth century there had been two, perhaps three, generations of troubadours and minstrels since Guilhem de Poitiers, and the songs they sang had fossilised into formulae. Poems began with the welcoming of spring after the lifeless winter. There was a beautiful woman who was loved even though she was unreachable. Sometimes she smiled. Sometimes there was the chill of a frown. Only her beauty was unchanging. The story was always the same. The singer was to be forever her faithful servant, obedient, entirely at her command.

It was a comfortably familiar story, but it had been sung as many times in the courts as the *Pater Noster* had been repeated in churches. The words changed, the music changed, the sentiments were static. Some troubadours added variety by complicated rhyme schemes. Others used arcane language. There were ingenious rhymes. But underneath the dressing there was the same tired body. Everyone knew the feelings were insincere. There was no genuine emotion, only rigid verbal patterns.

Bernart de Ventadorn escaped from the trap by appearing to be caught in it. Forty-five or more of his songs survive. Of them twenty or so have music, 'an astonishing number when one considers that Bernart de Ventadorn flourished in the mid-twelfth century, a hundred years before our first written records'.[41] (For his compact discs see Appendix 1.)

He did not compose in the obscurantism currently in favour nor was he interested in technical complexities. In contrast, his words were lively, humorous, varied with pleasant surprises. He was no deliberating technician vaunting a mastery of complex constructions. There was more of Shakespeare in him:

Lovers and madmen have such seething brains
Such shaping fantasies, that apprehend
More than cool reason ever comprehends.[42]

He lulled his audience into thinking that nothing had changed by beginning his songs conventionally, welcoming the arrival of spring and the happiness that his love of a fine lady gave him:

Can l'herba fresch' e.lh folha . . . [Poem XXXIX]

When green grass and green leaves grow
and the tree bears blossom,
when nightingales sing sweet and fine,
lifting their voices melodiously,
then I have joy from song and flower
and joy for myself and my beloved.
I am entwined with joy, joy everywhere,
A joy that is far beyond any other.

It was a trick. It was meant to delude his listeners. He knew how to awaken them to the realisation that, unlike any of his colleagues, he was sincere, just as other singers have known how to delude.

In 'Rose-cheeked Laura . . .', said by T.S. Eliot to be one of the most perfect of all poems, the Elizabethan poet/musician Thomas Campion, wrote:

These dull notes we sing,
Discords need to save them . . .[43]

Bernart de Ventadorn also introduced discords.

He involved his audience. He transformed them from external listeners into participants, like the actors and actresses in a drama, as they unconsciously recognised themselves in his words. From an impassive audience they became an orchestra, each one seeing his or her identity in the characters Bernart portrayed: the friend or the enemy; the true or the deceitful; the discreet or the gossip; the defender or the accuser; the faithful or the disloyal; the chaste or the carnal. In a superficially traditional format he used his listeners, much as Anglo-Saxon and Norman minstrels had done in their dramatic recitals. He persuaded them that he, quite differently from others, was sincere in his love for a beautiful woman. Best of all, he persuaded the woman.

His portrayal of the good and the bad in life are all there in his Poem XXXI:

Non es meravelha s'eu chan

Of course it's no wonder that I sing
Better than other troubadours,
My heart is more sincere towards love . . .

Then came the comparisons: the feeling and unfeeling:

Ben es mortz qui d'amor no sen

A man is dead if he does not feel love truly
The faithful, the disloyal

Per bona fe e ses enjam

In good faith, without deception
Honest lovers and seducers

A Deus! Car se fosson train . . .

Ah God! If only the difference between true love and false was obvious
Foul tongues and kind words

E.lh lauzenger e.lh trichador

Slanderers and frauds should have horns to expose their unworthiness.

And then Bernart revealed himself, honest, submissive, the most sincere of
admirers:

Bona domna, re no.us demn . . .

Good Lady, I ask nothing from you
But that you admit me as your servant
And I shall serve you as if you were my lord.
No matter what gift, big, little, comes to me,
I am at your command, ever trustworthy
To you, you so noble, gentle, courteous, joyful.
After all, you are not a ferocious bear or lion –
You will not kill me if I give myself to you.

'Give myself to you' was sufficiently ambiguous to avoid suspicion of
his being a philanderer surreptitiously creeping towards hidden
intimacies.

Poems like *Non es meravelha s'eu chan* were greatly admired by both her courtiers and Eleanor herself. The proof is in the *vida*: 'E plasion li fort las chansos . . .' (She was very pleased with Bernart's songs. She received him and made him welcome. He stayed at her court for a very long time).

For itinerant troubadours a great court was a *caravanserai* where one might linger a day or two, perhaps a week, but seldom longer. There was always another patron, another part of the musical world. 'A very long time' was probably months, even a year or more, a sojourn granted only to the most favoured of singers and most liked of men.

Noticeably, Bernart's songs were directed to Eleanor as his noble lady, grand mistress of her court, and they became more direct, reminding her of his unhappy past and his delightful today.

He sang of the false woman at Ventadorn:

Can par les flors . . . [Poem XLI]

When I think how I used to love
One who was false and merciless,
Such anger comes back to me
That I almost abandon my present joy.
My lady, for whom I sing and now live,
Wound my heart with your mouth
Through a sweet kiss of heartfelt love
To bring back joy and banish mortal grief.

As time became 'a long time', then, very gradually, underlying the crust of courtly love in his poems were the entreaties for physical love. In Poem XXVI *Lancan vei per mei la landa . . .* he wrote:

Sinful she is if she doesn't command me one night
To come to the room where she undresses, alone,
And make me a necklace of her arms
Beside her bed . . .

He rhapsodised about her 'white, plump and smooth body', 'well-formed, thin and smooth', 'fresh skin and high colour . . .', 'lovely, graceful, and engaging figure, making me rich when I was poor', very flattering for a woman, even a queen, in her thirties. She admired the praise, waited for more. In *Pois preyatz me, senhor . . .* Poem XXXVI, he groaned:

I shall die, I know,
Of yearning and desire

If that lovely lady does not call me
Near her, where she lies,
And let me hold and kiss her
As she presses closely to me . . .

Bernart, so near yet far, continued. In Poem XXXVIII, *Lo gens tems de pascor* . . .

It is grief. Why live
If day after day I can't see
My finest, truest pleasure
In her bed beneath the window,
From head to foot, white body
Like snow at Christmas,
And we two, lying against each other
Stretched out together, side by side?

Whether Eleanor ever granted him the final favour is unknown. It is unlikely. Whatever her inclinations, she was a great queen and he a low-born commoner. Not being social equals, they could not be sexual partners, unlike other reputed lovers of hers, Raymond of Antioch and Geoffrey of Blois, both noblemen of high rank.

If ever Eleanor and Bernart did make love, the memory was lost with their deaths. In life matters were decided for them. Concerned, hearing whispers, Henry II, King of England, husband of Eleanor of Aquitaine and Normandy, summoned Bernart de Ventadorn to England on the pretext of ordering him to abandon womanish serenades and compose manly martial music.[44]

Bernart hated England and its chilled, wet autumn. He wrote about his misery – *Faihz es lo vers tot a randa . . .* – and went on: "I am far from my lady like a magnet the fair one draws me to her, whom may God protect. If the English king and Norman duke so wills it, I shall see her before the winter surprises us.'[45]

Hardly had the reluctant musician been permitted to return to France than Henry ordered his wife to leave France. She abandoned her troubadour: *En Bernartz si remas de sai tristz e dolenz . . .* 'Bernart stayed behind, sad and mournful and he went to Count Raymond of Toulouse where he remained until the Count died'.

Years later in 1168 Eleanor returned to her homeland and held court in Poitiers at Guilhem's Maubergeon tower, which he had defiantly named after his mistress. Eleanor may have left England, affronted at Henry's well-advertised affaire with Rosamond Clifford.[46] The great hall is now the city's

Palais de Justice. Poets gathered there, Gaucelm: Faidit, Bertran de Born, even the more famous Chrétien de Troyes.

Hundreds of miles away, without hope, Bernart was abandoned. He mourned in *Ero.m cosselhatz, senhor . . .* Poem II

> With the tears I wipe from my eyes
> I write more than a hundred letters of love
> And send them to the most beautiful,
> The courtliest of all women in the world
> Many times I heartbrokenly remember
> What she did when we had to part:
> She covered her face –
> Because she could not tell me, 'Yes' or 'No'.

He went to Raymond V of Toulouse and, on the count's death, possibly visited the Viscountess Ermengard.of Narbonne. One of his later poems mentions the place, *Per aquella dolo*r . . . (Because of his grief Bernart retired to the Cistercian monastery of Dalon and ended his days there.) He is believed to have died there around 1194. It was some 4 miles from Hautefort in the Dordogne, the castle of the military-minded troubadour Bertran de Born, who died in the same monastery some time before 1215.

Preferring fiction to fact, Jean de Nostradamus had Bernart de Ventadorn die almost thirty years later in 1223, in Montmajour abbey near Arles in Provence. It was 200 miles east of Dalon.[47]

Et ieu, N'Uc de Saint Circ . . .

And I, Uc of Saint-Circ, wrote this down from what I was told by Viscount Eble of Ventadorn, who was the son of the viscountess that Bernart had loved. And he wrote the songs that you can read.

Like the sixteenth-century Nostradamus, Uc could make mistakes, even though his life overlapped with Bernart's. His Ebles was not the son but the grandson of the viscount whose wife had been charmed, perhaps seduced, by Bernart de Ventadorn.

EIGHT

I'll sing of those troubadours
Who perform in a mixture of styles, including
The worst of them who think they sing well.
They should go singing somewhere else.
The entire hundred has not a tune between them,

(Peire d'Alvernhe)

Since Peire d'Alvernhe has sung
Of troubadours now of the past
I shall sing, as well as I can, of those
Who have arrived more recently.
They should not be angry
As I criticise their shortcomings.

(The Monk of Montaudon)

A Melody of Troubadours, Twelfth Century

A wand'ring minstrel, I,
A thing of shreds and patches,
Of ballads, songs and patches,
And dreaming lullaby.

(W.S. Gilbert, *The Mikado*, I).

Today the castles are husks. Winds chill through their emptiness. There is no colour, no warmth from their roofless walls. Sparrows chatter where troubadours sang. Where there were tapestries there are only the droppings of birds, and where feet danced rhythmically to the music there is only the tap-tappings of falling rain. The castles are tombs whose ghosts have departed.

It was not always so. Peire d'Alvernhe wrote about a castle he remembered:

Lo vers fo faitz als enflabotz . . .

This song was made to a bagpipe's burping
At Puivert, while playing and laughing.
It was a time when there was music everywhere.

The twelfth century was the century of the troubadours in southern France. They were not confined to the Languedoc, although that was the heartland. The songs reached westwards to the hills of Provence, southwards into the Spanish domains of Aragon, Navarre and Castile, where the love of ladies had already been sung for centuries. Troubadours were welcomed as far north as the Auvergne, Limousin, Poitiers.

The eleventh century's brief and tuneless winter had ended with the arrival of the muddy, bawdy boots of Guilhem, Count of Poitiers. It warmed into full spring with the delicate yearnings of Jaufré Rudel, and spring became full summer with the words and melodies of Peire d'Alvernhe, Raimbaut d'Aurenga, Peire Rogier and, even more than them, Bernart de Ventadorn.

The warmth continued over the years as the troubadours who followed those splendid makers of music were mocked tenderly by the Monk of Montaudon, that contradictory person who drifted idly about the countryside with his songs of love, enjoying wine and song, if not women, while remaining a fully ordained cleric.

Two singers told the story of that century of love, the Monk and his predecessor, Peire d'Alvernhe. That troubadour had a *vida*.

Peire d'Alverne so fo de l'evesquat de Clarmon . . .

Peire d'Alvernhe came from the diocese of Clermont. He was clever, well-read and the son of a burgher. Physically he was attractive and he could sing and compose well. He was the first really good troubadour in the world and he wrote the finest tune in the poem that went:

De iostals iorns els loncs sers . . .

A time of brief days and long nights
When the clear air grows darker . . .

He wrote no *cansos*, those complex songs of courtly love, only simple poems. He was greatly respected and admired by all the good men, the great lords and ladies of his time and he was considered the world's finest troubadour until the coming of Guiraut de Bornelh.[1]

Little is known of Peire d'Alvernhe's life. He was writing in the mid-1150s, and it was rumoured at the time that he had been a Canon of the Church but had broken his vows. It was also accepted that he was an extremely good poet. He was an innovator, the maker of the first religious poem in Occitan, a poet of restrained verse, often with deep Christian sentiments. His was grave, pure poetry, composed, like Marcabru's long before him, quite deliberately in challenging metres and difficult rhyme schemes, a style known as *trobar clus* or 'obscure poetry'. 'Verbal gyrations', Bonner described it. He took himself seriously, claiming to be the first to write in pure diction.

Sobre.l vieill trobar e.l novel . . .

About the old-style poetry and the new
I want to explain to men of learning

So that generations to come can understand
That, before me, there was no perfect poem.

Qu'ieu so raitz, e dic qu'ieu soi

Premiers
I am the root, and I claim to be the first to write
In perfect speech.[2]

Peire d'Alvernhe praised himself highly in his songs but when criticizing
other singers, he also included himself:

Peire d'Alvernhe a tal votz . . .

Peire d'Alvernhe has such a voice that he can sing
Well whether the notes are high or low.
To his listeners he speaks highly of himself
As the master of everything. But it would be better
If he could make his verses plainer
Because hardly anyone can understand them.

It was his self-mockery that saved him from ridiculous conceit. The verse
came at the end of a long lampoon he composed, making fun of his
fellows:

Cantari d'aquestz trobadors . . .

I'll sing of those troubadours
Who perform in a mixture of styles, including
The worst of them who think they sing well.
They should go singing somewhere else.
The entire hundred has not a tune between them,
Not one of them knows a single note of music.

And the teasing verses ended with:

Lo vers fo faitz als enflabotz . . .

This song was sung to the sound of bagpipes
At Puivert's castle, with much laughter and pleasure.

He must have been accompanied by his minstrel. Even the most accomplished troubadour would have been unable to sing and blow the bagpipes simultaneously.

Unlike many of the smaller castles in the Languedoc Puivert, 'the green mount', is not a complete husk. Sixteen miles south of Carcassonne, it can still be visited. It stands a fair walk from the main road, but a car can be taken quite close to the entrance with only the gentlest rise to its impressive barbican. Inside, it is a shell. The spacious but empty courtyard is ramparted, but the southern wall has been destroyed. At the far end, however, is the original square keep, aligned on the cardinal points with an entrance facing exactly west.[3]

The *donjon* still stands more than 30 metres (100 feet) high. It is complete. It has a basement where grain and other foodstuffs were stored, a ground-floor guardroom beneath family rooms and a chapel. Above them is the castle's glory, its tall *salle des musiciens*. It was here that Peire d'Alvernhe and his fellows had gathered in 1170, singing to their minstrels' music, percussion, stringed, blown and wheel-turned. Eight of the instruments can be seen carved high on the walls.

The images are in stone lamp brackets, *culs-de-lampe*, where the illumination of flambeaux had burned. One jongleur plays a *cornemuse*, an early form of bagpipes whose bag was often designed as the body of a tortoise with the pipe's bottom end as its head. There is a musician with his lute similar to a mandolin and a cittern, a drummer with his *tambourin*, a violinist holding his *vieille à archet*, used when the jongleur was singing without any accompanying players, another with a *cittern* and plectrum. A sixth has the enchanting three-stringed *rebeck* and its bow. The adjacent bracket has a minstrel with a psalter, plucking its long strings, and finally comes a jongleur with his *orgue portatif*, a hand-organ akin to a guitar but with keys that tapped the strings by turning a wheel. Details in the carvings are difficult to see in the castle as they are well above head height, but there is a fine set of reproductions and an exhibition of musical instruments in the handsome Musée Quercorb in the nearby village.

Puivert's *salle des musiciens* was the venue for d'Alvernhe's teasing poem about the talents and demerits of his comrades. He described thirteen. The majority, like Guillem de Ribas and Gonzalgo Roïtz, are almost unknown. Four are not, the first being Peire Rogier followed by Giraut de Bornelh and Bernart de Ventadorn. Ninth in the poem but fourth of the better troubadours was Raimbaut d'Aurenga.

Like so many of d'Alvernhe's criticised singers Peire Rogier was deaf to the delicate cadences of words and music.

D'aisso mer mal Peire Rotgiers . . .

In that deficiency Peire Rogier also is guilty
And he shall be the first to be accused
For he sings too publicly of love.
He would be better off with a psalter
In a church, holding a candelabra
With an immense candle flaming in it.

Like d'Alvernhe, he seems to have been ordained only to abandon his vows and take up singing. He was encouraged to spend a long time in Narbonne at the court of Ermengarde, the viscountess. His *vida* said so: *Lonc temps estet ab ela en cort a se fo crezut . . .* (He was for a very long time with her and there were increasing rumours that she had granted him the intimacy of her love).[4] Ermengarde heard the murmurs. Rogier was no more fortunate than Arnaut Mareuil had been at Burlats. He was banished. To a modern ear it is surprising that he had been permitted to remain for so long. The poems of 'love' of his that survive seem emotionless and didactic rather than ardent and romantic.

Giraut de Bornelh, d'Alvernhe's second target, was a far better troubadour. He was admired by later Italian poets including Dante and Petrarch. Dante termed him a poet of 'rectitude', and in his *Trionfo d'Amore* Petrarch placed him *E quei che fur conquisi più Guerra . . .* (among those whom love could not subdue). His vida was as enthusiastic about his abilities.

Si fo deLimozi de l'econtrada d'Esiduoill . . .

Giraut de Borneil was from the Limousin near Excideuil, a rich castle of the Viscount of Limoges. He was of low birth but well educated and wise and, because he was a better troubadour than anyone earlier he became known as 'The Master Troubadour'.[5]

Alfred Jeanroy disagreed. 'This so-called "Master of the Troubadours" seems to us like an infatuated pedant, pompously spinning out his banalities . . . He reminds one of a tenor as pleased with himself as he is displeased with a public whom he cannot forgive for not going into ecstasies over his floral flourishes.'[6]

The condemnation had some slight truth. Bornelh was a master of poetical technique. He devised arcane rhyme patterns. He could write in the *trobar clus* and the *trobar leu*, the perplexing and the clear styles. That was his problem. Master of all ways of writing, he had no recognizable style of his own. Hearing one of his more than seventy poems for the first time, sung by another troubadour, one would not know whether one was listening to Rogier or Marcabru or Rudel or Ventadorn. There was no noticeably identifiable Bornelh.

He travelled widely in France and Spain, accompanied Viscount Adémar V on the Third Crusade and was present at the siege of Acre in 1191. He reached a crusader's ambition. He reached Jerusalem.

His *vida* had a *razo*, a gloss or afterthought:

Girautz de Borneil si amava una dompna de Gascoigna que avia nom N'Alamnda d'Estanc . . .

He loved a woman from Gascony called Alamanda of Estancs . . . She granted him smiles and fair words but nothing more except one of her gloves. To his dismay he lost it. 'My lady Alamanda, when she saw that he supplicated her much for her love, and knew he had lost the glove, grew angry about the glove, saying he had kept it ill' and withdrew entirely from him.

Heartbroken Guiraut entreated one of the lady's servant-girls, also Alamanda, to help him. She failed. 'The truth was that lady Alamanda had come upon another man for which she was scorned because the man was unstable and spiteful'.[7]

Peire d'Alvernhe derided Bornelh:

E.lh segons Girautz de Bornelh

And the second, Girault de Bornelh,
Is like a goatskin dried out in the sun.
His thin whining moans sound like
An old woman with a heavy bucket of water.
If he were to see himself in a mirror
He'd rate himself no more than a tiny eglantine.

It was the golden age of the troubadours, the later years of the twelfth century, when there was patronage everywhere, but Guiraut de Bornelh noticed signs of decay.

E vitz cortz amar . . .

And you saw the perfect singers,
Handsome boots, finely dressed,
Going from one court to another
With one thought, to praise ladies.

Now you hear nothing about them,
Of how their glory is ruined.
Where this corruption began
Of speaking badly of ladies
I cannot say. Whose fault? The ladies, their lovers?
Both. Because exaggeration removed sincerity.

On son gaudit joglar . . .

Where have they gone, the singers
That once were so eagerly welcomed?
Each lord who leads must have
Someone to guide him himself . . .

And Bornelh ended:

Era no m'ais! Per que . . .

I am not complaining. Why not? Don't ask,
It would be a shame to end my song on that sad note.

It had been an inbuilt weakness of the chanson d'amour that later troubadours, having inherited an established tradition of complimenting, even over-praising ladies, had to express their 'feelings' in increasingly elaborate and increasingly clearly insincere sentiments. Often the song of love became a song of falseness. But this was still the Golden Age.

The third of d'Alvernhe's victims was Bernart de Ventadorn, whose verse has already been quoted: *E.l tertz, Bernartz de Ventadorn . . .,* stating that he was shorter than Bornelh, that his father was a labourer and that his mother a castle menial collecting firewood for the oven. This did not detract from the poet's genius.

The last of the exceptional troubadours that Peire d'Alvernhe teased was Raimbaut d'Aurenga.

E.lh noves es En Raimbautz . . .

And the ninth is En Raimbaut
Who's much too proud of his own verse;
But I look down my nose at him,
For he knows neither joy nor warmth,
That's why, to me, he's no better
Than those flutists who go begging alms.

Of Rambaut his *vida* said:

Roembaez d'Aurenga si fo lo seigneur d'Aurenga . . .

Raimbaut d'Aurenga was the lord of Orange and of Courthézon and many other castles. He was clever, well-taught, skilful in weaponry, and talked well. He greatly liked fine ladies and honourable behaviour. He wrote good poems and songs but he preferred to compose in difficult, subtle ways.[8]

Raimbaut d'Aurenga III, 3rd Lord of Orange, was the first native troubadour of Provence. He was the son of a nobleman who died leaving enormous debts that his son was unable to settle. Raimbaut became a gambler, irresponsible, but a good poet. Although lacking funds, his favoured court at Courthézon entertained fine troubadours, Guirat de Bornelh, Peire Rogier, maybe even the finest of all, Bernart de Ventadorn.

Good looking, according to Rogier, with golden-brown hair and an attractive body, he was popular with ladies, especially in the complex verses he wrote for and about them.[9] From the early 1160s to 1173 he composed almost thirty poems, frequently elaborate in style and many fundamentally crude in their jokes. For a time he was in love with Marie de Vertfuoil of Lombardy, whom he called his 'jongleur', and then with the Countess of Urgell in Lombardy, although, in a comparable idiosyncrasy to Jaufré Rudel's, he never saw the beloved, simply adoring her for her many good works.

He is also said to have had an unsatisfactory affair with a passionate poetess, the Countess of Die. Preferring courtly pleasures, he wrote songs, often at the expense of ladies.

Si volatz dompnas guasanhar . . .
Datz lor del ponh per mieg sas nars

If you wish to win ladies and they
Repeatedly reply rudely to your pleas
Give them a punch on the nose.

As a poet he is best considered as a talented dilettante, technically brilliant with a lighthearted virtuosity but often shallow. Yet he could be ardently persuasive:

Bon aurai, dompna, grand honor

I shall be greatly honoured, Lady,
If you would grant me the favour
Of holding you in my arms
Naked beneath the covering sheets.[10]

Almost penniless he pawned lands. Many castles were his in name but it
was a divided claim. Kinsmen existed, and in Provence and the Languedoc
there was no statutory right of inheritance to the oldest son. All had a
share. Like many of these weakened landowners, he fought in several of
the endless, petty local wars against his overlord, Count Raymond V of
Toulouse. Such persistent internal feuding and social fragmentation was to
be disastrous when the Languedoc was later confronted by a single-minded
army of conquest.

The twenty-nine-year-old Raimbaut died suddenly on 29 May 1173 in
his castle at Courthézon, probably a victim of the influenza epidemic that
had spread through Europe. A chronicler wrote: 'many people coughed
out their souls.' Raimbaut's friend, the professional troubadour Guiraut de
Bornelh, wrote a *planh* mourning him and praising his work:

Dels vostres trobars esmratz

When they think of the poems you refined
And perfected, of your acts of kindness
Your fame, wisdom and splendid works
Even those people who suffer most
Will find themselves feeling pleasure.[11]

Raimbaut d'Aurenga, Rogier, Bornelh, Ventadorn, these were the men
whom Peire D'Alvernhe mocked at Puivert in 1170. They were the talented
minority.

Whichever court or castle they visited, they were eagerly welcomed
and abundantly rewarded for their concert with ornate clothes, horses,
rich equipment, costly gifts. In exchange for the romantic pleasure and
merriment they provided, they received generous largesse. There was
nothing inconspicuous or *chiaroscuro* about their arrival. Those famous
entertainers came with a technicoloured travelling troupe of minstrels,
a rainbow of red, blue, green and yellow knee-length tunics, flared
sleeves billowing at the elbows, some tunics plain, the majority striped,
the players wearing broad-brimmed hats, skull caps, others bare-headed,
legs warm inside multi-patterned, expensive stockings and boots of fine

leather, a motley of musicians playing pipes and trumpets to the beating of drums. The 'performance' began some distance from the court as a clarioned overture proclaimed their approach, the medieval forerunner of a Hollywood fanfare.

In southern France there were rich halls everywhere, the most luxurious being at Toulouse, Narbonne, Montpellier, Béziers and Carcassonne. There were commodious castles like Puivert, the nearby Coustaussa and Rennes-le-Château, the more distant Pennautier and Saissac, unusually situated on low ground, Aguilar, in whose region the Fitou vineyards flourish today, Padern, Tuchan, Cabaret and many others. There were strongholds, strategically placed, that would grow into monsters: Puilaurens, Peyrepertuse, Quéribus, Termes, fortresses so forbidding that they were nicknamed the 'Sons of Carcassonne', barricading the Franco-Spanish border. In peacetime their bastions were ajar for singers. The Languedoc was a golden paradise for the talented singer.

But such talented men were rare. For every Rogier or d'Aurenga there were ten, twenty, perhaps more with less virtuosity. They were, literally, journeymen plodding from small castle to wealthy burgher's house hoping to find an open door, an invitation. Only the brashest went to the courts of great lords risking a rough, even violent rebuff by a contemptuous doorman and his porters.

Some of the mediocre, the most pathetic of the nonentities, were Gilbert's things 'of shreds and patches', with a poorly strung harp and a stale repertoire of well-known songs. On a few occasions they were tolerated as players that would suffice until something better came. They existed but they did not succeed. Such was the troubadour on his horse at the banks of the Tarn, despairing of any patronage in the south, dreading the derision and contempt of the monetarily rewarding lands north of the cold river.

For the elite it was a good time. In the south of the country there was no tumultuous disruption, no savage war. There were sporadic local feuds over territory, like those in which d'Aurenga had sided with the Trencavels, viscounts of Béziers and Carcassonne, against the Pons, the powerful counts of Toulouse, skirmishes in which a retainer or two might be maimed or killed but life soon returned to equanimity and the leisurely existence that that land of sun and song had known for generations. Peacefully marrying off eligible daughters was a far more congenial method of placating land-hungry neighbours. And excellent troubadours transformed that good existence into a lotus-land of dreams.

Into that escapist world came the Monk of Montaudon, the odd man out among a collection of individuals. He was an ordained member of the

Catholic Church who had not sneaked away from his monastery. He had
been given permission. He was not the only troubadour who had begun
as a novitiate clerk. There were probably other intelligent boys who, like
Uc de Saint-Circ, had been intended for a clerical existence and taught
to read and write before rebelling against the prospect of a life in the
church and abandoning their studies.There were others – Peire Rogier and
Peire d'Alvernhe among them – who had taken Holy Orders and risen
to some status within the Church before deciding that a life of luxury in
castle courts was preferable to the drudgery of transcribing texts in cold
cloisters.

The Monk was different from any of them. His *vida* reported:

Lo monges de Montaudon si fo d'Alvernhe d'un castel que a nom Vic . . .

The Monk of Montaudon was from the Auvergne, from a castle called
Vic which is near Orlac. He was of gentle birth and was made a monk
in the abbey of Orlac. And then the abbot gave him the priorate of
Montaudon . . .

E tornat s,en ad Orlac al sieu abat . . .

He returned to Orlac, to his abbot, showing him how he had improved
Montaudon priory, and pleaded to the abbot to let him follow King
Alfonso of Aragon's advice, and the abbot agreed. For the king had
ordered him to eat meat [*manjes carn e domnejes e catntas e trobes . . .*]
court ladies, sing and write poetry.[12]

He can be imagined as a jovial person, a Friar Tuck *doppelgänger* among
a band of merry men, with a happy smile and much laughter, and with a
persuasive but sincere tongue. Good poetry was his profession and good
company, an abundance of food and drink, his essentials. Many of his
poems evoke an impression of being recited uproariously at table with
friends and wine. Whether it was red, white or rosé wine was no matter
as long as it was good and plentiful. He was funny, censorious of uncouth
behaviour and, at times, as earthy as Guilhem of Poitiers.

The Monk even wrote a poem in which he had the effrontery to argue with
God that women should have as much right to use cosmetics as the statues
of St Mary and other saints had to have painted faces. Unsurprisingly, in
verses by the Monk of Montaudon God Himself was not averse to using
colloquial language about bodily functions. Even in a condensed prose
version it chortles irreverently:

Autra vetz fui a parlamen . . .

1. The other day I happened to be in Heaven and heard the holy statues complaining about the make-up women were putting on. Only statues, they said, should have painted faces.
2. God replied firmly. 'Monk, images of sainted ladies should have colour. It's their right. So, off you go and tell women to stop using cosmetics or I'll stop them Myself.'
3. 'Lord God', I retorted, 'be more moderate. It's natural for women to beautify themselves. Neither You nor the carvings should grumble, especially them, because if they had their way there would only be frustrated, undecorated women down below and they'd stop making donations to those saints.'
4. 'Monk,' grunted God. 'You argue badly. Earthly humans have no right to enhance themselves without My consent. How can I be God Omnipotent when those below whom I make old keep making themselves look young? If that goes on they'd soon become as unchanging as Me.'
5. 'Lord, You speak from too high up. Using make-up won't stop until You do something about it. Either make women remain lovely until death or cause all make-up vanish.'
6. 'Monk, it's simply wrong for women to improve their appearance. You defend them but, remember, they choose to use astringents that make them look finer but it also mars their skin and, worse, it comes off when they have a piss.'
7. 'Lord, the women who make up take care to do it properly. They put colour and powder on so thickly that it can't vanish with their first piss. What's more, if You can't be bothered to make them beautiful why shouldn't they do it for themselves?'
8. 'Monk, don't you realise that facial cosmetics cause women indignity when they're forced to make love unnaturally. Do you think they really want to bend over so that their man won't rub against their faces?'
9. 'Lord God, let them all go to Hell! I can never satisfy that hole. Even when I think I've reached dry land I have to start swimming again!'
10. 'Monk, we'll leave them alone! Since pissing wrecks their make-up I'll give them something to keep them pissing for ever!'
11. 'Lord, whomever You do make urinate, please spare Helis de Montfort. She never uses cosmetics and she always gives generously to the statues.'[13]

And with that barbed in-joke about a lady as notorious for her powdered, painted face as for her penny-pinching purse, the end of the poem had men thumping the table with their splashing flagons while other cheerfully inebriated listeners tumbled from their benches in spluttering convulsions of mirth. The Monk returned contentedly to his laden platter.

Some twenty-five years after Peire d'Alvernhe's Puivert skit, he composed a pastiche on his own contemporary troubadours. Never spiteful, the Monk imitated Peire in nineteen chuckling verses. Like his predecessor he included several men who, today, do not have one *vida* between them.

Pos Peire d'Alvernh's cantat . . .

Since Peire d'Alvernhe has sung
About those troubadours now of the past
I will sing, as best I can, of those
Who have appeared much more recently.
May they not be upset and angry
As I gently criticize their failings.

La primiers es de Sanh Desdier . . .

The first is from Saint-Didier,
Guilhem by name, who sings not only
Spontaneously but most agreeably;
But what's good about a man who dares not
Ask for what he wants? One must
Conclude that he's of little worthiness.

His *vida* clarifies nothing: *Guillems de Saint Leidier so fo uns rics castellan de Veillac . . .*[14]

He was a rich lord from Velay and may have been the first to be mentioned by the Monk because of his great age in the 1190s. He was the composer of light but charming songs that were elegant, lacking irritating conceits. He is said to have been in love with the viscountess Margarida, wife of Heraclitus, Count of Polignac, of whom Saint Leidier was a vassal.

He wrote many songs of love to her but later turned his affections to a lovely countess, for which, in revenge, 'Margarida gave herself to Hugo Maraescala, a treachery which caused her former admirer to estrange himself from her for ever'.

Le segons de Sanh Antoni . . .

The second, the viscount of Saint Antonin
Has never been rewarded with love's joy.
He had bad luck, for the first
Lady he loved became a heretic.
Since then he's looked for no other one,
And then weeps night and day.[15]

Raymun Jorda fo vescoms de Saint Antoni . . .

Despite its name, Saint-Antonin-Noble-Val is a rather drab tourist town in the Aveyron near the castles of Bruniquel and Penne d'Albigeoise. Raymond Jordan, its viscount, loved the lady of Penne, but when her husband was apparently fatally wounded in a battle and she believed she would be a widow, she joined the Cathars and became one of their Good Women. Despite the sad story, Saint-Antonin with its fine church offers no information about its minor troubadour.

4. *E lo terz es de Carcasses . . .*

And the third is from the Carcassès –
Miraval – who pretends to be so courtly,
Forever giving away his castle. Yet he's
Never there more than one month in the year,
And never for the Feast Day. So why
Should he care if someone else claims it

With Raimon de Miraval the story is different. He was a fine troubadour with a wife who was a poetess. He achieved some notoriety by ejecting her. The Catalan poet Uc de Mataplana rebuked him for such unmanly behaviour:

Car per sos bels captenemens . . .

For it was because of her fine manners
And her fine poems that he removed
His courtly wife from himself . . .

Raimons de Miraval si fo uns paubres cavalliers de Carcases . . . [16]

Raimon of Miraval was a poor knight from the Carcassès who held only one quarter-share of a castle so small that it did not have even forty men. But for his poetry and his talk, and for what he knew of love, gallantry and of the courtesies that pass between lovers, he was greatly liked and admired by the Count of Toulouse . . .

His career bridged the transition from the golden age of the troubadours to one of slow but insistent decline during the debilitating years of the Albigensian Crusade.

It was Miraval who advised an impoverished but competent player, Bajona, that, if he wanted recognition and reward, to go first to the castle of Cabaret and then to the lord of Saissac, 'who is certain to present you with a fine light robe'. Should his colleague then go on to the finest and most generous centre of all, the town of Minerve, it was likely that he would be given a horse and a suit of clothes.

In essence, he was a poet of the court, insisting on the strict observance of good manners both by the woman and her lover. His poetry, always in the *trobar leu* style of instant clarity, constantly spoke of propriety, any lapse of which was cuttingly condemned. (For his songs on compact discs see Appendix 1.)

He was as pure in his own affections. He was a poet of the court, and a woman that he loved, Azalais de Bousseizon, was of one at Lombers. He loved everything about her and her court:

Per liels am fontanas e rius . . .

She makes me love springs and streams,
Woods, orchards, market gardens and hedges,
The ladies and the excellent and despicable men,
The wise and the foolish men, the simpletons,
All of the noble region where she lives,
And the surrounding countryside.
For my thoughts are so much in that direction
That I do not believe that
Any other land or people exist.

In Poem 1 he wrote:

D'amor es totz mos cossiriers . . .

Love it is that occupies me
Because love is my one concern,
And miserable tongues will say
That a knight should think of other matters.
I say, that is not so,

For it is out of love, whatever others say,
What is best whether foolish or wise
And whatever one does for love is good.

And in Poem 10

Chansoneta, ves midons vai corren

Run, little song, to my lady
For she has worth and keeps her youth.

Miraval was the oldest of four brothers and two sisters, an undistinguished family in which Raimon was a poor knight hovering socially between the despised bourgeoisie and the desirable gentry. Born around 1135, he began writing his courtly verses thirty or so years later.

The castle at Miraval-Cabardès was as undistinguished as the family. Today it is a ruin above the banks of the River Orbiel. The village road from Carcassonne, twisting through Conques and Lastours to Mas-Cabardès and northwards through the wilderness of hills in the Carcassès, bends abruptly between the church and Miraval's castle, stands on a knoll, not even a hillock, neither high enough nor steep enough to deter a healthy cow, let alone a band of armed men. It was abandoned in 1209 when Simon de Montfort's crusaders approached it.

Early monkish contemporaries like Guillaume de Tudela, his 'anonymous' successor, the Cistercian monk Pierre des Vaux-de-Cernay, and the later, less reliable Guillaume de Puylaurens, chronicled the campaigns. Those events, the sieges, ambushes and battles, have been described in many subsequent works, the most accessible being listed in the Bibliography.

In his Poem 5 the Monk lampooned a penniless knight from the Auvergne:

Lo quartz Peirols, us Alvernhaz . . .

The fourth, from the Auvergne's called Peirol.
He's worn those clothes for thirty years
And is more dried out than a burnt stick,
And his singing has gone flat and stale.
Since he took up with Clermont harlots
He hasn't produced a single worthwhile poem.

He was a troubadour who suffered ill luck even though he had been knighted. The Dauphin of Auvergne had a sister, Sail de Claustra, with whom Peirol fell in love. The Dauphin interceded for him, and, delighted with his songs, *li volia ben e.ill fazia plazer d'amor . . .* (she 'gave him the pleasure of her love'), to the Dauphin's knowledge.

But, like Mareuil, Rogier and de Ventadorn, such a relationship could not endure. The Dauphin became irritated at the affection she offered Peirol, suspecting improper liberties, 'so he dismissed the singer, telling him to go, giving the man neither clothes nor arms nor money so that Peirol could not maintain the status of a knight 'e vene joglars . . .' (and became a jongleur).[17]

E.l cinques es Gauselms Faidtz . . .

And the fifth is Gaucelm Faidit
Changing from lover to husband of a lady
Who had quite a following. Since then
We haven't heard his trills and cries
But his singing was never highly appraised
Except in his homeland, Uzerche to Agen.

Faidit, the fat glutton, had, of course, married a prostitute, hence the sardonic, 'quite a following!'

E.l seizes Guilllems Azemars . . .

And the sixth is Guilhem Ademar –
Never was there a worse singer.
He accepts old clothes as a reward
And dedicates his songs to a lady
Already with thirty or more of his rivals;
I always envisage him poor and miserable.

Guillems de Ademars s fo de Jauvaudan d'un castel que e nom Maruois . . .

Guillem Ademar came from the town of Jauvaudan near which there was a *donjon* called Mereuis. He was a gentleman, son of a knight who was not powerful or rich. The lord of Mereuis knighted him . . . but Guillem lacked the means to support such a rank and, instead, became a jongleur . . .

There has been confusion about 'Mereuis' near 'Jauvaudan'. There is a ruined castle with a six-storeyed square donjon at a Meyreuis between Hautefort and Biron in the Dordogne. It was not his birthplace.

The correct Meyrueis is a town 30 miles to the south-east on the arid limestone *causses* of the mountainous Cévennes in the Languedoc. It is in the Gévaudon region, the 'land of tyrants', once heavily wooded and inhabited by packs of dangerous wolves. One, the *Bête*, is said for three terrified years around 1765 to have killed more than fifty boys and girls guarding their flocks. Today the small town is famous for its production of *Bleu d'Auvergne*, an exceptional cheese similar to Roquefort, less salty and made from the milk of cows. Guillem Ademar was born there. And its lord knighted him. Little more is known of the troubadour, some clearly written poems by a singer of the second class, almost unremembered and seldom quoted in anthologies.[18]

Such a dismissive reference could not be applied to one of the finest of all troubadours, Arnaut Daniel.

Ab Arnaut Daniel son set . . .

With Arnaut Daniel that's seven. In his
Whole life he's sung nothing but a few
Bewildering words that no one understands.
And ever since his 'hunted the hare with the ox'
And 'swimming against the rising tide'.
His songs have been totally valueless.

Daniel even laughed at his own elusive lines. In *Ans qe.l cim . . .* he wrote 'I know so much that I can stop the incoming tide / And my ox is faster than a hare'. Hi *vida* told little of his genius:

Arnautz Daniels so fo d'equella encontrada don fo . . .

Arnaut Daniel came from the same place as Arnaut de Mareuil, Perigord at Ribeyrac castle. He was gentle, educated, loved poetry and abandoned his education to become a troubadour. He developed a poetic style of 'scarce rhymes', that is, lines that were hard to understand and learn.[19]

Of all the poets satirized by the Monk, he was pre-eminent. Dante was a great admirer of his work. In his *Purgatory* he wrote of:

Miglior fabbro del parlar materno . . .

A better workman in the mother tongue.
His verse of love, his prose romance, outclassed

Us all – and let fools babble on who say
He was by the man of Limoges surpassed . . .

an aside that referred to Guiraut de Bornelh.
 Petrarch also admired him:

Fra tutti il primo Arnaldo Daniell o. . .

Daniel is the supreme poet,
The very finest poet of love,
The short song with a deep meaning . . .[20]

He was brilliantly inventive yet followed the long tradition of courtly
poetry. Almost a century after Guilhem of Poitiers had introduced the
fashion of beginning a poem of love by welcoming the onset of the fertile
spring after the sterility of winter, Daniel could use the identical theme to
celebrate the discovery of love after long years of an empty life. (For his
compact discs see Appendix 1.)

Chansson do.ill non son plan e prim . . .

A song of calm, fine words I'll sing
Now that willows are budding
And the highest of hills
Are coloured with
Their growing flowers
And leaves become green
And sounds and songs of birds
Come out of the shadowed woodlands.

with a final quatrain of

Bella, qui qe.is destuoilla . . .

Fair lady, wherever you may depart
Arnaut will go there instantly
Where he will honour you,
Because your worth grows ever more.

His poetry was delicate, often elusive, but attractive in stating his desire
for his beloved lady and the sad impossibility of ever gaining her true
affection:

Tant l'am de cor e la queri . . .

I love her nobly and long for her so much
That, through my great desire, I dread that
I'll deprive myself of her . . .

and

La jorn quez ieu e midonz nos baisem . . .

The day when my mistress and I kissed,
And she shielded me with her lovely blue mantle
That they might not see it, the slanderous,
The snake-tongued gossipers . . .

and

Del cors li fos, non de l'arma . . .

Would I were hers in body, not soul!
And that she let me secretly into her bedroom!
For it hurts my heart more than a rod's blow
That her servant, though knowing where she is,
Does not go in . . .[21]

Eighth of the Monk's singers was a Catalan, Tremolata, for whom there is
no *Vida*. Then came:

E.l noves, Arnaut de Maruelh . . .

The ninth is Arnaut de Maruelh
Whom I always see downcast
For his lady is without heart, pitiless.
It is wrong of her not to favour him,
For his eyes are always crying for mercy,
The longer he sings the more the water flows.

There were many reasons for a well-born lady such as Azalais of Burlats
to keep her distance from an over-amorous admirer, even an enticingly
tongued but low-born troubadour. Discreet intimacy was difficult in the
bustle of castle life. Difficulty became danger if intimacy were discovered,
even suspected, by a possessively outraged husband. The outcome could be

lethal, as the reported fate of Guilhem de Cabestanh attests even if his story is a fable. In real life there were other illicit Romeos whose deaths were fact.

There was also propriety. A married woman of rank and respectability had rigid standards about what was acceptable socially, and she would as soon handle a poisonous snake or walk naked through her court as make love with a vassal. It was a class barrier to be discovered to their disappointment and chagrin by Arnaut Mareuil at Burlats, by Peire Rogier at Narbonne, by Bernart de Ventadorn at Ventadorn and perhaps also at Angers. Words and wooing were welcome. Sexual intimacy was not.

For his tenth poet the Monk chose *Salh d'Escola es lo deze . . .*, who had a brief *Vida*: *Saill d'Escola si fo di Barjarac . . .* – from Bergerac, he was the son of a merchant, a jongleur and a maker of pleasant *chansonettes*. The eleventh was Guilraut lo Ros: *Guiraudos lo Ros si fo Tollosa* (Guiraudet le Roux was from Toulouse), the son of an impoverished knight. He went to the court of Alphonse and fell in love with the count's daughter, for whom he wrote many songs of love.[22]

E lo dotzes sera Folquetz . . .

> And the twelfth will be Folquet
> Of Marseilles, a little merchant
> Who made an idiotic vow when he swore
> He'd never write another song;
> But then he's done it time after time
> And perjured himself.[23]

Folquet of Marseilles had a career that was a reversed image of the Monk's. That cheerful parodist had been a respected prior in the Church only to become a troubadour. Folquet had been a respected troubadour who decided to take Holy Orders. He was an unusual priest. He had been a rich merchant of Marseilles and a famous troubadour who had given up monetary fortune, family and fame to join the Church. So deep was his spiritual change that when in Paris he heard a minstrel singing one of his love songs he was so ashamed that he imposed a harsh penance upon himself.

He rose to become the bishop of the greatest city in the Languedoc, Toulouse. If not a fanatic, he was certainly fervent in his conviction that if Cathars would be converted they should be condemned to the horrors of the Hell that they had earned. Of his sincere piety there was no question. But with it went a single-minded righteousness, and this led one of the finest of troubadours, Peire Cardenal, to condemn him and all Catholic clergy for their hypocrisy.

The thirteenth to be laughed at by the Monk was his cousin, *E lo trezes es mos vezis . . .,* Guilhem Moizes. Despite that distinction he has no *Vida.*

Peire Vidals es del derriers . . .

Peire Vidal's the last: not only
Is he lacking one or two marbles
But this serf and former furrier
Had better get a tongue of silver,
For ever since he was made a knight
He hasn't shown any common sense.[24]

His *vida* recorded that

Peire Vidals si fo de Tolosa, fils fo d'un pelicer . . .

Peire Vidal was from Toulouse, the son of a ferrier. He sang better than any man alive and was a good troubadour. He was also one of the maddest of men because he believed that whatever he wanted would come to him. No one was as good as he was in making words and music and none so crazy in his talk of feats of arms and love and in his malicious criticism of others . . .

He dressed in black and completely shaved his head, mourning the death of his great patron, Count Raymond V of Toulouse, in 1194.

He was the most original of the troubadours, in his poems constantly changing his identity behind a series of masks, the warrior, the lover, the patriot, metamorphosing in disguises that concealed the man behind the words. In one poem, *Baron, de mon dan covet . . .,* he was a mirage of boasts, skills in battle and the admired lover of ladies:

Ben es proat et auzit . . .

It is well-known and accepted
That I am both worthy and distinguished
And because God has blessed me so richly
It is improper that I should be corrupt.
There's a hundred ladies who long to have
Me if only they could catch me.
But I am one who never boasts or pretends
Nor talks too much about myself.
I merely kiss ladies and unhorse knights.

But in another he could only speak gently of his lady:

E s'ieu sai ren dir ni faire . . .

If I am able to do or say some things
The thanks should be hers, because she
Gave me the wisdom and the craftsmanship.
It is because of her I am courteous and a poet
Everything I do that is proper and understood
Came from her lovely body,
Even these dancing words from my heart.

Vidal is said to have loved a beautiful but flighty woman, Auda, the wife of
the lord of the castle of Pennautier She was also known fancifully as *Na
Loba* or 'Louve', the she-wolf of Pennautier. Little is left of her castle, only
the square keep standing as the corner of a later building.

Et ab joi li er mos treus

I go to her with joy
Though wind and snow and sleet.
The She-Wolf claims that I am hers
And, by God, she's right:
I belong to her
More than to any other, even to myself.

Vidal's biographer termed him 'the most foolish man in the world' who
fell in love with every woman he met. He was infatuated with Loba. He
is reported to have dressed himself in the flayed hide of a wolf hoping
his appearance would lure Loba to his side. Instead, his disguise was
camouflage enough to deceive peasants, who set their savage hunting-
dogs, mastiffs and greyhounds, on him. Badly wounded, he was carried
to Cabaret near Pennautier, where he was tenderly nursed by his beloved
lady, who laughed at his idiocy yet tended him with every courtesy. But,
like so many love stories, the ending was one of pathos. The attractive
but emotionally peripatetic Na Loba turned her affections to the other
troubadour, Raymond of Miraval, and then to two or three other noblemen,
before becoming the mistress of the Count of Foix.
     The madcap story had not ended:

E fo vers c'us cavaliers de San Zili . . .

A knight of St Gilles had Peire Vidal's tongue cut out because the troubadour told him that he was the lover of his wife. And Sir Hugh of Les Baux took care of him and had his wound tended.

When he was cured he went overseas where he married a Greek woman in Cyprus. He believed that she was the niece of the Emperor of Constantinople and that in time he would became emperor himself. So he spent all his money building a great ship as he intended to conquer the empire. He wore imperial arms, entitled himself emperor and his wife, empress.

He courted every woman he met, asking all for their love and they allowed him to say and do what he wanted because they believed him. Each one was dying for him. He had noble horses, carried noble arms and had an imperial throne. He considered himself the finest knight in the world and the one that ladies loved more than any other.

That is what one version of his *vida* claimed, probably finding the 'information' from the fantasies in his own imaginative poems. (For his songs on compact discs see Appendix 1.)

The selected troubadours of the Monk of Montaudon continued with the fifteenth, Peire Laroque. Despite the distinction of being chosen he is unknown. The Monk then ended with himself:

Ab lo semesme n'I a pro . . .

With the sixteenth that will be sufficient.
He's the lapsed Monk of Montaudon
Arguing, quarrelling with everyone.
He forsook God in favour of good living. And because
He wrote verses and songs like these.
He should be hanged, left swinging in the wind.

Est vers fe.l Monges es dis lo . . .

The Monk wrote and recited this poem
At Caussade for the very first time.

E trames lo part Lobeo . . .

And then took it quickly beyond Lobeo
As a present for Lord Bernard.

It was the Monk's home territory. Caussade was some miles to the north-east of Montaudon, his birthplace. Loupian was midway between Agde and Montpellier, the lordship of Bernart-Aton, Viscount of Nïmes and Agde.

It was the conclusion of those melodies of troubadours. They were all men. Among those verses many women had been mentioned. Not one was notable as a trobairitz. Despite that absence there had been many of those poetesses in the decades when Peire d'Alvernhe and the Monk of Montaudon were composing their songs.

1. The 'Pavilion d'Adélaide' at Burlats near Castres where Arnaut de Marueil serenaded the lady Azalaïs. *(J.M. Burl)*

2. Bust of the greatest of the trobairitz, the Countess of Die, in the far east of the Languedoc near the Alps. *(J.M. Burl)*

3. The site of the house of Héloïse and Abelard near Notre-Dame, Paris. *(J.M. Burl)*

4. The tomb of Héloïse and Abelard in the Père Lachaise cemetery, Paris. *(J.M. Burl)*

5. The pedestal of the Countess of Die under its fountains. The foothills of the Alps are in the background. (© *Lilet*)

6. Puivert castle in whose square tower so many famous troubadours sang. (*Author*)

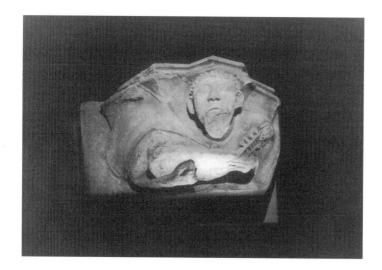

7. Carving of
a musician
with bagpipes
on a sconcer
in the Hall
of Musicians,
Puivert. *(Author)*

8. Musician with
his harp. *(Author)*

9. A musician
with a tambourine,
Puivert. *(Author)*

10. The statue of the Saxon queen, Ethelfleda, outside Tamworth castle.
(Author)

11. The fortified walls of Carcassonne. *(Author)*

12. The castle of Villerouge-Terménès where the last of the Cathar Good Men was executed. *(Arthur Brown)*

13. The five castles of Lastours. The earliest, Cabarets, in on the extreme left. *(Author)*

14. Fontevrault abbey and the restored royal tombs. Eleanor of Aquitaine lies to the left of her husband, Henry II. *(Author)*

15. The striped towers of the castle of Angers where Eleanor had one of her 'courts of love'. (Author)

16. The ruins of the cramped castle of Miraval-Cabardès, home of the troubadour, Raimon of Miraval. (Author)

NINE

The Countess of Die and Other Ladies

Dompna met mout mal s'amor

A lady must value love very cheaply
If she hunts for a man of wealth,
one who is not an underling.
If she does that she is a fool.
For it is said in Velay
that love and money do not go together
and the woman who chooses riches
throws away her honour.

(Azalaïs de Porcairagues, *c.* 1180)

An Age of Remarkable Women, around AD 1200

Lady Azalais of Porcairagues was of the country of Montpellier, a noble lady and well taught . . . and she knew how to make poetry.

(I. Farnell, from *Vida* LII, p. 271)

In the enormous Languedoc stretching almost from Poitiers in the north down to Carcassonne and Foix in the south, and from Bordeaux in the east to Nice in the west, an area of some 8,000 square miles, there were hundreds of pleasure-loving places: affluent courts, great castles and scores of minor forts with liberal patrons. They could be found in the cities of Toulouse, Béziers and Narbonne, in the castles of Saissac, Cabarets, even in tiny fortlets like today's forgotten Miraval. And anywhere where accomplished singers performed they were welcomed and rewarded.

So were some women. It could be a good time or a bad one. For some of the more fortunate the years around 1200 were an age of freedom. The crusades had left many high-born wives in charge of great estates, sometimes for years, and that responsibility was accompanied by the liberty to enjoy discreet liaisons in the absence of their husbands.

For others little changed. Before the concept of knightly chivalry, men often treated women roughly as no more than desirable objects. It was still a period when marriages of convenience were customary, particularly among the upper classes as they arranged alliances between families. Young women had little choice. Men did. Many husbands regarded their chosen wives as a combination of capable housekeeper, hostess and the means of producing heirs. Mistresses were for pleasure.

The general impression of down-trodden, physically abused wives of the Middle Ages, spinning and weaving, meekly obeying every command of their husbands, is not always misleading. An unknown trobairitz complained about the husband to whom she had been allotted:

Si anc fui belha ni prezada . . .

Once for beauty I was widely known
But my world's into drabness grown.
Because he's wealthy and has power
I was married to a man both vile and sour.

Happily, there were many exceptions. There were good marriages.
There were women famous for their learning. There were capable women
who controlled their lives. There were women who could compose music
and write poetry. There were many strong women: Cathar noblewomen;
even higher-born ladies, duchesses such as Eleanor of Aquitaine; queens
as powerful as Blanche of Castile, wife of Louis IX of France. There were
learned women: Héloïse, lover of Abelard (see Appendix 3), and there were
excellent women troubadours, the *trobairitz*. .

Yet even well-placed, rich and educated women were not invariably
accorded an equivalent status with men. The influential widow
Esclarmonde of Foix, sister of the count there, was one of the most famous.
She founded a house for Cathar women in Pamiers, and, when a clerical
Cathar/Catholic debate was held there in 1207, being educated and
confident, she spoke. Appalled at such female presumption, a Cistercian
monk, Frère Étienne de Minsèricorde, rudely rebuked her. 'Go back to your
distaff and spinning, woman, it is not proper for you to speak in a debate
of this nature.' The boor spoke from the misogynous Pauline dogma: 'Let
your women keep silence in the churches . . . if they will learn anything,
let them ask their husbands at home: for it is a shame for women to speak
in the church.'[1]

There were great ladies like Blanche of Castile, a granddaughter of
Eleanor of Aquitaine. In 1200 Eleanor escorted the girl to Paris to marry
Louis VIII of France. Years later Blanche ransomed her husband from his
disastrous crusade and, when as a widow she was Regent of France, by a
combination of craft, conciliation and conquest, she crushed conspirators
and by a skilfully arranged marriage of children created the unification
of France. 'She was the wisest of all the women of her time, and all good
things came to the realm of France while she was alive.'[2]

There were women celebrated for their learning. Héloïse, who died only
a few decades before 1200, as a young woman could both read and write,
unusual achievements for anyone of her time, and extraordinary in a
woman. She was fluent in Hebrew, Greek and especially in Latin, and it was
in that language that she wrote some of the most passionate love letters
that the world has ever known (see Appendix 3). The medieval French poet
François Villon mourned her passing in one of his most elegiac poems, the
'Ballade des Dames du Temps Jadis':

Où est la très- sage Héloïse
Where's Héloïse, the learned nun . . .

Mais où sont les neiges d'antan?
But where are the snows of yesteryear?

(Trans. Dante Gabriel Rossett)[3]

And there were patronesses who encouraged the troubadours and trobairitz, welcoming them into their courts. Among the finest were three noblewomen far from each other in Poitiers, Ventadorn near Tulle in the Limousin, and Narbonne on the cost of the Gulf of Lyons and the Mediterranean.

In spite of the three hundred meandering, decaying roads between Poitiers and Narbonne, many troubadours and jongleurs went to all three courts, the poorest often going on foot, many making a 30-mile detour at Tulle to visit the Viscountess Marie at Ventadorn. Her *vida, Bone azetz audit de ma dompna . . .*, proclaimed, probably correctly, that she was 'the most sought-after lady there ever was in the Limousin', her gigantic castle perched on a crag frowning on the arid Corrèze wilderness below.

Like her two sisters, she had been married off to one of the neighbouring viscounts, Ebles V, himself a patron of the singers. His second wife, she inherited a tradition of troubadour hospitality generations old begun by Ebles II, contemporary of Guilhem of Poitiers, who had developed his own poetical 'school' there. Marie enthusiastically encouraged the continuity of the custom and many of the best singers enjoyed her hospitality: the Monk of Montaudon, Gaucelm Faidit who fell from her favour, even the miles-distant Savaric de Mauléon. For her kindness and generosity she was lauded in words and song by many of them.[4]

Marie herself composed poems and one was a *tenson* or 'debate' between herself and her platonically respectful lover Guy d'Ussel, one of whose castles was only a few miles away. Her words delicately expressed the problems of courtly love.

Gui d'Ussel, be.m pesa de vos . . .

Guy d'Ussel, I'm troubled by the hurt it brings
To learn you're giving up your song.
Please never let love go. It must be wrong,
And since you know about such things
Please tell me what a lady is allowed to do
For her lover, from you to me, from me to you,
As much as to each other? I must be told
According to the codes of love we hold.[5]

Our problem, centuries later, is that we are detached from those long-ago people. Yet their emotions and their physical bodies were as human as today's. What is remote from our understanding are the laws of their society, which seem as incomprehensible to us as those of South Sea islanders to Captain Cook, even though he saw them.

Without considerable care, Marie de Ventadorn, Eleanor of Aquitaine and Jaufré Rudel become waxworks of the mind. But they were people. Only suspension of disbelief can reincarnate them. Marie was not playing a part. She was a living person naturally following the laws of her society.

Far to the south another great patroness, Ermengarde, held court in Narbonne. Her gifts to talented singers were prodigal. The troubadour Raimon de Miraval told a jongleur, Bajona, to go to her court because, if his work pleased the lady, she would present him with a well-built horse, a fine saddle from Carcassonne and a shield engraved with the bearings of Narbonne.

Ermengarde was well acquainted with a detailed knowledge of the law, and in his satirical *De Arte Honesti Amandi* the chaplain Andreas Capellanus had her solving four complex problems of courtly love. First, was a woman who had a lover but then married right to deny her lover his usual consolations? Secondly, were feelings stronger between lovers than between married couple? Thirdly, a woman, once married, had married again but then divorced her second husband; could her first be allowed to regain her love? And, fourthly, a good man courted a woman who was then wooed by one even worthier; which should she chose? To which the viscountess replied: 'It is left to the woman to choose whether she will listen to the good man or the better one.'

There were whispers, never more than that, that Ermengarde had the most discreet of affairs with the troubadour Peire Rogier, who had been for a very long time, far longer than others, at her court. Whispers can become shouts. She dismissed him, *et el s'en amet dolens e pensius* (and he went away full of sadness and sorrow).[6]

Perhaps the most glittering of all courts was Eleanor of Aquitaine's at Poitiers. Powerful in her own right through descent, also queen of England through her marriage to Henry II, she entertained lavishly, feasting, singing, dancing, encouraging troubadours to come to her as frequently as they dared. Among those entertainers were the almost unexpected trobairitz whose emergence brought riches of tenderness and femininity to an already artistic world.

The few decades just before and after the year 1200 were times of a flourishing of fine poetry from women. It was almost an age of emancipation. Great women writers of poetry are rare. Since the long ago classical centuries of the Greek poetess Sappho and her followers, such women were few. Then, suddenly, there were many: accomplished troubairitz like Marie of Ventadorn; anonymous ones; Castelloza, Bietris de Romans, and, probably finest of all, the Countess of Die. It was quite a small group, no more than about twenty, and they were spread over many miles of southern France, from the Limousin to the Auvergne and the foothills of the Alps, and southwards as far as Provence and the sea.

Theirs was not always the poetry of idyllic love. Their emotional words expressed many of the varying concerns of women: their marriage; clothes; rejection; loneliness; even love for another woman. Despite the conventions of courtly love and mutual regard between man and woman composed by the troubadours, not all wives respected their husbands as lords and masters. One discreetly nameless bride quite explicitly hated her enforced existence. In colloquial langue d'oc the troubadour, Peire Duran described the despair of his lady:

. . . *flac cors c'anc non si desnoiri*

His flabby body that was never washed,
Whether armoured on horseback or standing;
He has besmirched my mind and hopes,
my sweet speech, my frolicking, youthful fun;
his ill will, too, plus his nasty ways;
he's withered my grace with his sour breath.[7]

This was far from the perfection of Courtly Love in which the *domna*, 'lady' or 'mistress', the dominant lady, had to be obeyed. 'In all, things [agree] to the 'commands of ladies.'[8] 'Thou shalt ever strive to ally thyself to the service of Love'. In his 5th Dialogue, 'a Nobleman to a Noblewoman', Andreas Capellanus described the *domna*'s inviolable status: In its extreme form it demanded from the lover total subservience to the lady's whim, and a grovelling humility: she is so far above him that he can only worship at her shrine.[9]

Many trobairitz did write of ethereal courtly love in straight-forward terms: *Si.m for grazitz* . . . (I'd be encouraged . . .). The fourth verse read:

Bel doucs amics . . .

If you knew my mind, sweet handsome friend
Your handsome, noble, learned heart
No longer would lament: for you're the one
Who's made me happier today than ever.[10]

But trobairitz poetry was not always about such dispassionate love. It could express many different feelings: anger; indignation; desire; rejection; loneliness. The intense sensations described in their poems are so familiar to people today that they move from the early Middle Ages into modern times.

The Countess of Die wrote with wistful sensuality about the man she had foolishly sent away:

> *Bon voltra mon cavallier*
> *Tener un ser en mos bratz, nut.*

> How I wish I could hold my knight
> In my arms, one evening, naked.[11]

There was also the sadness of rejection, a bitterness experienced by Castelloza, a woman of the Auvergne who was in love with the nobleman Armande Breon. Although she took almost foolhardy risks to entice him, he abandoned her:

> *Despois vos vi, ai fag vostre coman*

> Since I first saw you I have been
> At your command. And yet, my would-be friend
> It's brought me nothing.
> You have sent me neither
> Message nor messenger . . .[12]

Desire, rejection. There was a third: despair. Clara d'Anduza lived in one of the most important towns in the Languedoc. She complained angrily at the petty scandalmongers who repeated from house to house, from street to street, that she had a lover. They forced him to leave the town.

> *Quar vos qu.ieu am mais . . .*

> For you whom I loved more dearly than anyone
> They've separated you from me, sent you away
> And since I have no hope of seeing you again
> I fade in grief, in torment and resentment.[13]

One poetess wrote indignantly about the insulting clerical criticisms of the pretty clothes that young, well-brought up ladies liked. Such unworldly men condemned the wearing of rich, expensive materials adorned with little balls and pointed tongues so that 'their wearers look like devils in a painting'. St Jerome had already deplored such feminine extravagance. 'Beware of the wantonness of those girls who decorate their heads, let their hair fall onto their foreheads, polish their skin, use cosmetics, and wear tight sleeves, dresses without folds, and shiny shoes.'

Sumptuary laws, especially for the middle classes, were strict, and not always disregarded:

> No *bourgeoisie* shall have a carriage; they shall wear neither gold nor precious stones, nor crowns of gold or silver. Those *bourgeois* who are neither prelates nor dignatories shall not have a wax torch. A *bourgeois* who is worth two thousand Tournois crowns or more may have a dress made of 12 sous and six deniers, and his wife a robe of not more than 16 sous.[14]

Rich ladies shrugged at the pettiness. Long hair in two braids held in place by a shining clasp, long, rich gowns of silken samite interwoven with gold thread, embroidered at neck and wrists, laced at the side down to the feet, all under an ermine-edged robe. It was luxury enhanced by a braided girdle of crimson silk. The pious alms-purse and the chamois-leather gloves were delicacies, as was the modest veil that could be drawn aside for acceptable kisses. It was ostentatious wealth for the privileged.

Even convents of nuns were guilty and were forbidden to wear 'mantles of black or purple *brunetta*, fur coats or other exquisite and precious furs', and they 'should have no tight-fitting or stitched-on sleeves, no necklaces, no clasps, no golden or silver rings, no gold fringes, no silk belts, nor any other kind of worldly adornments'.[15]

An unknown trobairitz rankled at such petty prohibitions whether widespread or local, imposed by small-minded councillors, friars and miserable preachers who banned rich clothes trimmed with gold or silver. Nor did she want to be compelled to wear veils or wimples down the sides of her face to her shoulders.

De ma camiza blanc'ai tal pessamen . . .

I grieve for my white blouse,
Embroidered with silk colours,
Jonquil, vermilion and black mixed together,
White, blue, gold and silver.
Alas! I dare not put it on.
My heart feels like breaking.[16]

Trobairitz songs were of every variety. Some were plaintive. Known as *albas*, 'dawn songs', they could be erotically sad, as two lovers dreaded the coming of day: *Or ne hais riens tant com le jour . . .* (I hate nothing so much as day . . .).[17] Another, even better, is:

> *En un vergier sotz fuella d'albespi*
> *Tenc la dompna son amic costa si,*
> *Tro la gayta crida que l'alba vi,*
> *'Oy Dieus, Oy Dieus, de l'alba!*
> *Tan tost ve'*

> In a mayflower blossomed garden lay
> A lady and her lover enjoying Cupid's play
> Until a crier called the break of day.
> 'Ah God! Ah, God! How soon the dawn
> Appears'.[18]

By four hundred years it anticipated Romeo and Juliet as they argued whether the songbird they could hear was the reassuring nightingale or the dreaded lark.[19]

Perhaps at the extremes of feminism were women who refused to be the acquiescent playthings of men. There is even a hint of lesbianism in a *canso* addressed to a lady, Mary, by the female troubadour Bieiris, or Bietris, de Romans. Little is known of her despite her startling poem. She has no *vida*. The town of Romans is close to Valence and not far from Die and Orange, but of the woman herself there is only speculation. She may perhaps have been the sister or sister-in-law of Alberico de Romano, a troubadour from northern Italy, but that is guesswork. Some critics have argued, almost in desperation, that 'she' was a man because no other lesbian poem exists from this period, but that is masculine guesswork.

Her poem is not pornographic. It is tender, beginning *Na Maria, pretz e fina valors . . .* (Lady Maria, your virtue and distinction . . .).

> *Per que vos prec, si.us platz que fin' amors*

> And I beg thee, permit this true love
> So ardent, but in true humility
> Give me your help, all else above.
> Grant me Lady, I beg of thee
> What I most seek – my joy and bliss,
> For in you my heart and longings lie
> And only with thee will I gain this.
> For you I yearn, pine, for you I'd die.[20]

As Bogin observed, if it really was written by a woman, 'it is probably unique in the literature of the Middle Ages'. She added generally about many of poems of the trobairitz that some 'are so personal that is difficult to imagine that they were sung before an audience'.[21]

If that were true of Bieiris de Romans and some others, it is also entirely relevant to the intense poetry of the mysterious Beatritz, Countess of Die, whose name was not Beatritz, who may never have been a true countess and who possibly did not come from Die.

Die is a small town in the Drôme valley midway between Montélimar and Gap. It is a bleak region, 'as old as the rocks of Provence', with edelweiss growing on the mountainsides. It is close to the foothills of the Alps. Despite modern poetical optimism about the proximity of the countess and her lover, Raimbaut d'Aurenga, Die is not close to Orange. Because of intervening rough hills and mountains, a medieval traveller either rode or trudged almost 50 miles to Montélimar and then a further 30 southwards before reaching Orange.

Today Die is best known for its Clairette de Die, a light, scented sparkling wine of Muscat and Clairette made by the traditional *Die Méthode Dioise Ancestrale.* It is bottled during fermentation, which creates bubbles in the wine, and its semi-sweet Muscat flavour is an anomaly in a region of heavy, nondescript reds.

Despite myths, Die is not charming. It is undistinguished, unassuming, with a few interesting parts. It does have a long, quite notable history, and for the visitor there is a modern, attractive Office de Tourisme alongside a medieval tower and a length of old Roman ramparts. In Roman times Die was an important settlement of some 12,000 inhabitants, the *Dea Augusta Vocontiorum,* at the confluence of the Drôme and Meyresse rivers. The present eastern gateway had been the Roman triumphal arch. Three stretches of Roman wall overlook the Drôme, and with effort and some care one can walk along them. The Notre-Dame cathedral, partly demolished in 1570 and partly restored in 1673, has a porch supported by four sturdy granite Roman pillars from the temple of Cybele, a dark and rough pair alternating with two palely smooth.

Cybele the 'Great Mother' was a Phrygian goddess whose barbaric cult spread across the Empire, even to Catterick in England. In self-induced trances her priests leapt and howled to the raucous music of cymbals and drums, using an ancient stone knife to castrate themselves. Relics from her temple are displayed in the museum.

For Die and 'her' famous medieval trobairitz it is significant that the vernacular tongue of the Diois region is quite different linguistically from that of troubadour lands. The poems of Die's countess are written in a very localised Occitanian

Her four known songs are so personal that she has been called 'the Sappho of the North', although that term might be more applicable to Bieiris than to the countess. Yet for an artiste of such tenderness history has been harsh. She has been given three men to love instead of one, two or three different husbands, a 'Life' of inflated nonsense and a *vida* so short as to be near extinction, almost uninformative.

Her justifiable fame as a writer of sensitive, emotionally unreserved poetry rests on four *cansos* or lyrical songs arranged I–IV, of which these are the first lines:

I.   *Ab joi et ab joven m'apais*
      I flourish on joy and youthfulness

II.   *A chantar m'er de so qu'ieu non volra*
      Although I do not wish to, I must sing.

III. *Fin ioi me don 'alegranssa*
      Happiness brings me fine, true joy

IV.   *Estat ai en greu cossirier*
      Of late I've been in much distress.

There is also a *tenson* or 'debate', *Amicz et gran cossirier*, perhaps wrongly attributed to her and her supposed lover. (For compact discs see Appendix 1.)

The countess had two written lives, the *vida* and a much later one by Jean de Nostradamus, the sixteenth-century 'biographer' of the troubadours. He was as bad at recreating the past as his famous brother, Michel, was of predicting the future. Perhaps misreading an already faulty manuscript or from mere carelessness, even deliberate invention, Jean compiled a preposterous story of more than five hundred words in which the grand lady presided over a Court of Love and was in love, but only in a distantly courtly manner, with the troubadour Guillem Adhemar. Frustrated in his uncouth advances, he pined and died of longing for her. She and her mother mourned his passing. The older woman had an ostentatious mausoleum erected for his burial. The countess retired to a convent.[22]

The truth was different. There was a historical Adhemar from near Florac in the Languedoc. The son of an impoverished knight, he could not afford to maintain the status of even a minor nobleman and, instead, became a mediocre jongleur. He was mocked by the Monk of Montaudon in his satire about poetical contemporaries.

E seises Guilhems Ademars

And the sixth is Guilhem Ademar –
The worst of all the jongleurs by far.
He'll take cast-off clothes as payment,
So desperate for funds that any rival is no bar,
Against thirty better singers he'll spar,
Tunelessly squawking in his shabby raiment.[23]

Even if in jest the Monk had exaggerated, Guillem Adhemar would still have been a most unlikely candidate for the love of a nobly born woman.

The Countess of Die had a much earlier written and more reliable *vida*, perhaps by Uc de Saint-Circ around 1320 and based on erratic titbits of local information he had picked up around 1280 several decades after her death: *La Comtessa de Dia si fo moiller d'En Guillem de Peitieus, bella domna e bona. Et enamoret.se d'En Rambaut d'Aurenga, e fez de lui maintas bonas cansos* (The Countess of Die was the wife of Sir Guillem of Poitiers, a beautiful and good woman. She was in love with the well-born Raimbaut d'Aurenga and wrote him many fine songs).[24]

Its thirty-one words contain several considerable errors. The identities of both her lover and her husband were mistaken, and 'many' is an overstatement for 'four'. Raimbaut d'Aurenga III, third lord of Orange, did exist, the first native troubadour of Provence. He was the son of a nobleman who died leaving enormous debts that Raimbaut was unable to settle. His casual attitude towards life, money and women was described in the previous chapter.[25] D'Aurenga's raffish character appealed to many women, 'the rake *par excellence* of his day . . . ready-witted, full of animal spirits, a devoted friend, a bitter enemy, and a reckless, rollicking, jovial prince . . .'.[26] Such a 'devil-may-care' personality could attract some adventurous, unhappily married young wives.

Discreetly, some contented lovers proclaimed their achievement. With confidence, Arnaut Daniel could announce, 'We two shall bed, my lady'. Bernart de Ventadorn wrote of his woman's 'white, plump and smooth body' and demanded, 'Lady, let me have my way'. Peire Vidal was delicately explicit:

Dona . . .
E s'en grat servir vos pogues
Entre.l despulhar e.l vestir

If I could serve you to your pleasure
Between the time of undressing and dressing

Until quite early in the twentieth century it was believed, with no doubt, that Raimbaut d'Aurenga had an illicit romance with Beatritz, Countess of Die, had discarded her and had then shamefully justified his behaviour. A debating poem, a *tenson*, or argument, between them explained what had occurred.

> *Beatritz*
> *Amics, en gran cossirier*
> Why do you give me so much pain?

> *Raimbaut*
> *Domna, Amors a tal mestier*
> My pain is as great as yours!

And so it continued, woman and man speaking alternatively for eight more verses:

> *Amics, s'acsetz un cartier*
> *Don', quar yst lauzengier*
> *Amicz, nulh grat no.us refier*
> *Dona, ieu tem a sobrier*
> *Amicz, tan vos sai leugier*
> *Dona, je mais esparvier*
> *Amicz, creirai vos per aital*
> *Dona, aissi m'auretz leyal*

> You don't care about me.
> I avoid you only to quell gossiping tongues.
> I can take care of myself.
> If the slander grows, we are lost. I love you!
> You are just frivolous and uncaring.
> I care only for you. There is no one else.
> I have to believe that you will always be loyal . . .
> I shall forever be loyal. I think only of you.[27]

Even as late as 1976 in his spacious overview of troubadour times Jack Lindsay wrote that the *tenson* that Béatrice, Countess of Die had with Raimbaut d'Orange was genuinely between them. Despite today's near-obligatory vogue of revisionism, he may have been justified.[28]

There are vital questions to be asked. Why was d'Aurenga mentioned in the countess's *vida*, and which one of two d'Aurengas was he, III or IV? Why, after centuries of anonymous disputants in the *tenson*, was the woman suddenly called Beatritz in late-nineteenth-century versions? Her *vida* did mention Raimbaut d'Aurenga, but for her there was only a title, 'La Comtessa de Dia', who was married to 'd'En Guillem de Peiteuis'. There was no Christian name.

The inventive Nostradamus mentioned her many times. As well as his imaginary 'Life' of her, there were also frequent references to the countess, usually 'of Die', occasionally as 'of Dye', but, despite her medieval *vida*, never as 'Dia'. And nowhere did he give any first name.

Among the many uncut pages in his *Troubadours* of 1873, John Rutherford mentioned 'Countess Die', the 'Provençal Sappho' and the story about Adhemar, but she was given no Christian name. With his brief 'Countess Die', omitting the definite article, he may quite unknowingly have come very close to the truth.[29]

She remained nameless until nineteenth-century German scholars began assiduously examining a tedium of medieval genealogies, searching for a Countess of Die, not only of the right period and place but also married to a Guillem of Peitieus. Eventually, they found one. She had a Christian name. She was the daughter of Guigues I, Dauphin of Vienne, and she was married to Guilhem I of Poitiers, Count of the Valentinois. Die, in the local district of Diois, is about 40 miles south-east of Valence, the region's major city. She was called Beatritz, She had a son, Adhemar, whose name apparently explained the *vida*'s claim of an improbable association between his high-born mother and a threadbare troubadour. The identification seemed conclusive.

'Biatritz' was added to the literature of the countess in a biography of 1893 by Sernin Santy, whose *Comtesse de Die* was dismissed by Jeanroy as a 'publication sans valeur'. Santy probably obtained his information from Schutz-Gora's heavyweight 1888 German compendium of Provençal biographies.[30] Because such scholarly research had recovered the long-lost 'Beatritz', enthusiastic readers accepted her as the original poetess.

That belief has been questioned for decades. Critics noticed that the original *tenson* contained neither a Beatrice nor a Raimbaut, only a 'friend', *amicz*, and a 'Lady', *Dompna*. The names were added centuries later. There were other problems.

Wilhelm emphasised, 'nowhere in Raimbaut's work is a Beatritz or a Countess of Dia mentioned. Pattison insists upon the possibility that Raimbaut III wrote the entire poem, since feigned tensos' occur in the works of several other troubadours.[31]

The first biographer of the Countess of Die, whether Uc de Saint-Circ or another, may have seen how the first line of her *canso*, Poem IV, *Estat ai en greu cossirier* (much sorrow has come to me from my love of a knight) was almost identical to the first line of Raimbaut d'Aurenga's *tenson*, Poem 6,

Amics, en gran cossirier (Friend, I suffer great anguish), and so, speculatively, included d'Aurenga in the lady's brief *vida*.[32]

It may be no more than poetical coincidence, but it is noticeable how closely the first verse of Poem IV does echo the sentiments of the beginning of the *tenson*, as though there had been telepathic plagiarism by one or other of the two singers, who are supposed to have had little or nothing to do with each other.

Estat ai en greu cossirier

My foolishness has caused me deep despair
Over a knight I drove away. He was my own,
And now I want it understood by everyone
That I sincerely loved him beyond care.
   Now by my foolish pique I am betrayed
When, peevishly, I would not make love to him.
   Wherever I am, day, night, I regret that whim,
Whether dressed, or sleepless in a lonely bed I'm laid.

There are also similarities between the *tenson* and another of her poems, No. III, beginning *Fin ioi me don' alegranssa* . . . The word *lauzengier* 'scandalmongers') occurs twice in both. In the poem the woman would not be scared away by malicious words that were meant to harm her like foul fog obscuring sunlight. A resentful man would never stop her enjoying herself while she was young. 'As for you, gossiping, jealous husband', I shall indulge in whatever I fancy despite your displeasure. There is no direct reference to a possessive husband in the *tenson*, but it is implied in the third verse when the lady despairs *quar no m'en puesc estraire* (because I cannot free myself). Strangely overlooked, the Debate and both poems appear to contain too many similarities to be fortuitous.[33] Their repeated emphasis on youthfulness also is significant.

The acceptance of Beatritz as the Countess of Die who composed those forlorn songs endured for hardly a century. Since 1952 there has been another, now generally accepted candidate in place of the persistent misidentifications of the past that had given her three lovers instead of one, a medley of husbands and the near-heresy that she came from the insignificant town of Die. In his detailed study of the poems of Raimbaut III, shoddily published for such important research, Pattison concluded that the wife of a Count of Valentinois could never have been known as a Countess of Die.

Concerning the claimed husband of that wife there were five possible candidates. There was the Count of Valentinois but the name of his wife is unknown. So is that of the wife of Guillem de Peiteius, a vassal of the viscountess Ermengarde of Narbonne. The three remaining possibilities could be ignored as improbabilities.

More positively, Pattison came upon a genuine Count of Die, Isouard, who had a son, Pierre, and a daughter, Isouarde, whose honorary title, by accepted usage, would have been 'countess of Die'. Some time before 1184 she was married to Raimon d'Agout, which would have made her date of birth in the late 1160s or early 1170s. She would have been a contemporary of Raimbaut IV, the grand-nephew of Raimbaut III and a far less accomplished troubadour than his forebear. Cautiously Pattison suggested that Isouarde was the original Countess of Die.[34]

The interpretation has much to commend it and one objection that makes it doubtful. As Isouarde was married to Raimon d'Agout rather than a Guillem de Peiteius, it was puzzling that whoever wrote the *vida* of the Countess of Die chose to refer to a Guillem but not to Raimon d'Agout, when that man was independently named in that collection of 'Lives' itself, mentioned as a patron much praised by Gaucelm Faidit.[35]

Meticulously continuing his quest for the countess, Pattison also discovered a lady with the Christian name of Dia.[36] She was a member of the well-born Montdragon family and was living in 1166 at the same time as Raimbaut III. Her feudal title of Comtessa Dia could easily but wilfully have been 'improved' by some medieval copyist into the Comtessa of Dia, the precise wording given in her *vida*, a lady *enamoret se d'En Raimbaut d'Aurenga*.

The identification is feasible. The wealthy Montdragons had possessions in and around Orange and Courthézon, where Raimbaut III died, and other towns and villages of which he was the lord. It is probable that the two noble families met.

It was noticed by Bruckner and her colleagues in *Songs of the Women Troubadours* that Dia was born around the same time as Raimbaut d'Aurenga III's birth in 1144. Both lived in the second half of the twelfth century when fine singers such as Bernart of Ventadorn and trobairitz like Azalais de Porcairagues were composing. So, of course, was Raimbaut. If Dia and he met during the late 1160s, both would have been in their early twenties. She could have been married for almost ten years, attached by church law to a churlish husband.

It may be that Beatriz and Isouarde are the wrong women and that the almost unconsidered Dia was the real Countess of Die.

Reading the four poems is like looking into a private, very personal diary. The romance started happily in true courtly style. She sang happily. Poem I began:

Ab ioi et ab joven m'apais

> I thrive on youth and joy
> And joy and youth nourish me

And the verses continued

> I am happy that the man I love is so worthy and fine.
> It is proper and permissible for a virtuous lady to admit her love for a
>   good man.
> He is brave, he is noble, he is open-hearted

The ladylike admiration developed into womanly longing. The changed tone is noticeable in the second verse of Poem IV, lines 1 to 4.

Ben volria mon cavalier . . .

> I wish my knight could be caressed
> By me, naked, in my arms.
> He would be enraptured by my charms,
> Resting in comfort on my breast.

And continuing in the unrhymed lines 3 to 6 of the third verse:

E que iagues ab vos un ser . . .

> If only I could lie with you for one evening,
> Embrace, kiss you, show my passion.
> I long so wistfully to have you here
> For ever in the place of my husband.

These were almost girlhood dreams in the mind of a married woman. Whether or not these fantasies were fulfilled it seems that they did not last. There were arguments, reconciliations; she wanted more, he kept a colder distance. What happened between them is unknown. Perhaps she had encouraged him until he reached the status of an *entendor*, the suitor who believed that he might gain his deepest desire. Perhaps he had then been rebuffed by a flirtatious Countess of Die who had proved to be another Guilhelma, the tantaliser and tormentor of Savaric de Mauléon, granting her would-be lover every favour but the last. If so, Die's countess regretted her misguided prudery. He abandoned her for ladies of less moralistic tendencies.

There is an alternative. It could be that d'Aurenga, gifted dilettante, lover of noble ladies, had been successful in his pursuit but subsequently discovered her sincere love for him was too demanding and turned to less insistent conquests. He may even, like Jaufré Rudel, have chosen someone to court whom he would never see, the *domnas d'Urgel*, the Countess of Urgell, as his *vida* states,[37] famed for her goodness but far away, almost unattainable, in northern Italy. That would be as plausible an interpretation of the Countess of Die's poems.

It would explain both the *tenson* and the most plaintive of all her songs, Poem II

> *A chanter m'er de so q'ieu no volria*
> I must sing of something that I do not wish . . .

It is the one poem whose melody is known, and it has been recorded on many compact discs. The writer possesses six (see Appendix 1). The performances differ. Playing times vary from a brief 2 minutes 46 seconds to an extended 14 minutes 50 seconds, which includes a spoken *vida*.[38]

In some versions, inappropriately, the poem is sung by a man. Most are by women. Several are accompanied by a group of musicians with viols, tambourines, drums, pipes and the three-stringed rebec with its bow. On one or two the background is a single instrument, perhaps a lute. One, very lovely rendition is sung by an unaccompanied chanteuse. All of them are quiet, slow and sorrowful.

> *A chanter m'er de so q'ieu no volria*
>
> I do not wish to but I am forced to sing
> In bitterness about a love to which I cling.
> I loved a man more than any other thing.
> But to my merit, courtesy, he was disobliging,
> Also to my beauty and my noble birth.
> I've been tricked, deceived, he dishonouring
> Me, despising me as though I had no worth.

The distant displeasure against 'a man' changed to direct accusations against 'you' in the following verses 2 to 6:

> 2. *D'aisso.m conort car anc non fi faillenssa* . . .

Although you have hurt me I have one consolation. I have never done you any wrong. But I excel you. You are valiant, I am faithful in my love.

Mi faitz orguoill [but] *francs vas totas autras*

I am hurt because you are haughty and cold to me but affable and charming to everybody else.

3. . . . *c'autre'amors vos mi tuoilla*

I have reason to weep. You have turned against me. It is unjust that another lures you away by her false promises of pleasure. Remember what bliss it was for us in the beginning.

Q.en ma colpa sia.l departimens

Please God! Let it never have been my fault that I am to blame for this unhappiness.

4. *c'una non sai, loindana ni vezina*

I am troubled and in fear. You are so fair, so attractive that there is no woman, near or far, who, if she looked for love, would not turn to you. Surely, my friend, your own discernment should show you where true worth can be found. Remember our agreement.

5. . . . .*mos pretz e mos paratges e ma beltatz*

My merits, my high rank, my loveliness should be enough. That is why I am sending you this song.

. . . *vos m'etz tant fers ni tant salvatges*

I need to know, my great and noble friend, why you have become so cruel and harsh to me?

Then there was anger and resentment.

6. *Mas aitan plus vuoill li digas, messatges,*
Q'en trop d'orgoill ant gran dan maintas gens

But tell him, song, this in particular. Let him understand excessive pride has brought down many other, better men.

It was the final poem. The Countess of Die disappeared from trobairitz history.

There is one last irony. If Dea of Montdragon was the woman who wrote the poems, or the unlikely Beatritz was the poetess, or the persuasive Isouarde composed the songs, the town of Die may have had nothing to do with any one of them.

The town, however, had not forgotten how famous the poetess had made it. From the Office de Tourisme one can walk a short distance up the path just inside the Roman walls and come to a pleasantly open square, the place de l'Hôtel de la Ville, near the cathedral. There, proud on a granite column at the centre of an ornamental pond is a bronze head, stylishly wimpled, of the 'Sappho of Provence', fountains playing around her, her face outlined against the background of the massive Alpine cliffs of Glandasse. Imaginary image it may be, a geographical optimism, but it is fitting that she should have a memorial in the Shangri-La that history has given her.[39]

There were many other singers. In Provence and across the whole of the Languedoc, where there were courts there was music. Where there were courts, troubadours went. Some were weary, walking with a harp or a drum on their back as they wandered from hopeful castle to hopeful fort. Others rode proudly with a versatile jongleur toting his orchestra of musical instruments, going to Narbonne, Montpellier, Roussillon, Carcassonne, Toulouse.

There were dozens, scores of this band of musicians. Amongs them was the elite whose names were known and songs sung throughout the province: Guiraut de Bornellh, Bernart de Ventadorn, Gaucelm Faidit, Arnaut Daniel, Peire d'Alvernhe, and amongst those professional entertainers were aristocrats like Raumbaut d'Aurenga.

There were, as yet, no professional trobairitz, only high-born ladies like the elusive Countess of Die who sang their poems in the privacy of the courts of family and friends.

Abroad the Second Crusade had ended in failure. Jaufré Rudel was dead. The Third and Fourth Crusades were to follow shortly. Such remote events in the Holy Land hardly interrupted the gaiety of life in the Languedoc, where Toulouse was a Mecca.

The new count, Raymond VI, was a generous patron and in the evenings his court was a splendour of entertainment: food, drink, jugglers, acrobats, singers. It was the finest of courts in that land of song and sun.

In the daytime it was a court of argument over religion. Belief in the Cathar faith flourished. In towns and across the countryside the Cathar faith was strong. Very early in the thirteenth century, after the failure of Bernard's attempts to convert the unconvertible, Pope Innocent III had appointed St Dominic in 1206 to succeed him, but even when that saintly zealot dressed as simply as the Cathar Good Men, lived as abstemiously as they, travelled on foot in coarse robes and preached the Catholic word of God in everyday words to people, he also found that words were insufficient. The heresy was too deep and too widespread. 'Sweetness and blessing have failed', he informed the Pope. Physical force would be needed if the evil of heresy was to be exterminated. Abandon words. Bring war!

The Catholic Church fumed impotently against it. Preaching directly to the people had failed. Persuading the powerful to put down the heresy seemed more promising. High-ranking papal legates were despatched to Count Raymond VI, urging him to expunge the unfaithful mockers of the Trinity from his realms.

Among the legates was Pierre de Castelnau, proud, implacable. Richly apparelled, escorted by a cavalcade of priests, bodyguards and servants, he was a man whose arrogance and self-importance made him overbearing. His imperious manner did not endear him to the highest nobleman in the entire south of France.

Presumptuously and unilaterally Castelnau organised an army to suppress the Cathars of Provence. Unsurprisingly, Raymond VI refused to lead it. The Pope, Innocent III, sent a furious letter condemning him for such defiance. Fearing that papal anger might provoke some form of military action, Raymond arranged a trucial meeting with Pierre de Castelnau and others in the town of Saint-Gilles near the Rhône. The talks between two stubborn men were unsuccessful, and late in the evening of 9 May 1208 Castelnau and his retinue departed to camp overnight by the river. At dawn next morning an unknown assassin killed the legate.

Like the murder of Thomas â Becket at Canterbury in England in 1171, the crime shocked the Catholic world. Pierre de Castelnau was canonised on 10 March. The same day the Pope sent a letter to the King of France, Philippe-Auguste, urging him to assemble an army of 'Soldiers of God' to eradicate the Cathars.

Even in their earliest years when troubadours were singing of love and ecstasy there were stirrings of an heretical movement that would culminate in the extinction of the Cathars.

After the ineffective urban debates between Catholic priest and Cathar Good Men had failed by the beginning of 1206, Pope Innocent III had appointed the fine preacher Dominic Guzman to go on a further mission of conversion. In the Languedoc the years around 1200 were years of contradiction.

There were persistent conflicts between Cathars and Catholics. In contrast, unclerical songs of love were widespread. Domestically, women were bound to their husbands' demands. Yet, artistically, the musical words of women troubadours, the trobairitz, were heard and applauded across the south of France.

TEN

BERTRAN DE BORN

S'amdui li rei son pro ni coratjos . . .

If both kings are brave and full of spirit
We'll soon see fields strewn with fractured
Helmets, shields, swords and saddlebows,
And men hacked through from neck to groin,
And riderless warhorses running wild,
And lances through chests and ribs
And joys and crying and celebration,
The losses great, the victory splendid.

Trompas, tabors, senheras e penos . . .

Trumpets, tabors, banners, pennants,
Banners, black and white, chain-mailed chargers
We shall see. Life will be good for robbers.
We'll ransack the cellars of moneylenders.
Laden packhorses will not journey safely
Even in daylight, nor travellers without fear,
Nor fat merchants coming here from France.
But for those daring death, rich plunder.
       (Bertran de Born, *Miei-sirventes* . . . (A Half-Sirventes))

Bertran de Born and the Love of War, *c.* 1140–1200

E perché tu di me novella porti . . .

And so that you can carry news of me
Know I am Bertran de Born, the one who gave
Such ill advice to the young king's majesty.

(Dante, *Hell*, Canto 28, 133–5)

The end of the twelfth century and the beginning of the thirteenth saw no military invasion of the Languedoc. The threatened Albigensian Crusade against the heretical Cathars had not begun. But there was warfare elsewhere in the south of France, 100 or more miles west of Toulouse. One unusual troubadour welcomed it.

Bertran de Born was a minor knight, part-lord of the castle of Hautefort, by troubadour coincidence just south of the fortress of Excideuil, the homeland of Guirault de Bornelh.

It was a dangerous region. Hautefort stood on the northernmost borders of department of the Dordogne some miles east of Périgueux; 40 south of Limoges in Haute-Vienne, and 100 miles south of Poitiers in Vienne. It was an area of insignificant petty rivalries between families but also one of constant Anglo-French conflict. Undisciplined soldiers and plundering mercenaries ravaged any town or village left unprotected.

Bertran de Born welcomed the disruption. He was an exception among the sundry band of singers, one who preferred the battle to the boudoir, his poems often exclaiming the charms of his lady in a few lines, many more extolling the excellence of his lance.

To any audience who did not know him, his songs seemed to repeat the customary enjoyment of spring after winter and the expected declaration of love of some distant but adored lady. It was a pattern begun by Guilhem of Poitiers at the onset of the twelfth century and established as a convention by Jaufré Rudel. De Born followed his own preferences. (For his compact discs see Appendix 1.)

Guilhem of Poitiers had written:

Pus vezem de novel florir . . .

Now when we see the meadows once again
In flower, and the orchards turning green,
Streams and fountains running clean,
The breezes and the winds . . .

and Jaufré Rudel had improvised:

Quan lo rius de la Fontana . . .

When the waters of the spring
Run clear once more,
And the flower blooms on the eglantine
And on the branch the nightingale . . .

Theirs were fine introductory verses, familiarly comfortable prefaces to
elaborate variations on amorous verses.

Bertran de Born's technique was deceptive. It promised the expected and
provided the unconventional. One song began:

Be. m platz lo gais temps de pascor

I am gladdened by the merry season of Easter
Bringing out leaves and flowers,
And I have joy to hear the cheerful sounds
Of the musical birds that make their songs
Sound through the woods,
And I am delighted to see the meadows . . .

The listeners probably did not yawn, but they knew what was to come. It
did not. The verse continued with de Born seeing meadows not rich with
flowers but

Covered with tents and fine pavilions,
And very great is my pleasure
To see all over the countryside
Armoured knights and war-horses.

Fighting to him was a way of life and a necessary one for his survival. Yet
to him warfare had strict codes:

Bela m'es pressa le blezos . . .

Pleasant to me is a throng of shields
Covered in blue and scarlet hues,
Of ensigns and banners of varied hues,
Tents and bivouacs and fine pavilions,
Lances shattered, shields pierced,
Shining helmets split, blows given and taken

No.m platz companha de bascos . . .

A brigand's band does not please me,
Nor that of greedy whores. I'm repelled
By bags of English and French silver
When they come from fraud.
One should hang a mean captain,
And the rich who sell instead of giving.
A man should not court a greedy mistress
If cash can get her into bed.

Bertran de Born was a minor knight but because of his passion for conflict
he mingled socially with great nobles. He had known Henry II, king of
England, his sons, Henry the Young King, Richard Coeur de Lion, Geoffrey
of Brittany, he fought against Richard and then joined him, and he had
encouraged the Young King to rebel against the old one, his own father.

De Born's *vida*, of which there are two versions, was one of the longest
with no fewer than nineteen supplementary *razos* as additions to the main
life.

Razos were a mixture of facts, half-truths, misidentifications, and
guesswork. As most were compiled more than 100 years after most of
the troubadours whose 'histories' they wrote had died, the surprise is not
that they are unreliable but that they exist at all in that time of general
illiteracy.

In their details the *razos* are often as untrustworthy as the legends of
Robin Hood, whom guesswork has placed in the time of Richard Coeur de
Lion, the contemporary of Bertran de Born. The association is historically
very dubious.[1] As general sketches, however, the *razos* almost certainly
contain genuine pieces of information. As an example, Bertran de Born's
vida stated that:

*Bertrans de Born si fo uns castellans de l'eveqet de Peregors, seigner d'un
castel que avia nom Autafor . . .*

Bertran de Born was the constable of a castle in the Perigord, lord of the castle of Hautefort. He was constantly at war with his neighbours: the Count of Perigord, the Viscount of Limoges, with his brother, Constantine, even with Richard the Lionheart when that prince was Count of Poitou. He was a valiant knight and warrior, educated, well-spoken, a good lover and troubadour, but he knew too well both how to bring calm and to encourage trouble . . .[2]

The few certain facts known about him are that he was born in the early 1140s, had two brothers, Itiers and Constantine, was twice married, the first wife presumably having died young, and that he had five children.

Some forty-five of his songs survive. They can be dated between 1181 and 1197. He wrote good verses, sang well and was congenial company. In contrast, he quite deliberately encouraged noblemen to quarrel with each other, not for its own sake but for his personal gain. Knights like him needed an income and battles provided it. 'I would that the great men should always be in violent disagreement,' he wrote. He relished the excitement, the danger and the profits of war.

Ee autresi.m platz de senhor . . .

I am delighted with a lord
When he heads the attack . . .

Massas e brans, elsm de color . . .

Maces and swords, coloured helmets,
The useless shields hacked through.
We'll see when fighting begins,
Many liegemen together striking
Some lost in the bewilderment of battle,
And horses galloping, riders wounded or slain.
Once fighting's started make every nobleman
Think only of destruction of arms and legs.
A dead man's worth more than alive and beaten.

Baro, metez en gatge . . .

Barons, put up as pawns
Your castles, villages and cities
Before you stop fighting each other.[3]

And de Born added:

Ie us dic que tan no m'a sabor . . .

I tell you there is not so much flavour
In food or wine or sleep
As when I hear men shout, 'They're there! On!
Smash into them . . . '

In his magisterial biography of Henry II W.L. Warren wrote that the importance of men like de Born was of 'representing the attitudes a class of men whose collective influence on the situation in Aquitaine should not perhaps be underestimated: those whose fortunes depended on winning favours from the major lords – or their wives. Troubadours such as Bertrand de Born were the spokesmen, the propagandists, for the interest of *la petite noblesse* – the constables of castles, the holders of minor fiefs, the landless younger sons of knightly families whose only asset was their training in the craft of arms'.[4]

Bertran de Born was not always in armour. Like other troubadours he visited courts: at Toulouse, Limoges, and, perhaps somewhat reluctantly, even in the Christmas of 1182 to Henry II's English gathering at Argentan which, being in the far north of France near Caen and the Channel ports, was usually a hall of dull, sober faces. Fortunately, it was a time when the exiled Henry the Lion, Duke of Saxony was also there. With him was his English wife, Matilda, daughter of Eleanor of Aquitaine, queen of England, and as lively as her mother. Even de Born 'admitted that the presence of Duchess Matilda added sparkle and gaiety to a court which normally depressed him by its serious and sober attention to business'.[5]

Ja mai non er cortz complia . . .

A court with no one laughing or joking
Is incomplete. A court with no rich presents
Is just a paddock full of munching barons.
From the boring and vulgar court of Argentan
Her smiling, kind face, the good companionship
Of the Saxon lady saved me.

Despite the lady's charms it is unlikely that he lingered in northern France very long. He had other interests, great friends who were rivals in love: Richard, Count of Poitou, later to be King of England; his brother,

Geoffrey of Brittany; King Alfonso of Aragon; and Raymond V, Count of Toulouse. They all, including Bertran, professed their ardent love of Raymonda of Montagnac. In several *razos* she was misnamed 'Maheut'. Razo 37 recorded:

Bertrans de Born si s'apellava 'Rassa' . . .

Bertran de Born and Count Geoffrey of Brittany called each other *Rassa*, and this count was a brother of the Young King and of Richard, Count of Poitiers. Both Richard and Geoffrey were in love with Maeut [Raymonda] de Montanhac, as were also Alfonso of Aragon and Raymond, Count of Toulouse. But she turned them all away for Bertran de Born whom she had taken as her lover and counsellor. And he, in order to make them cease courting her, wanted to tell Count Geoffrey whom it was he loved, and praise her in such a way as to make it appear that he had seen here in the nude and possessed her [*q'el l'agues vista nuda e tenguda . . .*], 'he had seen her naked and had held her in his arms'. He wanted people to know that his lady was Maeut, the one who had turned away Poitou – that is to say, Richard who was Count of Poitou – and Geoffrey who was Count of Brittany, and King Alfonso who was lord of Saragossa, and Count Raymond who was lord of Toulouse . . . and for these reasons he wrote the *sirventes* which says:[6]

Rassa, domn'ai qu'es frescha e fina . . .

Rassa! A lady I have who is fresh and pure
A graceful and happy young girl,
Golden of hair tinted with ruby,
Her skin white as hawthorn flowers,
Her soft, supple arms, her firm breasts.
Her back as lively as a young rabbit's,
Her pure, fresh complexion,
Her high merit. It's warm praise.
Connoisseurs know she is the best.
And know which part I prize the most.

The stanza's first lines were conventional, but the jerkiness of the fifth dismayed his four listeners:

E sembla conil de l'esquina . . .
like the hop, hop, hop of a little rabbit is her lithe back.

To compare such up-and-down movements, rhythmic undulations, with those of a young rabbit, a *lapron*, that candid imagery was as close as any troubadour had dared to describe human copulation. And 'which part I prize the most' convinced his friends, all men of higher rank than de Born, that the lady was his, had been taken, and would never be theirs. Whether it was poetic licence or fact, it disheartened the hopeful suitors.[7]

For them retribution was sweeter than revenge. They laughed in derision when the fickle woman suddenly abandoned de Born. Half in despair, half in retaliation, he composed another song that praised the attractions of other fine ladies, each with attributes that outmatched his dismissive woman:

Domna, puois de me no.us chal . . .
Lady, since you do not care for me . . .

And he itemised the virtues of other women that he admired: the gentle look of Cembellis, 'the entrancing lure' of a lady of unknown identity, the merry talking of another, the hands and neck of Guiborc de Montausier, Viscountess of Chalais; the hair of Agnes de Rochechouard, the perfection of the lady Faidida's teeth, the gaity and poise of the beautiful Mirallis. There was an even worse contrast. He had found someone comprehensively better than she whom he had once considered the 'Good'. He had discovered the lovely Guischarda de Beaujeu, wife of Archambaud of Comborn.

A mo Mielhs-de-be deman . . .

Of my Mielh-de-be I entreat the sight
Of her well-shaped, glorious young body,
Which, as anyone can see, 'Better-than-Good',
Would be pleasant to hold warm and unclothed.

Regrettably, none of them, not even Guischarda, wanted him.

Despite his final miserable rejection by Raymonda, there was still something malicious about de Born's temporary conquest that had humiliated his friends. It was made worse because he had not only seduced the woman they desired but had also intentionally fomented resentment between them. Similar discords existed in the English royal family.

Anger and dissention was almost hereditary in the Plantagenet family of Henry II. His sons already were in hatred of their father because of his treatment of their mother. By 1182 Eleanor of Aquitaine had been a captive for nearly eight years even though Rosamund Clifford, Henry's lover (see Appendix 4), had died six years earlier, having retired to a nunnery when the king rejected her in favour of yet one more mistress, the Capetian princess, Alais, sister to Philip of France,

The sons loathed their self-centred, adulterous father. Now there were disagreements between themselves. Power, status and territory were the touchstones. Henry, the Young King, had been made Count of Anjou and Maine by Henry II. Richard became Count of Poitou in 1169 and its duke ten years later, Geoffrey, the next-born, had Brittany. Only John 'Lackland', the youngest, received nothing.

As a father Henry II had been enigmatic. According to the monkish chronicler Giraldus Cambrensis, Gerald of Wales, the king was

> the kindest of fathers to his legitimate children during their childhood and youth, but as they advanced in years looked on them with an evil eye, treating them worse than a stepfather; and although he had such illustrious and distinguished sons, whether it was that he would not have them prosper too fast, or whether they were ill-deserving, he could never bear to think of them as his successors.

The blame, Gerald knew, was with the corrupt woman that Henry had married, herself descended from an immoral union, and who had scandalous sexual relations with Geoffrey of Anjou while she was still married to Louis VII, and then proceeded to leave her husband for Geoffrey's son, Henry.[8]

Her own sons, however, loved and respected their mother and hatefully resented Henry's treatment both of her and of them. The reaction was predictable. 'From the Devil we came', declared Richard, 'and to the Devil we'll return', with one of his many oaths that caused Bertran de Born to call him, *Oc-et-Non*, 'yes and no', in a biblical reference to Richard's habit of swearing. He told a minstrel to go to Richard;

a'n Oc-e-No t'en vai viatz . . .

Fast to my Lord Yes-and-No
And tell him he has lived in peace too long.[9]

Bertran de Born persuaded the Young King to turn against Richard. He needed Richard to be weakened because Bertran's brother, Constantine, had claimed Hautefort, de Born's castle, as his own and Richard supported him. De Born's *Razo*, no. 44, declared:

Bertrans de Born, si com eu vos ai dich . . .

Bertran de Born, as I've said, had a brother, Constantine, who was a gallant knight of arms but not one who sought fame. He wished ill-fortune to his brother and assisted those who felt the same. At one time he wrested Bertran's castle from him but Bertran regained it. So Constantine asked the Viscount of Limoges to assist him, and similarly King Richard, and they attacked lord Bertran and pillaged his lands . . .[10]

To counter such a perilous union of enemies, Bertran reminded the Young King that Richard had illegally built a castle at Clairvaux on the precise boundary of his brother's lands. It was a threat and an insult.

It was to disturb a deadly swarm of hornets. War began. Henry II supported the Young King. Philippe-Auguste, the French king, always eager to lessen the power of England in France sent mercenaries to assist Richard. According to Warren:

> The discontent was fanned by Bertrand de Born, a man of knightly family from the Limousin, and a troubadour whose particular claim to fame as a composer of topical ditties [*sirventes*] of unusual pungency and impertinence. Bertrand was in dispute with his brother about possession of the minor castle of Hautefort, and gives the impression that this private quarrel was the cause of rupture between Richard and the viscount of Limoges, and that the incitements to war conveyed by his *sirventes* were a major influence in the formation of a sworn conspiracy of the barons of the Aquitaine against their overlord.[11]

Warren considered that de Born had hugely exaggerated his role in the dispute, which was in reality a mere triviality. No chronicler mentioned him. It was not quite true. Bertran de Born was referred to by the cleric, Geoffrey of Vigeois, although only as a minor footnote.[12] Far stronger confirmation of the troubadour's part in the family quarrel came from a very convincing source, the Italian poet Dante Alighieri.

Dante consigned de Born to the ninth chasm of Circle Eight in Hell, the place of torment for Sowers of Discord who were constantly beaten by a demon with his sword. Because Bertran de Born had criminally separated father from son he was to be punished by having his head separated from his body.

Looking down into the Inferno onlookers could see:

Un busto senza capo andar, si come . . .

A trunk without a head come walking there,
Just like the others of that dismal clan.
It held the severed head up by the hair,
Swinging it like a lantern in his hand,
And, pointing at us, moaned in its despair.
It made for itself a lamp and scanned
And they were two in one and one in two.
How this can be He knows who had it planned.
When just below the bridge, when going through,
It raised its arm up high with the whole head
And to our ears, its words the closer drew.
'Look, you the breathing come to see the dead.
Take a good look at my grievous penalty.
Is any else as harsh as this?' he said.
'And so that you can carry news of me,
Know I am Bertran de Born, the one who gave
Such ill advice to the young king's majesty.
What Ahithophel launched was not more grave.
Absalom against David he incited .
I made fathers and sons as foes behave.
Because I parted persons once united,
I carry my brain divided from its source.
Upon this trunk. In this I am requited.
The law of retribution takes its course.'[13]

In his *De vulgari eloquentia,* however, Dante did term Bertran de Born the troubadour as pre-eminent in the poetry of warfare.

As a result of Bertran de Born's urging, the Young King took advantage of the widespread unrest to demand Richard's homage for his effrontery at building a castle at Clairvaux on Henry's land. The hot-blooded Richard refused. Negotiations failed. Geoffrey of Brittany joined in the dissent. So did Raymond V of Toulouse. Philippe-Auguste sent mercenaries who destroyed, robbed and raped through the territory.

Al temps qu'En Richartz era coms de Peitieus . . .

at the time when Richard was Count of Poitou when he was not yet king, Bertran de Born was his enemy because Bertran was very friendly with the Young King who was at war with Richard. And Ademar, Viscount of Limoges, the viscounts of Ventadorn and Gumel, the Count of Perigord and his brother, the Count of Angoulème and his two brothers, Count Raymond of Toulouse, the counts of Flanders, Barcelona, Gascony, Bigorre, Dijon, Gaston of Bearn, all these were persuaded by Bertran to abandon Richard and rebel against him.[14]

The ruthless Richard was accused of raping the wives and daughters of his subjects, and 'after the ardour of his lust had died, he handed them over to his knights as common prostitutes'. It was helpful propaganda for his adversaries, but it was an almost incestuous struggle, described by a nineteenth-century French historian as 'a war of succession, with this especially odious circumstance, that the father whose heritage the sons were disputing was not yet dead and he took part in the conflict'.[15]

Henry II and Richard fought back vigorously against their opponents. Henry besieged Limoges. Richard marauded mercilessly through Poitou and 'had those he captured drowned, butchered, or blinded, knights being made to suffer in exactly the same manner as foot soldiers'.

Henry, the Young King, escaped from Limoges but lacked his bellicose brother's intensity and had no plan of campaign. He meandered without purpose. Sacrilegiously, shrines were plundered to pay his lacklustre soldiers, and, finally, a fever he caught in the hot summer developed into dysentery. Anticipating death, he chose to lie on a bed of stones and ashes in repentance for his many sins. Wearing his unused crusader's cloak he died in. Martel on 11 June 1183.[16]

Le plaintz qu'en Bertrans de Born fetz del rei Jove . . .

Because of the Young King's excellence, and because of the grief that all men felt at his death, Bertran de Born composed a threnody, *Mon chan fenis al dol et ab mal traire*, 'My singing ends in my wretched misery . . .[17]

Si tuit l idol e.lh plor e.lh marrimen

If all the tears and grief and misery
And the anguish and the pain and the misfortune
That one ever heard of in this sad world
Were put together they would seem as nothing
Beside the death of the young English king,
Whereat merit and youth remain grieving,
And the world obscure, dark and gloomy
Deprived of joy, full of sadness and sorrow . . .

Dolen e trist e ple de marrimen . . .

Grieving and sad and full of memory
Stand the courtly retainers left behind,
And the charming troubadours and jongleurs'
Death hath for them too deadly a foe
For it has taken from them the young English king . . .

The poem's fifth stanza continued:

Celui que plac p.el nostre marrimen

To the One whom it pleased to in our misery
To come to the world and save us from evil,
And who received death for our salvation,
As to a charitable and just lord,
Let us beg mercy, that the young English king
Be pardoned, if it please Him, as He is true pardon
And that he be placed with honoured Companions
There where never was pain nor will be sorrow.

With the Young King's death, the coalition collapsed. De Born raged,
'I am making a *sirvente* against the cowardly barons', because he was
unable 'to make a single one of them run or even trot', against Henry II
and Richard.

Henry, Richard and Alfonso of Aragon bombarded and wrecked the walls
of the rebellious headquarters of Limoges. The city once taken. Henry II
went to Rouen for his son's burial. Richard stayed for his long-awaited
retribution. He advanced on Bertran de Born inside his castle of Hautefort.
The unforgiving Richard, furious that de Born had sided with the Young
King, besieged the fortress. Alfonso, King of Aragon, Born's erstwhile
friend, joined him.

Learning of Alfonso's arrival and hoping for some assistance, Born sent
him food and wine, with the naïve request that Alfonso should advise
Richard to move the heavy catapults of trebuchets and mangonels that
were already weakening Hautefort's defences. Instead, and predictably,
Alfonso told Richard, who immediately increased the numbers of siege
machines.

Bertran de Born was outraged at the treachery of his old friend and
ally.and composed a *sirventes* condemning such unexpected, unjustified
disloyalty.

Sirventes . . .

Since the gentle season of flowers
Spreads forth, gentle and gay,
A desire has entered my heart
To compose a new *sirventes*,
So that the Aragonese may know
That their king
(and of this they can be sure)
Came here beneath an evil star,
Dishonoured, a mere mercenary.[18]

It did not disturb Alfonso. Nor did it deflect Richard from his determination to break into Hautefort and capture his unfaithful troubadour.

Lo reis Enrics d'Engleterre si tenia assis En Bertran de dedins Autafort . . .

Now King Henry of England held Bertran de Born besieged inside Hautefort and fought against him with his siege-weapons, for he hated him because he believed that it had been Bertran that had been the cause of the enmity between him and his son. So he had come to Hautefort to deprive de Born of his inheritance . . .[19]

There are obvious mistakes. Henry II was in Rouen, not at Hautefort. That siege was commanded by his son, Richard, Coeur de Lion, who took the castle and had the wounded de Born brought to his tent.

En Bertrans ab tota sag en fon menatz al pabaillon del rei Enric . . .

Bertran and all his men were led to king Henry's pavilion. He was very badly received. The king said, 'Bertran, Bertran, you have said that you never needed more than half your wits, but now you will need them all.

'My lord', replied Bertran, 'I did say that and I was speaking the truth'. The king replied, Now it seems you have lost your wits completely. My lord, said Bertran, You are right. They are all gone. Why is that?, asked the king. My lord, said Bertran, when your son, the valiant Young King, died, I lost my wits, my judgement and my mind.

And when the king saw Bertran's tears and heard what the troubadour had said and sung about his son, he was much grieved, and he was close to fainting.

When he recovered he called out, crying, 'Bertran, Bertran, it was only right that you should lose your wits for my son because he loved you more than any other man, and for love of him I shall set you at liberty, and grant you your belongings, your castle. I shall grant you my love and my favour'.

And Bertran fell to his knees, giving the king his thanks and his deep gratitude. And the king went away with his entire army.[20]

Bertran de Born became a devoted follower of Richard who became king of England in 1189, went on the Third Crusade, was captured and ransomed in Austria.

After Richard's triumphant but brief return to England he went back to protect his possessions in France. Bertran de Born wrote a poem of rejoicing:

Ar ven la coindeta sazos . . .

Now the warm season has arrived
When English ships will come to French ports
And the bold, worthy king will land,
King Richard. The like there never was.
Then we'll see gold and silver in plenty,
Siege-weapons constructed,
Loaded for bombardment,
We'll see great towers shiver and collapse
And enemies captured and imprisoned.

It was one of his last poems. It was not prophetic. History is seldom kind. Within a short few months Richard was killed at Chalus.

It was probably shortly after that tragedy that Bertran de Born retired to the Cistercian abbey of Dalon, only 4 miles east of Hautefort, the same retreat that another fine troubadour, Bernart de Ventadorn, had chosen.

Exactly when Bertran de Born died is not known. It was certainly before 1215. By that time invasion of the Languedoc by a destructive army of Catholic crusaders was already six years old.

ELEVEN

RAIMON OF MIRAVAL AND GUY OF CAVAILLON

D'amor es tottz mos cossiriers . . .

Love is all that concerns me
Because my one real care is love.
Condemning tongues will say
A knight should think more of other matters
But I say that that is incorrect.
From love comes, whatever others say.
What is best both for foolishness and wisdom,
And all that's done for love is good.

Raimon of Miraval, c. 1190

The Death of Courts and the Loss of Castles, 1209–1233

> The splendour falls from castle walls
> And snowy summits old in story;
> The long light shakes across the lakes
> And the wild cataract leaps in glory.
> Blow, bugle, blow, set the wild echoes flying,
> Blow, bugles, answer echoes, dying, dying, dying . . .
>
> Alfred, Lord Tennyson, *The Princess*, IV, 1–6

What had been a gradual decline in the world of troubadours became a collapse in the thirteenth century. Patrons and courts were lost. The greatest of all patrons died. In April 1204 Eleanor of Aquitaine was buried in Fontevrault abbey. Through military conquest Occitanian courts of love became, one by one, French-speaking castles of hate. Those early years precipitated the decline of the musicians.

Tiredness was another reason. The formula of winter's frigidity warming into the fecundity of spring, the time when singers' thoughts turned to a yearning for the woman they loved, had become a cliché. Repetition transformed romance into routine, a succession of stale words.

Late in the twelfth century, Raimon of Miraval (*c.* 1135–*c.* 1215), the singer teased by the Monk of Montaudon for repeatedly giving away his castle, converted such staleness brilliantly. Whether he knew Andreas Capellanus' *Art of Courtly Love* is unknown, but in his conventional songs he converted that Art of Love into art for art's sake.[1]

He would, he asserted, obey his lady in whatever she demanded, accept her orders unquestioningly, always fulfil them. Understandably, such noble sentiments were accepted in every court both by wives and husbands. In his *sirvente*, XXXVIII,

Aras no m'en puosc plus tardar . . .
he was explicit about his own invariably courtly standards

Mas eu n-om vuoill far entestar . . .

I do not want to beat myself on my head.
To my lady I am unfailingly loyal
And know exactly how to honour her.
If my lord should remark, 'It is raining',
I shall agree that the weather is just like that,
Because I would have been untrue to my lady
If I contradicted her husband in anything.[2]

Topsfield described such idealism: 'Raimon's poetry accords with the tastes of a noble society which in its splendour and luxury walled itself in from contact with the rough reality of life outside.'[3] (For Miraval's compact discs, see Appendix 1).

Miraval's actual life was less idealistic. He had loved the Marchioness of Minerve – *Te la Marquez' aders de Menerba sai jos . . .* (all that is youthfulness and of value is the lady of Minerve) – but left her when he discovered someone of even more merit, *Mais d'amic*, his 'more than lover', probably the notoriously wanton Louve of Pennautier, 'Loba', with whom the foolish Peire Vidal had been infatuated. A *razo* of his described her:

> *Mas el si amava una doma de Carcases, que avia nom Loba de Peiinautier*
> *. . .*

> He loved a lady of the Carcassés, Loba [the she-wolf]. She was very beautiful, gracious, very anxious to be known and admired, and all the lords of that region, and those from elsewhere, loved her: the Count of Foix, Oliver of Saissac, Peire Rogier of Mirepoix, Aimeric of Montréal. But Raimon of Miraval loved her most deeply, and by his songs and praises made her famous.[4]

Miraval was infatuated: *S'a dreg fos chantars grazitz . . .* (If my song is truly appreciated I shall sing more often). And in verse 6 he sang:

> *Domna, vos m'etz del tot guitz . . .*

Lady, you are my guide in everything,
For I am foolish or wise at your command.
My longing is so deep that a year is a day,
But the long delay brings me anxiety
And my song seems to be without reason
Because when one woos with sincerity
A demand to wait three years is too long.

In gratitude she welcomed his songs, promised him her love, bound him to her with a kiss. But she was false. His razo continued: *Mas ella non le avia amor . . .* (But she had no love for him. She was in love with the high-ranking Count of Foix and she gave herself to him in mind, spirit and body . . .).[5] Rather strangely, the gossipy Jean de Nostradamus did not mention her.[6]

Miraval found calm after the turbulence by serenading two other ladies. The first was Azalais of Boissezon, wife of Bernard of Lombers near Albi. He extolled her. His poem

Era ab la forssa dels freis . . .
Now with the chilling cold the entire world trembles

had the conventional introduction, but then its sixth verse, *S'a Lombers corteia.l reis . . .*, introduced the lady:

If the king comes to the court at Lombers
He will find everlasting joy because of that.
Although he is incomparable in every skill,
For every one of his he will discover two more.
The incomparable courtesy and nobility of the lady Azalais,
Her delicate complexion, her fine blonde hair,
Give delight to the entire world.

'Dompna', he continued, *'tant vos sui verais . . .'*;

Lady, I am so loyal to you that
I wish to assist you in all courtly matters.[7]

He succeeded too well. He wrote songs that proclaimed her beauty and virtue and sent them to every influential person that he knew. Intrigued by the enthusiastic descriptions, King Pedro of Aragon sent messengers to Lombers, wrote letters, presented gifts of precious jewels. A monarch, courageous warrior, and experienced womanizer, he came to the lady's court and very smoothly seduced Azalais.

Si que la nueit ac lo reis tot so que'illl volia . . .
that night the king had of her all that he desired.[8]

Next day the entire castle's servants and the king's retinue chattered about what had occurred. Miraval heard the tittle-tattle. He was broken-hearted. Naively he had only written so fulsomely to Pedro and other nobles of considerable standing in the expectation that such familiarity with royalty would both impress and conquer Azalais. Resentfully he quitted Lombers with the bitter comment: 'He who gives the most can enter first!'[9]

Undeterred by his misfortunes with the faithless Loba and the too easily traduced Azalais, he found hope of solace with a woman of less social status, Ermengarde of Castres, wife of a well-to-do freeman. What followed was not an affair but a farce of marital musical chairs. Being married, the virtuous Ermengarde refused to yield to Raimon unless he abandoned his wife, Guidairenca, evicting her from his castle.

Mas si el volia laisser sua moiller . . .

Straight away he went to the castle and told his wife, a poetess, that one poet in the household was sufficient and she must go to her father's house as he would no longer have her as his wife. As it happened she favoured a knight, Guillem Bremon, for whom she had composed lyrical songs.

At Raimon of Miraval's words she affected sadness and said she would get in touch with her relatives but, instead, wrote to her knight saying she would marry him and depart from the castle at Miraval.

Sir Guillem was delighted, assembled his retainers and went to the castle. Guidarenca told her husband that her kinsmen had arrived. He was overjoyed. Then his wife said that the company belonged to Sir Guillem Bremon and that Raimon should present her to the knight to become his wife. He consented. Bremon produced a ring, took her in wedlock and rode away with her.[10]

Raimon of Miraval returned ecstatically to Castres, only to discover that he had been deceived yet again. The giggling Ermengarde had married Oliver of the great castle of Saissac.

Despite his many disappointments Raimon of Miraval continued to sing but with less pleasure in his life.

Lonc temps ai avutz conseriers . . .

For long I have suffered worries and concerns
Without diversion, my songs and my joy
Being so diminished. But now I have changed.
So much has love betrayed me
That no song, Spring weather,
No flowers now give me any pleasure.

It was Raimon's own, very private world, as Jack Lindsay observed in an earlier historical context, his personal *Song of a Fallen World*.[11]

Miraval consoled himself that he still had his castle and the patronage of the wealthiest, most powerful lord in the Languedoc, Count Raymond VI of Toulouse. But within a few years he was to lose both.

Enraged by the murder of his legate Pierre de Castelnau, and frustrated by the continuing existence of the heretical Cathars in the Languedoc, Pope Innocent III called for a military crusade against them. Inspired by the promise of absolution of their sins, remission of their debts, the opportunity to slaughter infidels and the chance of acquiring land, castles and riches, French knights and their retainers enrolled in their thousands. In 1209 an immense army straggled southwards along the banks of the Rhone.

Montpellier was passed, safe as a papal protectorate. The next city, Béziers, notorious for its heretics, was defiant, its walls strong. It remained secure for just one day. Next morning, 22 July, some young, over-confident squires decided to attack the closest enemies, a shanty town at a distance from the tents and pavilions of knights and counts, a motley of ramshackle shelters, lean-to boards and sacking belonging to a rabble, scoundrels, thieves and cut-throats, vermin that followed every armoured host.

Parasites perhaps, poltroons never. Grabbing knives, axes, pitchforks, even swords, the ruffians attacked the reckless group, who fled for shelter. They were too late. Unable to repel the pursuing rabble, they had no time to slam the heavy gates. The undefended inhabitants of Béziers were slaughtered.

Aroused by the racket of clamorous bells and distant screams, realising with astonishment that the impregnable city had fallen, knights hurried to their armour with one question. How to distinguish between Catholic and Cathar? Arnaud Amaury, Abbot of Citeaux, with the monomaniacal bigotry of biblical belief, commanded:

Caedite eos. Novit enim Dominus qui sunt eis
Kill them all. God will know his own.[12]

What criminals had begun knights ended. Thousands of citizens were slaughtered in the sanctuary of Sainte-Marie-Magdeleine church. Nowhere in the city was anyone spared. The killing took just three hours of pitiless bloodshed

In a letter to Innocent III, Arnaud Amaury exalted at the bloodshed. 'Neither age, nor sex, nor status had been spared.' How many had died is unknown. It was a multitude. The city had a population of some 10,000, but to that number were added crowds of refugees from villages. The purge had been transformed into mass murder.

A Catholic trobairitz of the Dominicans, Gormonda of Montpellier, made an unconvincing and very long apology for a massacre that had occurred on the precise Feast Day of Saint Mary-Magdalene herself. She is supposed to have been a lapsed Cathar. It could explain her vehemence.

I   *Greu m'es a durar'*

>   It's hard to bear it
>   When I hear such false belief . . .

XX   *Roma.l Glorios*

>   Rome, may the Glorious One
>   who pardoned Mary
>   (whose gift
>   we surely hope for)
>   Magdalen, kill the rabid fool
>   who sows so much false speech.
>   he and his treasure
>   and his evil heart;
>   and when he dies may he die
>   in the torments
>   suffered by heretics.[13]

Guiraut Riquier of Narbonne was one of the last of the troubadours, born around 1230 over twenty years after the tragedy. He was a man who lamented the passing of Languedoc's courtly, artistic life and the degeneration of belief, 'Evil's so proud they've put Good up for sale'. He composed a *canso* about the carnage at Béziers. Of his 101 surviving poems, the melodies of 48 are still known. The tune for this one is lost. The bitterness remains.

>   Béziers has fallen. They're dead.
>   Clerks, women, children. No quarter.
>   They killed Christians too.
>   I rode out. I couldn't see or hear
>   A living creature.
>   I saw Simon de Montfort.
>   His beard glistened in the sun.
>   They killed seven thousand people,
>   Seven thousand souls who sought sanctuary
>   In Ste.-Madeleine.

The steps of the altar
Were wet with blood.
The church echoed with their cries.
Afterwards they slaughtered the monks
Who tolled the bells.
They used the silver cross
As a chopping-block to behead them.[14]

Four early monkish contemporaries: Guillaume de Tudela and his 'anonymous' successor who was arguably Guy of Cavaillon, knight and troubadour; the Cistercian monk, Pierre des Vaux-de-Cernay; and the later, less reliable Guillaume de Puylaurens, chronicled the Albigensian Crusade. Its sieges, ambushes and battles have subsequently been described in many works.[15]

Of those early chronicles the most vivid because of its poetical imagery, is *La Chanson de la Croisade Albigeois*, 'The Song of the Albigensian Crusade', begun by de Tudela. It consisted of 214 rhymed verses of varying length known as *laisses*. The first 130 *laisses*, almost 3,000 lines, recording the events of AD 1208–12, were written by de Tudela. The continuation, perhaps by Cavaillon, was almost three times that length, extending the 'history' to AD 1218. It is exciting to read, even in translation:

Guillaume had written well and conscientiously but his successor 'can toss showers of words into the air and catch them again, can make the morning air shimmer before our eyes as the knights ride to war along the riverbank with the sun glinting on their armour and on the waters of the Garonne. More than this, he has great economy of style, never any hint of longwindedness or padding, and his command of dialogue is such that we read on in amazement, thinking, for example, "How brave of that man to speak to Sir Simon like that!" before we catch ourselves up and remember that the whole conversation can only be invented.[16]

Leaving the smoking ruins of Béziers the crusaders reached Carcassonne by the first of August and besieged it. The defences were daunting, rampart within rampart, towers, an iron-grated barbican guarding its formidable castle.

There was one weakness. The fortification was on a high, steep spur of the hilly Corbières but it had been compromised. The city was almost a quarter of a mile east of the river Aude and the crusaders instantly took control of the Pont Vieux across it. Carcassonne became dependent on its internal wells during that long, hot summer.

The army attacked. Sappers protected by their covered 'cats' tried to undermine the walls. Catapults bombarded. Stalemate followed. The approaches to the citadel were too steep for the cumbrous gigantic trebuchets and the enforced range was too far for their missiles. The lighter mangonels and petraries were used but to little effect on the sturdy walls. Human assaults were driven back by crossbowmen.

During the impasse Pedro II, King of Aragon arrived with a token retinue of 100 knights. He was concerned that the lands of his vassal, Raymond-Roger, Viscount of Béziers and Carcassonne, could become those of a defiant, unsworn baron from northern France. He told the young Viscount that the crusaders were prepared to allow him and eleven of his men to leave the city under safe conduct. Everyone else would be killed.

Raymond-Roger refused to abandon his subjects whom the prelate had cursed as a nest of heretics. 'I would suffer myself to be flayed alive. He shall not have the least of my company at his mercy, for it is on my account that they are in danger'.[17]

The siege was resumed. It was a critical time. For many knights and their feudal levies the forty days of obligatory service were ending. Then the siege would have to be abandoned. Inside Carcassonne there were different misgivings. The wells and cisterns were failing in the sultry weather. A parley was arranged.

On 14 August under promise of safe-conduct Raymond-Roger and nine others entered the crusaders' camp. The conditions under which the inhabitants would be freed were decided. It was in the minimum of clothing and with no possessions.

The Bible permitted treachery. Despite the crusaders' sworn vows, Arnaut Amaury disregarded them. Raymond-Roger was a leader of heretics. Therefore he should be fettered and imprisoned in one of his own damp, dark and maladorous dungeons.

Next day the citadel's inhabitants were expelled, 'naked . . . bearing nothing but their sins', applauded Pierre des Vaux-de-Cernay. Guillaume de Tudela noted that they were 'quite unprotected, they rushed out pell-mell in their shirts and breeches, nothing else, not even the value of a button were they allowed to take with them'.[18]

Inexplicably, not one Cathar of the heretical haven of Carcassonne was arrested. It is a mystery. The crusade was against Catharism and it was to be merciless. In his letters Innocent III was explicit. 'You must try in whatever ways God has revealed to you to wipe out the treachery of heresy and its followers by attacking the heretics with a strong hand and an outstretched arm'. But no one was wiped out. All went free except Raymond-Roger, the Viscount. He died, in chains, of dysentery some months later. With his death and the capture of Béziers and Carcassonne the troubadours had lost one of their wealthy patrons and two of their greatest courts.

Carcassonne became the crusaders' headquarters. Simon de Montfort was appointed commander of the crusaders who remained in the Languedoc. He had already been on the Third Crusade and then joined the Fourth but in 1204. being a devout Catholic, had refused to take part in the sacrilegious pillage of Constantinople, a Christian city.[19]

Five years later he willingly joined another holy crusade, the one to exterminate the heretical plague of Catharism.

Petty disagreements, feudal disputes, family feuds had for generations been part of the southern way of life. Quarrels, came, flickered and went out. Military invasion did not. The armoured soldiers of the Albigensian Crusade, led by a master of battles and sieges, Simon de Montfort, came, conquered and remained. Fighting, confiscation and destruction in the Languedoc came early in the thirteenth century and lingered for several corrosive decades.

In a brief two years of ruthless campaigns to the north of Carcassonne towns and castles were captured and French crusader lords installed. Towns such as Lavaur and Minerve were besieged, taken, and their Cathar occupants, hundreds of them, burnt at the stake. Castles were attacked: Aguilar, Alairac, Bruniquel, Coustaussa, Puilaurens, Saissac. Raimon of Miraval's own at Miraval-Cabardès was hurriedly abandoned as crusaders advanced on it. Worst of all for the helpless troubadours, two of their finest courts were lost at Termes and the singers's Mecca, the famous fortress of Puivert.

There was little resistance. In September 1211 the southerners did assemble a fighting force at Saint-Martin-Lalande near Castelnaudary but the battle became a rout when the titular leader, Count Raymond VI of Toulouse, most generously described as hesitant, more realistically condemned as spineless, lingered cowardly in his fine tent while the courageous Count of Foix and his son fought ferociously against de Montfort's military machine.

So did Savaric de Mauléon with his mercenaries. 'There was panic in the Toulousian army', recorded William de Tudela, 'in the meadows below Castelnaudary, every man was anxious to retreat. *Savarigs crida n'aut: Senhors estat tuit quei'* 'Savaric shouted aloud, 'Stay calm, my lords, don't move! No one take down or fold his tent, or you are all dead men!' 'Ah, Lord God of glory, by your most holy law', said each man to himself, 'keep us from shame, do not let us be disgraced. The battle was lost even though, we outnumbered them ten to one, I promise you'.[20]

Raimon of Miraval became a *faidit*, a dispossessed knight of the Languedoc, dependent on the generosity of patrons to maintain him. He had known the court and the counts Raymond V and VI of Toulouse for twenty years. In 1213 he and his reconciled poetess wife Gaudairenca were there one again. So was Pedro II, the King of Aragon. Raimon praised him in Poem XXXVII. He was optimistic that his troubles would not last long now. Pedro, his successful rival for the favours of Azalais but now agreeable supporter, would bring succour.

> I. *Bel m'es q'ieu chant e coindei . . .*
>   It pleases me to sing and be agreeable

But in verses VIII and IX he was optimistic about his future:

> VIII *Tro-l fieu vos agues rendut*
>   *De Miraval q'ai perdut.*
>
>   Until I return to you
>   The lands of Miraval that I have lost.

> IX   *Mas lo reis m'a covengut . . .*
>   *Que-l cobrarai anz de gaire*
>   *E mos Audiart Belcaire:*
>   *Puois poiran dompnas e drut*
>   *Tornar ei joi q'ant perdut.*
>
>   But the king has promised me
>   That I shall soon get it back
>   And my Audiart will regain Belcaire:
>   Then both ladies and their lovers
>   Will go back to the joys that they have lost.

'Audiart' was Miraval's affectionate nickname for Count Raymond VI, whose minor castle in the Aude had also been taken by the crusaders. His was the optimism of a romantic. History proved it unrealistic.[21] It was an optimism that the battle of Muret put an end to shortly afterwards.

Fought just south of Toulouse in 1213, Simon de Montfort outflanked the uncoordinated army of Raymond VI, who characteristically did nothing, the Count of Foix and the soldiers of Aragon. Pedro was killed. It was rumoured that the king had spent the entire night with a woman and by the morning was so exhausted that he was unable to stand during the reading of the Gospel. The 'anonymous' chronicler who succeeded William de Tudela brilliantly evoked the fighting in *Laisse CXL*.

Tuit s'en van a las tendas per majas las palutz . . .

Across the marshes and straight for the tents [the French] rode, banners displayed and pennons flying. Beaten gold glittered on shields and helmets, on swords and hauberks, so that the whole place shone. And when the good king of Aragon saw them, he and a few companions rode fast to confront them. All the men of Toulouse came hurrying up, paying heed neither to count nor king. They had no idea what was happening until the French rode up and converged on the king once he had been identified. And he shouted, *Eusol reis!, mas noi est entendutz*, 'I am the king' but no one heard him and he was struck and so severely wounded that his blood spilled out on the ground and he fell his full length dead.

Muret is just a few miles south of Toulouse. Today the battlefield is marred by houses and streets, and pierced by a dual carriageway. The only memorial, wrongly placed, is a worn and weathered pillar on the outskirts of the town.[22]

It was the beginning of the end for troubadours in Occitania. There had been happy nights in great halls, people in the darkness around a bright fire playing chess, conversing, a minstrel singing and playing. Once time there had been so many patrons around Béziers and Carcassonne, recited Raymond of Miraval, that it would have taken forty verses to name them all. It was ending. Now there was to be a decline into defeat that culminated with Muret.

Miraval's *vida* states that after the battle, lost of all hope, the troubadour retired to the Cistercian abbey of the Ladies of Citeaux at Lerida in Catalonia. He died there shortly afterwards.[23]

Fighting continued. Like figures in the Bayeux Tapestry, chain-mailed knights and their soldiers systematically overran, burned, mutilated, confiscated. Over brief years the green dots of towns and villages in the Languedoc became red and French, as scarlet as the crusaders' Cross. Resistance weakened. Helpless southern lords submitted in hope of keeping their estates. The defiant became *faidits*. There were ambushes and treacheries. For wandering troubadours there were still the Catholic courts of Provence, of Aragon, Navarre, Castile, but their heartland was being lost.

Raymond VI, Count of the still-unconquered Toulouse, as always dithering, was excommunicated for failing to be zealous in his persecution of heretics. Dying unblessed, his corpse was denied burial, and for years his coffin was left neglected and exposed in the open air.

His son, Raymond VII, was different, decisive, a fighter, and he fought the invaders, often successfully. Toulouse continued to withstand sieges.

At Beaucaire in 1216 Raymond and loyal followers like Guy of Cavaillon trapped a French garrison in their usurped castle. De Montfort came to their rescue but was resisted. He was unable to defeat them. The *Chanson's* account of the fight that followed is a graphic account of brutal medieval warfare.

So evocative are the descriptions of hand-to-hand fighting, the noise, the movement, so enthusiastic about the excitement that, like Bertran de Born, the writer must have been not only an eye-witness but an actual participant. If so, he was a mounted knight to have seen so much of the field of battle.

Laisse 165: i l'abat el trebucha que I remas lo saureus . . .

Broadswords and maces came into play, daggers and knives: danger and death returned. Stones, darts and lances came in a blizzard like snow, arrows and bolts, halberds, pikes, javelins and axes flashed through the air. Bucklers were smashed, both rims and crystal bosses, hauberks and mails, helmets and iron hats, shields with their banding, bridles and belts. Lance-heads and javelins crashed and clattered – a storm, a downpour of pelting hammer blows.

So close and bitter, so deadly was the conflict, the crusaders reined back their Arab mounts and turned away and the townsmen pursued them with blows and shouts, they struck and wounded both horses and men. Slashed off and scattered you'd have seen legs, arms and feet, men's guts and lungs, jawbones and heads, scalps and spilled brain matter. So hard they fought and struck and slew, they drove them off, drove them from roads, hills and open places, from grassland and reedbeds. The battle ended, the remains left lying there made a feast for dogs and birds.[24]

If de Montfort's men were caught they were hanged as traitors and left dangling to rot on trees visible from the city.

En Guis de Cavalho desobre un arabit . . .

Sir Guy of Cavaillon, riding an Arab mount, struck down William of Berlit that day and they hanged him then and there from a flowering olive tree.[25]

Inside Beaucaire the beleaguered and starving defenders were granted safe conduct but without their weapons. De Montfort retreated. It is all in the *Chanson's Laisse 171, Lo coms se part del seti de gran felnia ples . . .*

> In rage and fury Count Simon abandoned the siege. He regained his men but lost their equipment, as well as their mounts, pack-horses and Arab mules. His losses of all kinds were so heavy that there was plenty of carrion left lying for birds and dogs. And Beaucaire remained in the hands of Raymond, count, marquis and duke.[26]

Furious, de Montfort raced back to the unguarded Toulouse before the startled townsmen could defend it. He bullied and imprisoned its burghers, destroyed houses, demanded money, jewellery, precious objects, departed for the wedding of his son, left its cowed inhabitants in the charge of his brother, Guy.

There was an uprising. Fighting in streets and alleys where mounted men could not enter, using what weapons they could find, the citizens drove out the small French detachment and closed the gates on them. De Montfort was almost hysterical with rage on his return. He swore that he would smash into the city before his pack-horses could be unloaded. It is at such incidents that the *Chanson's* poet is so convincing, reporting conversation that he could never have heard. A knight rebuked de Montfort for his excessive boast:

'Senher coms,' ditz, n'Alas, 'vos no siatz aitls . . .'

> My lord Count, said Sir Alan, don't think in that way, for your oath is mere morning dew.[27]

Simon de Montfort never did re-enter Toulouse. Raymond VII, Count of the region, did, and for ten months from 1217 to 1218 his city was besieged by the crusaders. There were attacks, counter-attacks, then stalemate. It ended with de Montfort's death.

Ac dins una peireira que fe us carpenters . . .

> There was in the town a mangonel built by a carpenter and dragged with its platform from St Sernin. It was worked by noble women, and little girls and men's wives, and now a stone arrived just where it was needed.

E ferric si lo comte sobre l'elm qu'es d'acers . . .

It struck Count Simon on his steel helmet, shattering his eyes, brains, back teeth, forehead and jaw. Bleeding and black, the count dropped dead on the ground. [28]

Some of the *Chanson*'s imagery is lost even in Shirley's vivid translation. So is the self-inflicted tortuous rhyme-scheme in which, using *Laisse 171* as an example, every one of its 178 lines ends with '*–es*'. Only a very good and technically proficient poet could have composed the *Chanson*.

For centuries he remained a man without a name until recent critical analysis suggested that the knight, Guy, lord of Cavaillon, who had fought so bravely at Beaucaire and elsewhere, could have been the poet.[29] Being a troubadour as well as a nobleman, it is possible.

It is not for him, however, that Cavaillon, a pleasant town near Avignon in Provence, is famous, but for its fragrant, luscious melons, so succulent that Alexandre Dumas, nineteenth-century author of *The Three Musketeers*, promised the corporation a complete set of his books in return for a yearly present of the fruits.

Guy, the town's medieval lord, is less well known. He is mentioned several times in the continuation of the *Chanson* as a courageous knight and loyal companion of Raymond VII. Being a good poet he had a *vida*.

Gui de Cavaillo fo uns gentils bars de Proensa . . .

Guy of Cavaillon was a noble baron of Provence, lord of Cavaillon. He was a generous, courteous and gracious knight, well loved of ladies and everybody, a fine knight of arms. He made good verses and couplets of love and merriment. It was believed that he was the lover of Countess Garsenda, wife of the Count of Provence, a brother of the king of Aragon.[30]

He is known to have composed five or six *tensos* and a *sirvente*. There was also a *cobla*, two verses, one by a lady, the other by him.

Guy had fought with Raymond VI, and, when that Count was compelled to leave Toulouse and go to Spain in 1216, he named Guy as the first among the barons to care for his son, Raymond.

Raymond was been exhorted by Guy to restore *paretge*, an Occitanian word meaning not merely courtesy but the virtues of tolerance, hospitality, charity and justice.

Laisse 154. Oimais es la sazos que a grans obs <u>Paratges</u> que siatz mals e bos . . .

Now is the time when *paratge* urgently requires you to be bad and good, bad to your enemies, good to your people. For then men will think well of you, if you are generous to friends and strangers and if you bring your enemies low and prefer to say 'yes' rather than 'no'.

Simon de Montfort was covering *paratge* with shame. 'If worth and *paratge* do not arise again this year, then *paratge* dies, in you the whole world dies. You are the true hope of *paratge* and the choice is yours, either you show courage or *paratge* dies.'[31] Raymond VII was not Raymond VI. Honour was upheld.

Some time after 1218 Cavaillon was besieged by the French in his castle of Châteauneuf near Montélimar. No friend came to his rescue. He wrote two sardonic verses to the absent Sir Bertran Folcon who had fought with Raymond at Beaucaire but had become weary of the unending, inconclusively useless warfare.[32]

Doas coblas farai en aquest son . . .

I shall make a song of two verses
To send to Bertran of Avignon
He knows that I am at Châteauneuf
And the French are surrounding us
He remembers me and my loyalties.
Why so often I goad the spur,
Shout the war-cry, display my lion's emblem.
So I send these news to Bertran of Avignon,
    Yes! To Bertan!

     . . . . .

To Bertran Folcon I write, trapped in these walls
Asking him to come here so that one day
Armoured in mail, on our warhorses,
After the evening and having eaten quickly
We shall sally from the walls and across the moat.
With the French there is no truce
Until a havoc of blows is given and received.
For three months I have been imprisoned
he just loiters at peace, safe at home,
Far from us, giving not a single care, not one. .
    Bertran Folcon!

Guy was also the reputed, reluctant platonic lover of Garsenda de Foulcalquier, wife since 1193 of Amios Alphonse II, count of Provence, brother of Peire II, king of Aragon.

Between Cavaillon and her there was perhaps no kind of romance until her husband's death in 1209. After that she became Regent of Provence, and, despite the turmoil of attacks and sieges, encouraged troubadours to visit her court. One of them, Elias Barjol, a merchant's son from the Agenais region, loved her.

> *E N'Elias s'enamoret de la comtesssa ma dompna Carsenda . . .*

With another jongleur, Oliver, he went from court to court. Count Alphonse of Provence had them stay with him and at Barjol gave them wives and land causing them to be called Elias and Oliver of Barjol. And after the Count died in Sicily [in fact, Perpignan] Elias became enamoured of his widow and for her composed four good, pleasant songs.[33]

Garsenda was the highest ranking of all well-born troubairitz, a woman fortunate to live in a world were women were officially adored.[34]

One stanza of hers exists, a *cobla* whose second verse is believed to be the work of Guy of Cavaillon. She rebuked him for his timidity.

> *Vos que.m semblatz deis corals amadors . . .*

You seem a warm and full-hearted lover.
I only wish you were not so hesitant.
I'm glad that you are in love with me
But I am helpless against your uncertainty.
Its timidity brings you only harm. .
You dare not tell me what you wish
Yet a lady can never admit what she desires
For fear of betrayal and other people's scorn.

She came from a family that was one of the two most important in Provence and it is extraordinary that she dared write so openly even as cautiously as this. Her rebuke obtained a humorous reply, probably from Guy of Cavaillon.

> *Bona dompna, vostr'onrada valors . . .*

Lady, it's your noble status scaring me,
So high a birth causes hesitation.
It is only that makes me so fearful
Of admitting my love. I would rather
Serve you well than bring you dishonour.
But I will take the risk of courting you
And let my actions be my message,
With direct deeds to replace ambiguous 'pleads'.
One noble service rather than a hundred words.[35]

The death of Simon de Montfort had not ended the fighting. Eager to prove his manhood Prince Louis led a further crusade against the Cathars in the Languedoc. In 1218 Pope Honorius III had entreated the French king to permit his son to take the Cross against the heretics and the following May Louis left Paris, marching to attack an inoffensive market town, Marmande, already under siege by Simon's brother for six months. It was to be a second Béziers.

The prince led an invincible juggernaut of an army, bishops, great counts, hundreds of knights, thousands of archers and soldiers. Awed, Marmande surrendered. Its garrison was spared. The implacably fanatical bishops insisted that all others should be killed.

Murderously, soldiers obeyed their spiritual superiors:

Laisse 212. *Els homes e las femnas totz despulhatz e nutz . . .*

Lords, ladies and their little children, women and men stripped naked, all these men slashed and cut to pieces with keen-edged swords. Flesh, blood and brains, trunks, limbs and faces hacked in two, lungs, livers and guts torn out and tossed aside as if they had rained from the sky. Marshland and good ground, all was red with blood. Not a man or a woman was left alive, neither young nor old, no living creature, unless any had managed to hide. Marmande was razed and set alight.[36]

Delighted at his atrocity the prince turned on Toulouse. 'So huge was this throng of murderers that the full host numbered thirteen hundred thousand.' Their aim was genocide. Bertrand, cardinal of Rome, was as explicit as the obsessive Arnaud Amaury. In case even one Cathar should escape, 'Death and slaughter must lead the way, that in and around Toulouse there will remain no living man, neither noble lady, girl nor pregnant woman, no created thing, no child at the breast, but all must die in fire and flames'.[37]

It was the city's fourth siege and it was as unsuccessful as the others. After forty-five fruitless days, his feudal blood-smeared soldiers were entitled to return home. Louis burned his siege-machines, left 200 knights and returned to Paris.

There is a mystery. The *Chanson* contained nothing of that ignominious retreat. It had no celebration of Toulouse's triumph. The verses of *The Song of the Cathars Wars* ended abruptly before Louis' departure.

Laisse 214. Quel filhs de rei de Fransa ve orgulhozamens . . .

For now the son of the king of France comes in pride bringing thirty or forty counts and so many troops that no man alive can reckon up their thousands and hundreds. The cardinal from Rome too, he comes proclaiming that death and slaughter must lead the way, that in and around Toulouse there shall remain no living man, neither noble lady, girl or pregnant woman, no created thing, no child at the breast, but all must die in fire and flames.

But the Virgin Mary will save them from this, she who puts right all that is wrong, so that innocent blood will not be shed. They will not be afraid, for St Sernin leads them, and God, justice, strength, the young count and the saints will defend Toulouse for them. Amen'

Que Dieus e dreitz e forza el coms joves e sens Lor defendra Tholoza! Amen[38]

With that confident 'Amen' the *Chanson* ended. There was nothing about a siege, skirmishes, the drawn-out days of stalemate. If the poet had been there he would have continued the saga. If he had been absent he would surely have rejoiced at the slinking away of the humiliated French prince. But there was nothing.

That gifted writer of war and fighting may have been killed in some forgotten sally, his story left unfinished. If so, the 'anonymous' continuator of what Walter de Tudela had started was not Guy de Cavaillon. He was alive ten years later in 1229 when he accompanied Raymond VII, 'the young count', to Paris for the ultimate degradation of the Languedoc.

If there were an anonymous poet, what of him? Perhaps like Thomas Gray's

village-Hampden that with dauntless breast
The little tyrant of his fields withstood

his bones now rest in a long-lost grave somewhere in southern France.

'Oblivion is not for hire': philosophised Sir Thomas Browne, 'The greater part must be content to be as though they had not been'.[39]

The writer of the second part of the *Chanson* should rest content. Whether Guy of Cavaillon or some unknown genius he has not vanished. He lives in his brilliantly evocative lines.

TWELVE

PEIRE CARDENAL AND GUIRAUT RIQUIER

Monge solon estar dins los mostiers . . .

Once monks in monasteries were shut
To worship God, saints, martyrs, but
Now lusting into towns they strut
And seize some decent wife, no slut . . .

(Peire Cardenal, c. 1250)

Be.m degra de chanter tener . . .

I should cease singing,
Joy and laughter do not fit my song.
I am burdened by such thoughts
That surround me that I am only serious,
Reminiscing on my melancholy past
As for the present, see how it is depressed
By thoughts of my future.
I have reason for tears and deep disquiet.

(Guiraut Riquier, c. 1280)

Troubadours abandon a Hostile Languedoc, 1229–1321

Mirabar celerem fugitava aetate rapinam . . .

I mavelled at the flying rape of time.
A rose was born: but now that rose is old.
Even as I speak the crimson petals float
Drift downwards, and the crimsoned earth is bright.

(Ausonius, *c.* AD 309–92)

Fighting continued, defiance drained. Disheartened, Raymond VII entreated France for a truce. It was a plea from a desperate man who could expect little compassion. Their crusades had been costly in lives and money for the French. Any terms offered would be severe.

On Maundy Thursday, 12 April 1229, a royal tribunal was held in Paris attended by aristocrats, cardinals, archbishops. At the heart of the pageant on high thrones were the young king, Louis IX, and his implacable mother, Blanche of Castile, the Queen-Regent.

On the Holy Bible, Raymond VII, Count of Toulouse, swore allegiance to Louis IX and obedience to the Catholic Church. Draconian decrees were announced. The count vowed that he would catch and deliver heretics to the Church. The walls of Toulouse were to be dismantled in thirty places for almost two-thirds of a mile. The French king took possession of all undamaged castles in the Languedoc. Raymond also lost two-thirds of his territories, including Avignon, Carcassonne and Nîmes, and lands east of Toulouse.

The terms were brutal, but there was worse. At the insistence of Blanche, ever protective of her son and the French crown, Raymond's little daughter, Jeanne, was betrothed to young Alphonse de Poitiers, the king's brother. If, when Jeanne died, the marriage were childless, the county of Toulouse would become French.

The humiliation was not complete. Next day, Good Friday, inside a crowded Notre-Dame, excommunicated for his crimes, Raymond VII was bloodily scourged at the altar. After the whipping, he, Guy of

Cavaillon and other knights were imprisoned for six weeks in the Louvre prison. Only on 3 June was the excommunication lifted and he was freed.

Many troubadours disapproved. Bernard Sicart de Marjévols raged at the Treaty, the disgrace and the lands and cities that had been lost –

Ai! Tolosa et Provensa!
E la terra d'Argensa
Bezers e Carcassey!
Qo vos vi e qu'us vey

Ah, Toulouse and Provence!
And the land of the Agenais!
Béziers and Carcassonne!
How I knew you, how I see you now!

– and grieved at the obsequious grovelling of once-proud southern nobility who bowed and said 'Sire' to their strutting French usurpers.[1]

The war was over but it did not bring peace. Fighting men had been defeated, leaders humiliated, castles confiscated, dispossessed knights left to wander through an unfriendly land, and disheartened troubadours were drifting on the farther outskirts of a former land of song from which the sun had gone.

Cathars remained. Hundreds, probably thousands of them. Many in towns, more in the countryside, all over the Languedoc, and their Good Men visited them, proclaiming the faith, bringing comfort and consolation, preachers disguised as weavers, pedlars, shepherds, indistinguishable from ordinary people. The Catholic Church raged at the empty outcome of 20, 30, 40 years of the military crusade. Loathed heretics still existed.

Things changed. On 20 April 1233, impatient with the failure to exterminate an irreligious sect, Gregory IX ordered a general inquisition in southern France led by Dominican preaching friars. Trained in theology and law, they were ideally educated to investigate, interrogate and detect inconsistencies in evasive answers. They were persistent and they were ruthless.

The years that followed were tragic. Once Cathars had lived openly in the Languedoc, respected, seldom troubled by nearby Catholics, but now towns were becoming death-traps where malicious or terrified neighbours might betray them. Now they could only worship in secret. And, like packs of hunting dogs, inquisitors searched them out, with the prospect of purifying pyres to cleanse the impure flesh.

They especially sniffed, pried and bullied for information about the leaders, the Cathar bishops, the preaching Good Men, the Parfaits, 'the so-perfect ones,' they sneered, and when one was trapped, he was quickly condemned to death. *Caput draconis* (Behead the Dragon) commanded Blanche of Castile. Some inquisitors, almost insane in their obsession, dug up bodies of known unbelievers and burned them too.

What happened in thirteenth-century France could also occur in fourteenth-century England. John Wycliffe, translator of the first English Bible, died in the Leicestershire village of Lutterworth in 1384. In 1428 a zealous Church Council ordered that his skeleton should be exhumed, the bones burned and thrown into the River Swift. Whether Cathar dualist or a man who had opened secular eyes to the once-withheld mysteries of the Latin Bible, they had sinned and had to be removed from existence.

For the same perceived iniquity, an even better and poetical translator, William Tyndale, was half-strangled and then burnt alive in 1536. The murder achieved little. Much of Tyndale's writing was incorporated into the Authorised Version of the Bible in 1611.[2]

Persecution for different reasons continued in the Languedoc not with swords but with the arbitrary trials and punishments of the sinister Inquisition. The first Dominican inquisitors did not use torture. That method of forcing the truth from unwilling lips would not be authorised by Pope Innocent IV until 1252 and even then it was permitted only under strict conditions. No clergyman was to be present. No life or limb was to be imperilled. No blood was to be drawn. There was no rack, no thumbscrew, no bastinado, but there were other exquisite methods of extracting information from reluctant witnesses.

One by one the Good Men were caught and executed. Others lingered in hiding. Some went to the last of all Cathar retreats, the remote, small but almost unreachable castle of Montségur high on its steep peak. Even that was taken. Offered the choice of recantation or death, on 16 March 1244 more than 200 Cathars, Good Men, laymen, women, children, tied and chained, were contemptuously hassled down the mountainside and,

refusant la conversion a laquelle ils étaient invites . . .

refusing the conversion offered them they were shut in a fence of stakes and posts, the pyre was lit and there they experienced the fire of Hell,

gloated the complacent cleric and chronicler Guillaume de Puylaurens.[3]

It was misguided complacency. Not all Catholic clergymen were devout servants of God. Purity of soul varied. Some were blameless and without malice. Some were remorseless persecutors. Others were sexual predators of a shamelessly unholy nature. The talented troubadour Peire Cardenal reviled them.

He came from an important family in Puy-en-Velay, born around 1180. As his last poem has been dated to the early 1270s, he was unusually long lived. Some 96 of his poems are known, 15 of them dubious. Most were *sirventes*, bitter judgements about the decline of manners and the lack of standards, spiritual, financial and moral, among the Dominican friars. Married, he had several children.[4]

> *Peire Cardinal si fo de Veillac, de la siutat del Puei Nostra Domna . . .*

> Peire Cardenal was from Puy-en-Velay, Haiute-Loire, and of a noble. honourable family, the son of a knight and a lady. While he was still young his father entered him as a canon in Le Puy canonry, and he learned to read and write, and became familiar with books and singing. He changed from study to song . . . When he was a man he enjoyed the world's vanities because he was happy, handsome and young, and wrote many songs with lovely themes and melodies

A jongleur, Miquel de la Tor, accompanied him, playing on either the harp or the *orgue portatif*, a light instrument light that rested easily on the minstrel's knees. Its pipes, held in a triangular frame, were played with the fingers of one hand, while the other hand held the frame close to the musician's lips to blow into the mouthpiece. It was popular and adaptable, as it could be played slowly for laments or fast for dancing.[5]

Cardenal had fellow troubadours, interesting characters such as Aimeric de Belenoi, who was praised by Dante; Guilhem de Montanhagol, who fought a losing struggle, singing courtly lyrics to vanishing courts. Discontented with the decline of the Languedoc and its acidic destruction by the Inquisition, he went to the still-welcoming courts in Castile

Another of Cardenal's contemporaries was Sordello, an Italian, a good composer, highly regarded by Dante for his fearless criticisms of kings and princes. He was also notorious for his decadent life, involved in tavern brawls, a suspected rape, and a secret marriage for which he fled fearing a family vendetta. He was imprisoned near Milan in 1266, and it is rumoured that he died a violent death.[6]

Cardenal far exceeded them in words, music and passion. Of his sincere piety there was no question. He composed the most devout of poems in the Occitanian language to Sainte Mary:

Vera vergena Maria . . .

True virgin, Mary,
True life, true belief,
True honesty, true path,
True mother and true friend . . .[7]

But with that Christian devotion went a single-minded sense of right, leading one of the finest of all troubadours to condemn Catholic clergy for their hypocrisy. He was vituperative. He attacked the senseless carnage of the Albigensian Crusade, human vices, acquiescent nobility, venal clergy and the ruthlessly powerful Inquisition.

To express such candour without fear he must have had powerful patrons. The Counts of Toulouse, Raymond VI and VII, had long lost influence. There had to be other guardians. As Jeanroy observed: 'It is a pity we don't know where, in what circumstances or beneath what sort of protection were written the poems of this fearless pamphleteer, as well as those of many others, no less daring, whom the Inquisition probably pursued, and which exposed their authors to the direst of punishments'.[8]

Cardenal never hesitated to expose his contempt even of kings and their avaricious subjects:

Rei e comte, bailho e seneschal . . .

Kings and counts, bailiffs and seneschals
Take castles and estates as they want,
Plundering the poor. And the barons,
The majority of them, are no better.

Clerzia vol, trastor l'an per egal . . .

Through the year the clergy demand comfort,
Greedy, well-shod and finely clothed.
Great prelates scheme for advancement
And greedily raise their taxes[9]

Even worse was the hypocrisy of the 'holy' friars' . . .

Clergues se fan pastors

Clergymen pass for shepherds
But they're murderers

Dressed in their pious robes
They seem so saintly . . .[10]

He scorned their pretence of caring for the sick and dying:

Tartarassa ni voutor

By nature buzzards and vultures know
Where some decaying carcase smells
Even more quickly monks . . .[11]

As he wrote and fulminated in the middle years of the thirteenth century, there was a dynastic coincidence that had nothing to do with troubadours or with the Inquisition. In those decades history repeated itself. In 1193 Eleanor, Queen-Regent of England, had raised the enormous sum of £300,000 by extorting monies, rents, valuables, land-taxes, anything available, to ransom her son, Richard I, held captive in Austria.

Almost 60 years later, in 1250, her equally redoubtable granddaughter, Blanche of Castile, Queen-Regent of France, collected 800,000 trustworthy Byzantine gold bezants, half of the entire yearly royal income, to release her son, Louis IX, captured by Saracens in Egypt during the catastrophic Seventh Crusade.

It was a matter of little interest to Peire Cardenal. Worse than despotic kings, selfish nobles and ambitious bishops were the degrading activities of the holy Dominicans, the very clergy whose holy brothers were inquisitors. They befouled their Order. They raped.

Perhaps the most powerful of all his *sirventes* was the one beginning:

Un estribot farai
I'll compose an estribot . . .

Its third verse began:

Monge solon estar dins los mostiers serratz . . .

Once monks in monasteries were shut
But now they seek out women.

Two centuries later, far to the north in Paris, the criminal scoundrel but genius of a poet François Villon, in his parody of a benevolent legacy, said the same about White Friars, the Carmelites:

Carmes chevauchent nos voisines
Mais çela, ce n'est que du mains

Carmelites shag our neighbours' wives
So what? It's as trivial as a handshake![12]

Cardenal was not prepared to laugh at the impiety and degradation:

Monge solon estar dins los mostiers serratz,
On azoravan Dieu denan las magestatz;
E can son en las vilas on an lurs pöestastz,
Si avetz bela femna o es homs molheratz . . .

Once monks in monasteries were shut
To worship God, saints, martyrs, but
Now into towns they come to rut,
Grab some lovely wife, no slut . . .

He continued bluntly about the disgraceful immorality of Dominican
friars, the Black Monks, so arrogant with the power of the Inquisition
behind them that one threat from them, even false, could be a sentence of
death that no one dared oppose them, not even respectable women.

Cardenal was disgusted at the foul image of some paunchy monk
debauching a helpless woman and one can almost hear his shout of rage.
The remaining lines of his *sirvente* are so explicit that they are better left in
the original Provençal:

El seran cobertor, si.eus peza o si.eus platz.
E can el son desus e.l cons es sagelatz
Ab las bolas redondas que pendon al matratz,
Con la letras son clausas e lo traucs es serratz,
D'aqui eyson l'iretge e li essabatatz.
a D'aqui eyson l'iretge e li essabatatz.
Que juron e renegon e jogon a tres datz,
Aisi fan monge negre en loc de caritatz [13]

The eight outspoken lines demand a prose translation with no evasive
bowdlerisms.

El seran . . .
'they will do it anyway, whether you like it or not'.
E can el son desus . . .

'when he's on top'.
Cons es,
the Latin origin of *Con,* 'vagina', was explained in Chapter Four;
sagelatz,
'sealed'.
Ab las bolas redondas . . .
'round balls' or testicles
pendon al matratz
'hanging below the shaft'
matratz being a predecessor of the French *matraque,* 'truncheon' or
   'staff'.
Con la letras . . .

Its customary translation, 'when the letterbox', is nonsensical. There
were no such boxes in subliterate thirteenth-century France. *Letras* came
from a medieval scribe misreading the text. The correct word was *levras,*
today's French *lèvres,* 'lips'; *son clausas,* 'are closed'; *traucs es serratz.* The
traucs would in later French become *trou,* 'orifice', and *serratz,* 'closed', so
that a translation of the line would be, 'when its lips grip snugly and the
hole is plugged'.
   The following three lines refer to the outcome of the rape. Bastards,
heretics and cheats were born by their befouled and ashamed mother. Then
came Cardenal's sardonic jest:

Aisi fan monge negre . . .

So the Black Monks, God's holy fathers, generously provide this in
place of charity!'[14]

One can almost hear the growls of the *orgue-portatif* behind the half-sung,
half-shouted words of sorrow and contempt. Cardenal was nauseated by
the oppression and selfishness. His loathing remained undiminished up to
the time of his death in the 1170s.
   'And I, Miquel de la Tor, state that the noble Peire Cardenal, when he died,
was nearly a hundred years old.' He was the last of the patrician singers.
He was also almost the last of all the competent troubadours of southern
France. There were followers but many declined into mere minstrelsy, no
longer visiting rich courts in the Languedoc but eking a living wherever
they could.
   There were a few exceptions. Guiraut Riquier was one. In 1250 Blanche,
Queen-Regent of France, had amassed a semi-fortune to ransom her son,
a captive in Egypt. Four years later Riquier's first poem was written. The

exact year is known because in the majority of his songs, he meticulously recorded when it was created.

The accomplished troubadour-to-be, was born in Narbonne some time between 1230 and 1235. He stayed in the city for well over 30 years before seeking for a court and a patron in the diminishing musical world of the Languedoc.

Despite the disadvantage of having to find support and encouragement in an alien environment Riquier's poetical output was considerable including not only rhyming 'Epistles' but also 89 lyrics, 48 of them with a melody, a proportion larger than any other troubadour's. Many of his songs were composed in long-neglected forms such the *alba* or 'dawn song' and the *pastorela*, a pastoral fantasy about a lustful knight encountering a lonely shepherdess. Riquier's poetical ability was not great but it was always good.[15]

Unexpectedly, he has no *Vida*. This was probably because he was born between 1230 and 1235 and his first poem was not written until 1254. Riquier meticulously dated it himself.

It was too late for a *Vida*. Uc de Saint-Circ's *'Biographies'* had already been written and circulated. As mentioned in Chapter One, Saint-Circ probably wrote several lives of troubadours he had either known personally or had hard stories about.

> *En Italie ou il est exile, Uc de sant Circ invente et recite vidas et_razos sur les anciens trobadours devenus célèbres. On lui attribue un grand nombre des biographies (rédigées vers 1220) . . .*

In Italy where he had retired Uc de Saint-Circ collected and recorded 'Lives' and 'Glosses' about the old and most famous troubadours. To him are attributed a great many biographies edited and set down around 1220 . . .[16]

When he was some 55 years of age, married, settled down, writing no more poetry, he retired to Treviso near Venice and at last began what was to be his most important task. He had come from southern France, where he had known many of the greatest singers, so Italian troubadours must have asked him many questions about those famous men. Probably he happily reminisced about them, their works and their escapes, gossip and anecdotes. At some time it must have occurred to him to write down what he could recall of their lives. It was an easy task, but it has proved invaluable to later researchers. Among the facts were mistakes, uncorroborated anecdotes and omissions, but without Uc's work little would now be known about that almost mythical world of song.

The biographies that we known came from his quill are those of Savaric de Mauleon and Bernart de Ventadorn, his own *vida*, and 'perhaps the greater part of those [lives] which exist'. But not one for Guiraut Riquier.

That troubadour, sadly misplaced in time, found his needed patron at the court of Aimeric IV, viscount of Narbonne. He was mentioned in the fifth verse of the poem beginning *No.m sai, d'amor . . .*

Al vescomte N'Amalric de Narbona . . .

To Viscount Aimery of Narbonne
I send this song for he loathes base deeds
And praises merit. Courage pleases him
That he bears down on the basely rich
With their sins, and he favours joy
And laughter without deceit . . .

It is rather ordinary verse, and there is no evidence that Riquier ever received any special favours from his patron, although he remained with him until Aimeric's death in 1270.

Riquier left Narbonne for the first time that year. That far superior wordsmith Peire Cardenal was still composing and creating words and music up to 1272. The year before, Alphonse of Poitiers had died of a long, wasting illness contracted on the disastrous Seventh Crusade of 1250, where, with his brother, Louis IX, he had been captured, grimily imprisoned and ransomed.

His wife, Jeanne, daughter of Raymond VII, died three days later. They had had no children and that meant disaster for the southern 'land of sun, song and laughter'. By the terms of the draconian 1229 Treaty in Paris, Raymond VII, count of Toulouse, had been forced to accept that, if there were no surviving heirs, all his lands and property in the Languedoc would become a royal domain. In 1271 the French king, Philip III le Hardi, took possession of it all. It was the culmination of a protracted tragedy.[17]

The unsettled Riquier went to Spain and the once-wealthy domain of Alfonso X the Wise of Castile. He stayed for 10 inconclusive years, never firmly establishing himself as a firm favourite, despite holding himself in considerable esteem as a poet rather than a mere musician.

In 1274 he almost arrogantly explained to the king that there was unnecessary confusion between the terms *troubadour* and *jongleur*. The first, he stated, was a poet, the second just a player of instruments, and one should not confuse a *troubadour* with a *jongleur*, who could be a fellow as low as a scraper of a third-rate bow in taverns. 'Jongleurie was invented by men of sense and was provided with some favour to divert and honour the nobility by the playing of instruments', but the true poet should be honoured with the title *Doctor de trobar*. If Riquier were ever termed a jongleur rather than a poet, he would abandon his craft.[18]

Regrettably there is no adequate edition of Riquier's work, although there are critical essays and translations of his poem in many anthologies. There are plentiful compact discs of his music (see Appendix 1). A perceptive analysis of Riquier's poetry can be found in Cholakian. Much of it concerns the poet's 6 *pastorelas*.[19]

His *pastorelas* describe a series of meetings between a wandering knight and a young girl alone in the countryside with her sheep. The knight never changes. The girl does. The poems were written between 1260 and 1282. The first begins:

L'autre jorn m'anava . . .

The other day when I was walking
Along the banks of a river
By myself, happily contented,
Because love was telling me
To compose a song.
Suddenly, surprised, I saw
A young shepherdess,
Lovely, desirable,
Watching her sheep.

Then come extracts from the verses that followed, telling of their conversation:

Ni sabetz amar?: 'Girl, do you know how to make love? Because I can give you pleasure.'

Que.us fos fazedor: 'Because I am in love with you I don't see why we can't make love!'

Belh Deport m'albir: 'Think of my dishonour!' 'I could force you!' But then I remember *"Belh Deport"*, my distraction of a conscience, reminding me of knightly behaviour and the truthfulness of courtly manners.

Senher, mal si gara: 'You must go.'

Et iretz vo.n ara: 'Although I shall miss you.'

Toza, souvendier: 'Young lady, often

Aurai est semdier: 'I shall come this way again.'[20]

The following four *pastorelas* provided a series of metamorphoses.in which the youthful shepherdess became a young woman who later changed into a married mother with a daughter who subsequently grew into a desirable lady and finally wrinkled into an old woman in the final *pastorela* of 1282:

A sant Pons de Tomeiras . . .

At Saint-Pons de-Thomières
A day or two ago, drenched
By the rain, I came
To a place owned by two ladies.
I didn't recognise them
And was bewildered
Because the older one smiled broadly
And whispered something to the girl
Something that made both of them laugh . . .
Then I began to remember

. . . . . .
'You're the shepherdess that led me along . . .'

En Guiraut Riquier, lassa
Suy quar tant seguetz trassa
D'aquestz leugiers chanters.

Guiraut Riquier I am sorry
that you continue to repeat
Those silly songs.[21]

It is as though Riquier in his 'silly songs' was desperately attempting to bring back a long-vanished past by the resurrection of forms of song that the past itself had forgotten. And it is an irony that the form he most preferred, the *pastorela*, had been introduced over two centuries earlier by the censorious Marcabru, a contemporary of Guilhem, Count of Poitiers.[22] Marcabru was almost the forerunner of the troubadours. Riquier was certainly one of the last.

Some time after 1280 Riquier gave up hope of recognition in Spain, returned to France, found no patrons and dejectedly retired to his birthplace, Narbonne. In 1292 he wrote his last poem, a lament.

Be.m degra de chantar tener . . .

From songs and singing I should refrain.
Because to sing there has to be gaiety
But I am so cast down by worries.

Everywhere there is pain and desolation
I think of the past and its drawn-out emptiness,
And then consider the present emptiness
With the future prospect of empty years.
I have only tears.

And he wrote the saddest of all troubadour lines:

Mas trop suy vengutz als derriers . . .

But I have come too late . . .[23]

And Guirat Riquier disappeared from history.

The obsessive, relentless Inquisition continued to ferret for the few Good Men, preachers of the Cathars, who still existed. In 1308 the only substantial group of them was betrayed in Carcassonne by a Judas, a spendthrift Cathar turncoat. He gained money. They lost their lives. James Autier and eight associates were captured and burnt at the stake. A tenth committed suicide. With their deaths it was almost the end of their 'heretical' religion.

The following year their leader, William Autier, was discovered in December, perhaps in Toulouse. For months he was questioned, tortured and questioned again. After almost a year of torment, on 9 April 1310 he was burnt alive outside St Sernin cathedral. He requested to be allowed to say something 'if he were allowed to speak and preach to the people he would convert them to his faith'. He was denied.[24]

Eleven years later came the end. In 1321 the last of the Good Men, William Bélibaste, was treacherously lured from Spain, arrested, interrogated, tortured and executed at the castle of Villerouge-Térmenès, north of Carcassonne, in 1321. It was exactly 250 years since Guilhem of Poitiers had been born.

It had been a quarter of a millennium of brilliance in the courts of the Languedoc. Audiences had delighted in the words and wit and music of fine troubadours and trobairitz: Guilhem himself, Jaufré Rudel, Bernart de Ventadorn, the Countess of Die, Bertran de Born, Peire Cardenal, Guiraut Riquier, scores of others.

History is a wayward mistress. The only extant memorial to be seen of that world of song is the modern bust of the countess in a square in the town of Die. There is, however, one Mecca for the pilgrim.

Leave the *péage* motorway at Carcassonne and travel southwards past Limoux and its vineyards to the small town of Quillan. Turn westwards towards Lavelanet up the long, winding hill, the land falling away to the left, past Nébias to the ruined castle of Puivert, 'the green height', standing on its gentle slope. Leave the car. Walk up the short, easy slope, go through the barbican and across the long, spacious bailey to the oldest part, the twelfth-century square *donjon*. Above the ground floor, once the guardroom, is a door with two shields leading to the family quarters and a chapel. Go past it and up the stone steps. The floor above is the tall *salle des musiciens*, with its eight carved sconces for burning torches on its four walls. On each sconce is a carving of a *jongleur* with his instrument, a lute, a zither, tambourine, psaltery, bagpipes, two hurdy-gurdies, a tabor. All had been been played in this room.

In this place Peire d'Alvernhe and the Monk of Montaudon had sung and teased their fellow singers. Bernart de Ventadorn may have sung here while the lord, his lady and his guests listened.

Just stand. In the silence imagine hearing faint echoes from the stones, all that is left of the once Land of Song. Shelley sensed it;

> Music when soft voices die
> Vibrates in the memory.

Puivert is the enduring monument to that lost time in the land of song.

APPENDIX ONE

(a) Compact Discs
(b) Codification of Troubadours and Trobairitz

(1) Compact Discs

They are first listed alphabetically and then catalogued with the songs of individual troubadours itemised.

A *Cants de Trobadours et Troubairitz des 12th & 13th siècles.* Avinens.

B *Jaufre Rudel, 12th Siécle.* La Compagnie Medieval.

C *A Mediaeval Banquet.* (Six CDs.) Martin Best Medieval Consort.

D *Music of the Troubadours.* Alte Musik.

E *Richard Coeur de Lion. Troubadours et Trouvères.* Alla Francesca.

F *Troubadoure.* Ensemble Convivencia.

G *Troubadours.* Clememcic Consort.

H *Troubadours.* Gérard Zuchetto, Occitan Trob'Art Concept 6.

I *A Minstrel's Music. Music from the Age of Knights, Castles and Chivalry.* English Heritage.

J *Guillaume IX d'Aquitaine.* Bruce Duisit.

K *Music from the Middle Ages.* (Five CDs.) Studio der Frühen Musik.

L *Manuscript. Trouvères et Troubadours.* Ensemble Perceval.

M *Chants les troubadours. Art Ensemble.* (Zuchetto) Gallo.

N *Medieval French Songs.* The Unicorn (Trouvères).

O *Provence Mystique, Sacred Songs of the Middle Ages.* Apex.

P *Manuscript du Roi. Trovères et Troubadours.* Ensemble Perceval.

Q *Bella Domna.* (Trobairitz) Sinfonye.

R *La Doce Acordance. Chansons de trouvères.* Diabolus in Musica.

X *On the Banks of the Seine. Music of the Trouvères.* Chandos.

Y *Sinners and Saints.* (Historical background. Last one, pilgrim's song, the Devil.) New London Consort.

Z *Mediaeval Babes. Salve Nos.* (Traditional.) Salva Nos.

Book

Songs of the Troubadours and Trouvères (some CDs) (Rosenberg, Switten & Le Vot [RSV]). It includes CD Bard BDCD 1–9711, also available from Folger Shakespeare Library, and DC20003, Albany Music Distributors.

The Troubadours – Alphabetical Order

Anonymous

 A/6. Domna pos vos ai chauzida.

 A/7. Tuit cilh que son enamorat.

 A/11. Amors m'ard com fueoc . . .

 A/13. A 'entrada del temps florit.

 A/16. Can ai lo mond . . .

 D, 2. Domna, pos vos ay chausida (instrumental). L, 5.

 G/1. 'a l'entrada de temps clar;

 K. Various. Most are too late

 P, 16. Lasse, pour qui refusai . . .? Alas, why did I refuse him . . .?

Aurenga, d', Raimbault

 C2, 17. Pois sals sabers.

 H, 1. Ar resplan la flors enversa.

Béthune, Conon de

 E, 9. Bien me deüsse targier.

 P, i. Tant ai amé.

 R4. Bele douce dame chiere.

 R, 5. Se raige et derverie

 RSV, 225, 242–8.

Béziers, the massacre. C6, 1. See also Figueira

Blondel de Nesle

 C2, 8. L'amour don't sui espris.

Born, Bertran de

 C4, 3. Ges de disnar.

 C4, 5. Chasutz sui de mal en pana.

 C4, 15. Ai Lemozi.

Bornelh, Guiraud de.

 C1, 20. Rei glorios; D, 8; M, 3.

 C4, 2. Leu chansoneta.

 C4, 4. Si.us quer consel, bel ami Alamanda'.

 C5, 1. *Ditto*, Canso melody. C5, 19.

 D3 [1]. Non puese sofrir.

Cardenal, Peire

 C2, 18. Now I can delight in love.

 D, 3 [2]. Ar me puesc.

 K5, 1. Tartarassa ni voutor.

K5, 2. Ben volgra. Quascos plor e planh (death of Raimon Roger).

K5, 3. Razos es qu'ieu m'esbaudei.

K5, 6. L'afar del comte Guio.

O, 6. Deis quatre caps que a la cros.

O, 9. Una cuitatz fo, no sai cals.

Chanson de la Croisade Albigeois. C6,18; K5, 1b. (Tudela); P, 2

Coucy [Couci], Châstelain de

E, 5. Li nouviautz tanz.

E, 7. A vous, Amours.

R, 11, La douce voiz dou rossigol sauvage.

RSV, 249–55. CD, La douce voiz du rosignol sauvage.

Daniel, Arnaut

C4, 6. Lo ferm voler qu'el cor m'intra; H, 4.

C4, 7. Chanson do'lh mot son plan.

H, 3, 'en cest sonet coinde leri'.

Die, Contessa de

A, 15. A chantar m'er de so; C1, 3; C2, 15; G, 6. Vida; M, 6; Q, 14.

Faidit, Gaucelm

E, 14. K2, 4. Fortz chausa es que tot le major dan.

Figueira, Guilhem

K5, 4. D'un sirventes far. O, 8, 'Béziers . . .'.

Marcabru

C2,7. Pax in nimine Domini; RSV, 51 (CD).

Marueil, Arnaut de

A8. Le gran beutats el's fins . . . (instrumental).

Marvejols, Bernart Sicart

K5, 8. Ab greu cossire.

Miraval, Raimon de

D, 5. Bel m'es qu'ieu chant.

F, 4. Ar ab la forsa.

F, 5. Chansoneta farai vencut.

H, 5. Chans, quan non es qui lentenda.

H, 6. Un sonet m'es bel qu'espanda.

H, 7. Bel m'es lu'ieu cant et coindi.

H, 8. Cel que no vol auzir chansos.

H, 9. D'amor es totz mos cossieriers.

Poitiers, Guilhem IX, Duc d'Aquitaine; Count VII de Poitiers

J, 1. Companhon farai un vers qu'er covinen.

J, 2. Companho tant ai agut d'avols conres.

J, 4. Bon vuelh que sapchan li plusor.

J, 5. Companho non puosc mudar qu'eo no m'effret.

J, 6. Pus vezem de novelh florir.

J, 7. Mout jauzens me prec en amar.

J, 8. Farai un vers de dreyt nien; C2,2. The song of nothing.

J, 9. Farai chansoneta nueva.

J, 10. Ab la dolchor del temps novel.

J, 11. Farai un vers pos mi soneilh.

J, 12. Pos de chantar m'es pres talens.

Riquier, Guiraut

A, 10. Aissi com es sobronrada.

A, 19. Cristians vei perilhar.

A, 4. Pus astres no m'es donatz; RSV, 174. (CD.)

C, 6. Entire disc 'is structured around Riquier's life, offering works from each period selected from the 48 melodies that survive.'

D, 10. Humils, forfaitz, repres e penedens.

F, 11. Jesus Christ; M, 5.

F, 14. Si chants me pogues valensa.

K2, 3. Ples de tristor.

RSV, 172. B.em degra de chantar tener.

RSV, 176. Tant m.es plazens le mals de l'amor.

Rudel, Jaufré

B, 1. Vida. Prologue.

B, 2, 3. La passion de jeu.

B, 4. Les risques de la courtoise.

B, 5, 6. Reflexions.

B, 7, 8. La decision.

B, 9, 10. Le depart.

B, 11,(12?), 13. Le voyage et la croisade.

B, 14. Le doute.

B, 15, 16. La mort.

B, 17. Vida. Epilogue.

C1, 10. Lan can li jorn; D, 12; L, 8; M, 1.

C2, 14. Non sap chanter; I, 3.

C5, 3. Can so rossinhols . . .

C5, 9. Can lo rius de la fontana.

Ventadorn, Bernart de

A, 12. Can l'erba frescha . . .

A, 17. Ai tantas bonos chanços.

A, 2. Can vei la lauzeta mover. C4, 8, D, 11; E/13; M, 7; G, 4.

C2, 11. La dousa votz; I, 4.

C5, 6; K4, 8. Ab joi mou lo vers . . .

C5, 14. Tant ai mo cor . . .

C5, 18. Can par la flors.

K4, 9. Pois preyatz me, senhor.

Vidal, Peire

    C4, 10. Pois tornatz sui . . . H/2.

    G, 3, 1. Vida e razos.

    G, 3, 2. Barons de mon dan convit.

    H, 2. Mos cors s'alegr'e s'esjau.

    L, 3. Pos Vesem que l'Iverns S'irais.

    RSV, 110. Anc no mori per amor. (CD).

(2) Codification

The works of troubadours were codified in 1933 by A. Pillet & H. Carstens in *Bibliographie der Troubadours*, Niemeyer, Halle. Each troubadour was allocated an individual number so that, as examples, the Countess of Die was given number 46; Guilhem of Poitiers, 183; Peire Cardenal, 335. That number was followed by another for each individual poem so that the *A chantar m'er de cho qu-eu non volria* by the Countess of Die became number 2, and listed as 46.2.

In the present book the significant southern troubadours and trobairitz, and northern trovéres are arranged alphabetically by surname, giving their Pillet & Carstens number, followed by the page references. Where the name differs from today's accepted form the Pillet & Carstens nomenclature is added. References to male trovéres can be found in Goldin. For women trovéres see: Doss-Quinby et al. *Troubadours and Trobairitz*.

Troubadours and Trobairitz

D'Alvernhe, Peire de: 323, pp. 278–83.

d'Anduza, Clara: 115, p. 104.

d'Aurenga, Raimbaut: 389, pp. 346–51.

Bacalairia, Uc de: 449, pp. 404–5.

Béthune, Conon de. See: Goldin, pp. 333–47.

Blondel de Nesle. See: Goldin, pp. 364–73.

Born, Bertran de: 80, pp. 67–77.

Bornelh, Guiraut de: 42, pp. 202–15.

Capestanh, Guillem de: 23, pp. 179–81. 'Guillem de Capestaing'.

Cardenal, Peire: 335, pp. 291–300.

Castelloza, Lady of: 109, p. 101.

Cavaillon, Gui de: 192, p. 192. 'Gui de Cavaillo'.

Cercamon: 112, pp. 102–4.

Cœur de Lion, Richard de: 420, pp. 379–80. 'Richart I, von England'.

Coucy, Châtelain de. See: Goldin, pp. 349–63.

Daniel, Arnaut: 29, pp. 27–32.

Die, Countess of : 46, pp. 41–3. 'Beattritz de Dia'.

Figueira, Guillem: 217, pp. 182–5.

Gormonda: 177, p. 153.

Mauleon, Savaric de: 432, pp. 386–7. 'Savaric de Malleo'.

Marcabru: 293, pp. 256–63.

Maruelh, Arnaut de: 30, pp. 32–7. 'Arnaut de Maroill'.

Marie de Ventadorn: 295, pp. 263–4.

Miraval, Raimon de: 406, pp. 367–74.

Montaudon, Monk of: 305, pp. 268–72. 'Monge de Montaudo'.

Montanhagol, Guillem de: 225, pp. 187–9.

Péguilhan, Aimeric de: 10, pp. 8–16.

Pistoleta: 372, pp. 335–7.

Poitiers, Guillem of: 183, pp. 155–8. 'Graf von Poitiers'.

Riquier, Guiraut: 248, pp. 225–34.

Rogier, Peire: 356, pp. 311–13.

Romans, Bieitris de: 93, p. 88, 'Bieiris (?) de Roman'.

Rudel, Jaufré: 262, pp. 238–42.

St-Circ, Uc de: 457, pp. 410–17. 'Uc de Saint Circ'.

Sordello: 437, pp. 394–400.

Vaqueiras, Raimbaut de: 392, pp. 352–61.

Ventadorn, Bernart de: 70, pp. 50–60.

Vidal, Peire: 364, pp. 315–25.

APPENDIX TWO

Omar Khayyam, his *Rubaiyat* and Edward Fitzgerald

The *Rubaiyat* – a word meaning 'foursomes' because of the four-line verses, quatrains, in which it was written – was the work of a genius.

The Sufi philosopher, Omar Khayyam, contemporary of Guilhem of Poitiers (1071–1126/7) died in Naishapur in the south of Persia, now Iran, in 1131. He had been born there on 18 May 1048. The Islam city was the capital of Khurusan, the north-eastern province of Persia (Iran).

Naishapur was close to the Caspian Sea and near the borders of Afghanistan, far north of Baghdad, and even more remote from the Muslim shrine of Mecca by the Red Sea. Omar's birthplace was also well over 2,000 miles from the western European lands of the troubadours.

He knew many highborn people. It is recorded that one of his supposed school friends, the vizier Nizami al Mulk, was killed by the poisoned dagger of an Assassin. That occurred in 1092 when Omar was already over fifty years old and when the vizier had been his patron for years.[1]

Few facts are certain about Khayyam's life. It is probable that he been a highly respected court-astronomer and a brilliant mathematician. He was a polymath, turning from science to philosophy, author of many of the poetical *rubaiyats* attributed to him.[2]

His full name was Ghiathuddin Abdul Fath Omar ibn Ibrahim al Khayaam al Ghaq. Of well-to-do Afghan parents, his nickname of 'Tentmaker', had an ancestral derivation with no more significance than today's 'Baker', 'Carpenter' or 'Tiler'. As a pen-name its meaning can be paraphrased as a 'man who ignores worldly goods to allow himself to follow the Sufi faith'.[3]

It is said that he was presented with the prestigious Naishapur observatory in 1173–4 when he was hardly twenty years old, testimony to the reputation he had already gained. He was so esteemed that later he became one of only eight astronomers charged with the reform of the Syrian calendar.

The result was a revision that was almost as accurate as the 1582 Gregorian amendment of the Julian calendar 500 years later. The historian Edward Gibbon was impressed by it and the way in which 'all errors, either past or future, were corrected by a computation of time, which surpasses the Julian, and approaches the accuracy of the Gregorian style . . . It is certainly remarkable that the Persians should have introduced a calendar so nearly accurate, 500 years before such an improvement was thought of in Europe.'[4]

Khayyam was also a brilliant mathematician who wrote a treatise on algebra that included a method of solving cubic equations.[5]

Despite these intellectual achievements, it is for his *Rubaiyat* that he is acclaimed throughout the world today; a collection originally of some 111 rhymed four-line stanzas rhyming AABA. It may, in fact, have been an anthology of his and other poets' moralising verses. There were many later additions whose questionable enthusiasms were condemned by a French critic as 'revolting sensualities which I refrain from translating'.[6]

Many faithful contemporaries condemned his work as unorthodox, written by a corrupt Sufi, 'a materialist incapable of following the Sufi path to knowledge of the divine'. He was condemned as irreligious, a misguided follower of the true religion whose sentiments were less spiritual than intellectual. The *Rubaiyat* was condemned as 'a tissue of errors like poisonous snakes'.[7]

Khayyam's fame is justified and yet it was the paraphrase of the *Rubaiyyat* by Edward Fitzgerald, published anonymously in 1869, that has amazed, pleased and enriched readers ever since. The 'translation' was a marvel of improvisation. From an old Oxford manuscript of well over a hundred quatrains the otherwise pedestrian Fitzgerald, during a never rediscovered period of genius, transfused Sufi philosophy into a freely-rendered from birth to death fantasia of seventy-five verses as though briefly acquiring a 'gift of knitting cobwebs together, of weighing thistle-down, and weaving together a magic tapestry of dragon-flies' wings'. He was never touched with inspiration again.[8]

It was the scintillation of a brief genius. One simple comparison of three independent translations of the *Rubaiyat's* first quatrain displays the chasm between the meticulously accurate and a maker of magic.

> While Dawn, Day's herald straddling the whole sky,
> Offers the drowsy world a toast, "To Wine",
> The sun spills early gold on city roofs –
> Day's regal Host, replenishing his jug.
> Graves, in: Graves & Alli-Shah, 45.

or

> The Sun casts the Noose of morning upon the roofs,
> Kai Khosrü of the day, he throws a stone into the bowl;
> Drink wine! for the Herald of the Dawn, rising up.
> Hurls into the days the cry of "Drink ye!"
> Heron-Allen, 3.

Whereas Fitzgerald made music of the words;

Awake! For Morning in the Bowl of Night
Has flung the Stone that puts the Stars to Flight;
And Lo! The Hunter of the East has caught
The Sultan's Turret in a Noose of Light.

The melody never returned. Even in the second edition only nine years later there was a heaviness:

Wake! For the Sun behind yon Eastern height
Has chased the Session of the Stars from Night,
And to the field of Heav'n ascending, strikes
The Sultan's Turret with a Shaft of Light.

Three further editions of 1872, 1879 and 1889 offered even less loveliness.

Omar Khayyam died in 1131 and was buried in Naishapur, the city where he had been born. To Nizami, one of his disciples, he predicted that 'his grave would be in a spot were the trees would shed their blossoms twice a year'. It was a botanical impossibility but when Nizami visited the place in 1135 he found it beside an orchard wall from which pear and peach trees shed leaves and petals on the stone, covering the burial place.[9]

In death Khayyam was not left in peace. Orthodox Sufis on pilgrimages to Mecca trudged a long pious detour to visit his grave and spit on it.[10] The spittle has dried, the desecrators are forgotten.

The neglected tomb near the Imamzadeh Mahroq mosque some miles outside Naishapur was renovated in 1934 and rests beneath a towering, elegantly mesh-worked cone.

The Persian Sufi, Omar Khayyam, lives through the lyrical adaptation of a Victorian Christian gentleman.

APPENDIX THREE

A Love that Never Died. Song and Sorrow in Northern France

Hebet sydus leti visus . . .

The face of a joyous star is dimmed
By the clouding of this heart
And my laughing lips grow cold.
Banished from her, in place of my happy song
I must lament.
She who was near is hidden, far away,
In whom my heart's strength flowered,
In whom all of my life once lived.

(*Carmina Burana*, no. 169)

Following the quotation from the *Carmina Burana* this Appendix begins with the quotation from Ezra Pound with which Chapter Four ended. Half a line is added:

And Poictiers, you know, Guillaume Poictiers,
    had brought the song up out of Spain
With the singers and viels. But here they wanted a setting.

(Ezra Pound, Canto VIII)

Guilhelm, 7th Count of Poitiers, 9th Duke of Aquitaine, may have used melodies from Spain to accompany his poems but that fashion of lyrical music only slowly became popular in northern France. In those parts there were no troubadours and troubairitz, only trouvères, whether men or women.

At first, only gradually, towards the end of the twelfth century, what had been sung in Latin in courts and castles became written and performed in everyday French for other classes of society. A female trouvère's work was usually anonymous. Her poem could be a *ballette*, a *pastourelle*, a *chanson d'amour* or a *motet* but the musician was nameless. Male trouvères were not. Like other great nobles

Guy de Thourette, governor of the Picardy castle of Coucy, was writing from the late twelfth century until his death in 1202 on the Third Crusade. His words were French and known to be his.

Je m'en voitz, dame . . .
I am leaving now, my lady.

So were the lines of Conon de Béthune, warrior, diplomat and statesman of the same period. He went on the same crusade:

Ahi, Amours! Com dure departie,
Me convendra faire de la meilleur
Qui conques fust amee ne servie!

Ah, Love. How hard it will be to part,
As I must, from the finest woman
Who was ever loved and served!

Many other trouvères were men including Blondel de Nesle, one of the earliest and probably the father of the famous Blondel who searched Germany for his imprisoned king, Richard, Coeur de Lion.[1]

Even earlier than these and almost a contemporary of Guilhem was one in Paris who wrote in Latin. He was Pierre Abelard from the borders of Brittany, a philosopher whose incisive mind and insistence on logical analysis of Biblical texts bred dangerous enemies amongst the orthodox hierarchy of the Church.

Born almost at the edge of troubadour country, he was fewer than 100 miles from Poitiers. Paris was over twice as far. Being of good birth Abelard may even have visited Guilhem's court and attended some of the entertainment there.

Famous as a lecturer, attracting students not only from France but from Germany, Italy and Spain, even England, he also wrote calculatingly seductive and appealing love songs to a young, attractive, and very erudite woman, Héloïse.

Où est le très sage Helloïs

Where's Héloïse the learned nun . . .
For whose sake Abeillard, I ween,
Lost manhood and put priesthood on?
. . .
Mais ou sont les neiges d'antan?
But where are the snows of yesteryear?

> (François Villon, *Ballade des Dames du Temps Jadis*,
> translated: Dante Gabriel Rossetti)

Abelard succeeded. Héloïse and he lived and made love during a series of troubled events, both personal and political. Theirs were years when Guilhem of Poitiers was composing his romantic, occasionally bawdy rhymes. When Abelard was sixteen in 1095 the Turks captured Jerusalem. Héloïse was born around 1099, the year when Christian armies retook the Holy City during the First Crusade.

As a boy Abelard lived at Le Pallet near Nantes, a Loire region of vineyards but not those that were to produce the well-known Muscadet that optimists claim that Héloïse and he had enjoyed. They had not. Even when François Rabelais, author of the lavatorial *Gargantua and Pantagruel* drank Loire wine 500 years later, enjoying it with carp – the perfect fish accompaniment to Muscadet today – it was a thin and acidic wine that Rabelais tasted, unfit even for the lowest shelves of a modern mini-market.

A vicious frost in 1709 killed all those local vines. They were replaced by a white grape that with careful cultivation yielded the fine Muscadet de Sèvre-et-Maine sur lie. Quality varies. Even today there is far more poor Muscadet than good.[2]

Already known as a fine teacher and controversialist Abelard went to Paris around 1110 and by the unusual expedient of charging fees accumulated many remunerative disciples. He was highly regarded for his trenchant philosophical arguments that seemed dangerously close to heresy to many bishops.

Less impulsively, coldly plotting, he inveigled himself into a virgin's bed.

At the time that he was teaching in Paris Héloïse, a lovely woman in her early twenties, was living there at the home of an uncle on her mother's side, Fulbert, a canon of Notre-Dame. She was already well known for being fluent in Latin, Greek and Hebrew and was so remarkable in her width and depth of learning that it made 'her famous throughout the kingdom'.[3]

Aware of the general admiration for her the arrogant scholar turned seducer and quite callously decided to debauch her. In his later *Historia calamitatum*, 'The Story of My Misfortunes', he admitted it.

I considered all the usual attractions for a lover and decided she was the one to bring to my bed, confident that I should have an easy success; for at that time I had youth and exceptional good-looks as well as my great reputation to recommend me, and feared no rebuff from any woman I might choose to honour with my love.[4]

Determined to enrapture the girl he wrote her complimentary letters and composed graceful poems with delightful melodies that praised and named her. They were sung throughout the city. Those love-songs were written in Latin. In one of her letters to him she said so. 'The beauty of the airs ensured that even the unlettered did not forget you'. The classically educated Abelard probably considered vernacular French too common and barbaric for the expression of sincere feelings.

Neglecting his lectures he created songs of love to Héloïse, wooing her with them. His campaign succeeded. Years later she still remembered. 'When in the past you sought me out for sinful pleasures your letters came to me thick and fast, and your many songs put your Héloïse on everyone's lips, so that every street and house echoed with my name'. 'Every wife, every young girl desired you . . . queens and great ladies envied me my joys and my bed'.[5]

They exchanged passionate letters. That correspondence, lost for centuries, was discovered in 1471 and revealed how successful Abelard had been.[6] The correspondence was in Latin but there was little classical about her feelings.

Lumini clasirissimo, et solsticio suo . . .

'To her clearest light and solstice, never falling into the shadows of darkness, but always imparting the colour of radiance, she whom no sun but you warms by day nor moon by night, may you radiate more brightly, shine more brilliantly. Not diminish in the fervour of our love, be seasoned with salt and preserve your flavour'.

Farewell.[7]

He was no less ardent.

He persuaded her uncle to allow him to become her tutor, a position that Fulbert was delighted to agree to, even providing Abelard with a room at his house by the banks of the Seine. Abelard paid rent, 'for Fulbert dearly loved money' and the canon 'gave me complete charge of the girl'. 'I was amazed at his simplicity – if he had entrusted a tender lamb to a ravening wolf it would not have surprised me more'.

The brief year or two of uncontrolled lovemaking had a predictable consequence. In 1116 she became pregnant and sent Abelard 'a letter full of rejoicing to ask what I thought she should do'. He sent her secretly to Denyse, his sister, at Clisson in Brittany. There, she had a son.

The boy was named 'Pierre' after his father and, curiously, Astralabe, an instrument for measuring the angle of the sun. The 'solar' name also had a concealed meaning because it linked the sun with his mother, Héloïse or *helios*, 'the sun'. She had already termed Abelard 'her solstice'.

When a man, Astralabe became a monk. There were proposals that he should later be made a prebendary, an honorary canon, but nothing is known of the outcome.[8]

Reunited back in Paris Abelard and Héloïse placated Fulbert by promising to marry, but in secret, and the wedding was held in St Aignan's chapel on the outskirts of Notre-Dame. Both men, the new husband and the uncle were satisfied. Héloïse was not. She had no need to be a wife to love Abelard. She raged. Vehemently she vowed that 'God is my witness that if Augustus, emperor of the whole world, thought it fit to honour me with marriage, and conferred on me all the earth for ever, it would be dearer and more honourable to me to be called not his Empress but your whore'.[9]

> How oft, when press'd to marriage, have I said,
> 'Curse on all laws but those which Love has made'
>
> (Alexander Pope, *Eloisa to Abelard*, 73–44)

More than a century later her downright rejection of marriage so amused the poet Jean Clopinel, popularly known as Jean de Meung, that when he added a continuation to Guillaume de Lorris's *Roman de la Rose* he parodied it in sixty-four satirical lines. His book was so popular that it was the first in French to be 'chained' against theft in the Sorbonne library.[10]

Desperate to appease the still resentful Fulbert the couple agreed to separate, Abelard to his old lodgings, Héloïse to her uncle's house. The truce did not last. Fulbert, protecting his own honour, began telling people of the marriage. Learning this Héloïse defiantly and openly denied the story. He attacked her. Remembering the merciless powers that a man as head of a family could use at that time it is probable that the disappointed, humiliated and resentful Fulbert physically beat her.

Desperately she sent a message to Abelard who smuggled her to her old convent at Argenteuil 8 miles north-west of Notre-Dame in the Île-de-France. As a further precaution he persuaded Héloïse to disguise herself as a nun. 'I also made for her a religious habit of the type worn by novices, with the exception of the veil, and I had her clad in it'. Despite the disguise they still contrived to make love in that house of God.[11]

Learning of Héloïse's abduction and apparent religious conversion by which she had become irrecoverable, the furious Fulbert and relatives plotted a dreadful revenge on Abelard. The intention was doubly clever and ruthless. They could effectively deprive him of Héloïse. They could also ruin him.

Abelard was only a minor cleric but could become a canon. Fulbert, already a canon and well versed in the Old Testament, knew of a Biblical enactment, one that was still strictly observed in the Catholic Church. 'He that is wounded in the stones [testicles], or hath his private member cut off, shall not enter into the congregation of the Lord'. It offered Fulbert both revenge for the debasement of his niece and an ending to Abelard's hopes of clerical advancement.[12]

Where Abelard was staying in 1117 is uncertain. Quite possibly he was in hiding and may have accepted the protection of his patron, the powerful and wealthy politician Stephen de Garlande, who lived on the Île de Cité just across the river from Notre-Dame. If Abelard did hide there it was an unsuccessful safeguard.

Fulbert bribed one of the servants to open the doors to a group of ruffians and lead them to the room where Abelard slept. Seizing him, muffling his shouts of alarm, holding him down, they castrated him.

Leaving their victim shrieking in agony they fled but in the startled household two were caught, one of them the treacherous servant. Medieval retribution was swift, without pity and biblically apt. Both thugs were castrated, then blinded, and flung out of the house to grope along the streets at dawn.[13]

Physically abused the emasculated Abelard almost vengefully abused Héloïse in spirit. Peremptorily, without explanation, he commanded her to become a nun, a life for which she felt no rapport and for which she was utterly unprepared. Yet, believing herself responsible for her lover's downfall, she obeyed.

Once again she was taken to the Benedictine community of Argenteuil, There, at her husband's orders, she took holy orders. She cried. She had no vocation for the monastic life. At Argenteuil she had done no more than wear the habit of a nun. Now, uttering Cornelia's words on learning of the death of husband, Pompey:

> . . . O noble husband,
> Too great for me to wed, was it my fate
> To bend that lofty head? What prompted me
> To marry you and bring about your fall?
> Now claim your due, and see me gladly pay . . .
>
> (Lucan, Pharsalia, VIII, V, 94–8)

She became a nun, taking the veil.

Believing herself the cause of Abelard's tragedy 'she hurried to the altar, almost snatching the veil blessed by the bishop, and publicly bound herself to the religious life'.[14] Yet she never forgot the loveliness of Abelard's songs and the ecstasies of his lovemaking.

He did. Once certain that she had obeyed him Abelard became a monk at the royal abbey of St-Denis in which many kings of France were buried. Although it was only 6 miles from Argenteuil he never once wrote to Héloïse. Instead, almost defiantly, he antagonised his abbot, the king's chronicler, Adam Suger, by questioning the identity of the founder of St-Denis, rashly denying it was the person named by Suger, almost an insult to the abbot who had zealously overseen the rebuilding of St-Denis which was the first of France's great Gothic churches. Abelard, it has been said, was no friend to himself.

Years later, when a greatly respected abbess, Héloïse could still write to him reminding him of their shared bliss. 'While I enjoyed with you the pleasures of the flesh, many were uncertain whether I was prompted by love or lust; but now the end is proof of the beginning. I have finally denied myself every pleasure in obedience to your will, kept nothing for myself except to prove that now, even more, I am yours'.[15]

However popular Abelard's songs to her had been, many probably copied onto ephemeral wax tablets, if any were transcribed onto more enduring parchment the manuscripts have not survived.

There is, however, a possibility that one still exists in a collection of mainly anonymous Goliard or 'wandering scholars' songs preserved in the *Carmina Burana*, the popular name for *Codex Buranus*, a manuscript book found in 1803 in the Bavarian monastery of St Benedikt Beuern, hence *Burana*. Its collection of more than 200 lyrical poems, all to be sung, makes it 'a scholar's song-book'.[16]

One, number 169, describes the grief of a lover separated from his love. *Hebet sydus leti visus . . .*, 'the star's joyous face dulls . . .', is considered one of the finest in the collection. It has teasing hints about its composer. The lines,

cuius normen a Phoebea
Luce renitet . . .

she whose name is radiant
with Phoebus' light   (lines 11–12)

may refer directly to Héloïse. As early as 1891 the German scholar Ehrenthal thought that Phoebus, the sun god, was a pun on *Helios*, 'the sun', and Abelard's 'Héloïse'. The name of their son, Astralabe, contained a similar solar connection.

Such word-play is suggestive but even more significant is that although the poem's first three stanzas are conventional lines of love the final verse is quite different. It speaks of an intimate predicament, quite unlike any other poem in the entire *Carmina Burana*. It astonishes.

Tanti spaci . . .

Yet she, without a hope of solace, wastes away,
the flower of her youth grows dry –
if only this great gulf of space
were done away with, that this parting
might grant rights which are secure
to those who are joined!

It is both astonishing and revealing because Abelard and Héloïse, unlike most unhappy lovers, were actually joined in marriage, only to be separated after Abelard's castration and Héloïse's 'wasting away' in her reluctant taking of Holy Orders,

Perhaps composed quite shortly after those distressing events the poem mourned the separation after the pleasures, when 'they were able to steal hours of love' under the same roof.[17]

Their lives became independent of each other. After his physical mutilation Abelard turned monk but suffered mental hostility. His intellectual arrogance and insistence on logical deduction caused antagonism. He was criticised, almost persecuted, and at Soissons in 1121 was accused of heresy.

He returned to lecturing and established a remote 'cell' at the Paraclete oratory near Nogent-sur-Seine east of Paris. Students swarmed to him. It was there that he laid the foundations of the great priory of which Héloïse was to become abbess.[18]

Even in the rigidities of the early medieval Church there was still partisanship. Fulbert's malicious belief that castration would prevent any ecclesiastical preferment for Abelard was thwarted. Instead, he was invited to become abbot of the undisciplined church of St Gildas-de-Rhuys on the Arzon peninsula of Brittany.

Abelard was a failure. The obstructive brothers almost destroyed him by their indiscipline, even attempting to poison him when he drank from the chalice, something that only an ordained priest could do.[19] Defeated in his attempts at reform he retired to a life of contemplation at the Romanesque abbey of Cluny near Mâcon, at that time the largest church in the entire Christian world. Today only parts of it remain. He died there in 1142.

After a dozen dismal years as a dutiful nun at Argenteuil, never receiving a word from Abelard, life changed for Héloïse. The abbot Suger closed the nunnery, claiming that the sisters led 'a wretched way of life' and deplored their 'extraordinary levity' as though happiness and laughter displayed a lack of dedication.[20]

Already a prioress she was invited by Abelard to take any loyal nuns to the unused priory of the Paraclete. There, as its abbess, she efficiently increased its lands and wealth, had other houses established, and gained the admiring respect of all who knew her. Abelard praised her achievements. 'And such favours in the eyes of all did God bestow on that sister of mine who was in charge of the other nuns that bishops loved her as a daughter, loved as a sister by abbots, the laity as a mother.'[21]

An anonymous trouvère, perhaps a woman, understood such conflicts of emotion:

Bel Doette prist s'abbaiie a faire

Lovely Douette proceeded to build her abbey
Which is very large and will grow larger,
She wants to draw all men and women there
Who know the pain and woe of love.
Oh, what grief I feel!
For love of you I'll became a nun at St Paul's.[22]

Even as a dedicated abbess Héloïse never lost her love for Abelard. During the long years that followed they had their great correspondence, dispassionate but helpful from him, more emotional and receptive from her. Abbess she was but woman she remained. She told him so.

> At your bidding I changed my clothing along with my mind, in order to prove you the sole possessor of my body and my will alike. God knows I never sought anything in you except yourself. I wanted simply you, nothing of yours. I looked for no marriage bonds, no marriage portion, and it was not my own pleasures and wishes I sought to gratify, as you well know, but yours. The name of wife may seem more sacred or more binding but sweeter for me will always be the word mistress, or, if you will permit me, that of concubine or whore.[23]

Abelard replied coldly. 'Solitude is indeed all the more necessary for your woman's frailty, inasmuch for our part we are less attacked by the conflicts of carnal temptations and less likely to stray towards bodily things through the senses'. It was near to hypocrisy for a castrated monk to write so unfeelingly to a virile woman.[24]

Her reply was gentle but insistent that she was always of one mind.

> In my case, the pleasures of lovers which we shared have been too sweet – they can never displease me, and can scarcely be banished from my thoughts. Wherever I turn they are always there before my eyes, bringing with them awakened longings and fantasies which will not even let me sleep. Even during the celebration of the Mass, when our prayers should be purer, lewd visions of those pleasures take such a hold upon my unhappy soul that my thoughts are on their wantonness instead of on prayers. I should be groaning over the sins I have committed, but I can only sigh for what I have lost. Everything we did and also the times and places are stamped in my heart along with your image, so that I live through it all again with you. Even in sleep I know no respite. Sometimes my thoughts are betrayed in a movement of my body, or they break out in an unguarded word.[25]

That extract came from one of a collection of seven very long letters and a 'Confession of Faith' by Abelard addressed to Héloïse, 'my sister, once dear to me in the world'.[26]

The fragile correspondence probably survived after being copied from wax tablets onto parchment by Héloïse in the Paraclete and then, a century after her death, transferred to Paris. It was those long letters that the poet, Jean de Meung, transcribed and translated late in the thirteenth century. Two hundred or so years later Johannes de Vepria found the more intimate, much shorter but more numerous 'lost' letters that the lovers-to-be had written in Paris.

Learning of Abelard's death, and knowing his expressed wish to be buried in the Paraclete, Héloïse asked the abbot of Cluny, the generous Peter the Venerable, to allow the body to be brought to her priory. There it was reverently buried by the altar, and it is reported, although unproven, that the lovely *Requiescat in labore* dirge was composed by the nuns to be sung over the grave. The last of its six stanzas almost celebrates Abelard's death on earth and exaltation in Heaven.

Sanctae animae, favete!
Consolare, paraclete!
Audin sonat gaudia!
   Cantilena
   Et amoena
Angelorum cythera.[27]

An early thirteenth-century legend claims that when Héloïse died on 16 May 1163/4 twenty or more years after Abelard she had asked to be buried with him. As though by a miracle, when his tomb was opened, 'he stretched out his arms to embrace her'.[28]

Their lives had been disrupted. So were their remains in death. They had been buried together in a small church close to the river Auduzon, green with weeds. Three hundred years later in 1497 their tomb was removed from a certain damp and watery place, namely a chapel in the said monastery, 'le petit moustier', and taken to a more imposing church on higher ground where they were buried separately in two places in the aforesaid church of the Paraclete, Abelard on the right, Héloïse on the left.

They did not rest in peace. On 15 March 1621, the abbess, Marie de la Rochefoucauld, had the two burials moved once more, this time under the altar of a crypt of a small chapel. The crypt still exists just to the east of a more recent family chapel.[29] In it is a slab incised with two crosses.

A century and a half later during the French Revolution, when churches and holy shrines were being desecrated, often demolished, in 1792 the buildings of the Paraclete were pulled down with the exception of the abbess's residence. Just before the demolition the burials were taken surreptitiously to the church of St-Laurent in Nogent-sur-Seine.

There was no rest. In 1800 the graves were disinterred and carried to Paris by an artist and archaeologist, Alexandre Lenoir, who intended to display them inside a custom-built 'Romanesque' chapel but, in fact, bogus Gothic. It stood in the gardens of La Musée des Monuments Françaises on the rue des Petits-Augustins in St Germaine-de-Près.[30]

Within a few years tradition, respect and romance demanded an end to the unpopular sacrilege. In 1817 Héloïse and Abelard were given a final, lasting home in an imposing mausoleum of white marble near the bottom of the slope of the sprawling cemetery of Père Lachaise.

It has an epitaph from another abbess of the Rochefoucauld family, Catherine, in 1701. 'The love which had joined their spirits in life and which lives on through their most tender and spiritual letters, has reunited their bodies in this tomb'.[31]

Mark Twain wrote of the tomb,

> This is the grave of Abelard and Héloïse – a grave which has been more revered, more widely known, more written and sung about and wept over than any other in Christendom save only that of the Saviour'.

Little remains of them elsewhere in Paris. Fulbert's home on the corner of the rue de Chantres and today's Quai des Fleurs on the Seine near Notre-Dame was demolished in 1846. It was still standing, although in decay, in 1822 when it was claimed that the rooms where Héloïse and Abelard had slept could still be seen. Twenty years later the decaying medieval house was uninhabitable and was pulled down. In 1849 it was replaced by two linked houses, nunmbers 9 and 11.

Above the door at the centre of the new façade is a stone tablet engraved, *'Ancienne Habitation de Héloïse et d'Abelard. 1118. Rebatie en 1849'*. Over the window to the left of the door is a small bust of Abelard. One of Héloïse is placed on top of the window on the other side of the door.

Theirs was one of the world's most enduring romances and it is surprising that Dante never mentioned the sad lovers anywhere in his poems. Even Chaucer gave Héloïse only the slightest of glances:

> . . . And Helowys
> That was abbesse nat fer fro Parys,
>
> (Prologue, *Wife of Bath's Tale*, 677–8)

Héloïse remained more woman than abbess as an extract from the first of her long letters to Abelard shows:

> I would have had no hesitation, God knows, in following you or going ahead at your bidding to the flames of Hell. My heart was not in me but with you, and now, even more, if it is not with you it is nowhere; without you, it cannot exist.[32]

Helen Waddell, the classical scholar, translator and lover of medieval lyric poetry – 'there is enchantment in the very words' – attributed a poem, *Vel confossus partier* . . ., to Abelard. The words echo the eternal love between him and Héloïse.

> Low in thy grave with thee
> Happy to lie,
> Since there's no greater thing left Love to do;
> And to live after thee
> Is but to die
> For with but half a soul what can Life be?

So share thy victory,
Or else thy grave,
Either to rescue thee, or with thee lie:
Ending that life for thee,
That thou didst save,
So Death that sundereth might bring more nigh.

Peace, O my stricken lute!
Thy strings are sleeping.
Would that my heart could still
Its bitter weeping.

The Ballad of Fair Rosamund

When as king Henry rulde this land,
The second of that name,
Besides the queene, he dearly lovde
A faire and comely dame.

Yea Rosamonde, fair Rosamonde,
Her name was called so,
To whom our queene, dame Ellinor,
Was known a deadly foe.

(Thomas Deloney, 1607, lines 1–4, 17–20[1])

Today there are only ruins. The first is the castle where she was born, the last the chapel that held her dishonoured tomb. Between the first and last is her reputation.

The story of Rosamund Clifford, or 'Fair Rosamond', as she was known, is a mixture of memories and mistakes. She was the most enduring of the mistresses of Henry II, preferred by him to his queen, Eleanor of Aquitaine. Her history begins with three medieval contradictions and one certainty.

It is believed, without direct proof, that the King first saw her when starting a campaign against the Welsh in 1165-or 1166.[2]

Uncritically it was speculated that she was born around 1140. If so, she would have been in her mid-twenties at that meeting, when most well-born young women as old as that had been married for years. Contradicting so early a date the censorious monk and chronicler, Gerald of Wales, no admirer of hers, said that she was a young girl when she met Henry II.[3]

That suggests a more probable date of birth around 1150, the nubile Rosamund being no more than 15 or 16 when the lecherous eyes of a lustful, unscrupulous and long-married monarch first noticed her in her father's castle at Clifford, near Hay-on-Wye in Herefordshire on the Welsh borders. Henry had already 'passionately loved' Rohese, Countess of Lincoln, 'the most beautiful woman in England,' sister of Roger de Clare, Earl of Hertford. The king had also enjoyed an affair with Avice de Stafford. Husbands guarded wives, sisters and daughters against the royal lust.[4]

The fortress at Clifford was the westernmost of 5 castles of the Lords Marcher to protect the boundaries of England. Named 'Cliford' in the Domesday Book of

1087, 'ford at the bottom of a cliff', the name explained that for protection against a surprise attack the castle had been erected at the edge of a precipitous drop down to the river Wye. It barricaded access to the Upper Wye Valley.[5]

Rosamund was the daughter of Walter de Clifford, 'Rosamund, the faire daughter of William, lord Clifford'. She was one of a family of 6, 3 boys, 3 girls. Shortly after meeting her Henry II gave the Shropshire manors of Corfham, Carlinton and several others to her father 'for love of Rosamund, his daughter'.[6]

Their affair was little different from that of any other young woman and a married man. At first she was kept discreetly just outside Oxford at a hunting lodge near Woodstock. Later when Queen Eleanor was no longer favoured by the King, Rosamund was flaunted blatantly at court. Even in the Queen's absence Henry humiliated Eleanor by installing Rosamund in the Queen's apartments.[7] They were called *Camera Rosamunda*, a euphemism for the rooms of the King's kept woman.

The unusual difference was that over a period of more than 10 years Henry II was in England for only 3½.[8] It is possible that occasionally Rosamund accompanied him, secretly at first, openly once Eleanor had been imprisoned for her part in the rebellion of her sons against the King.

Of all royal mistresses she was the most discreet. For the long years she spent at Woodstock there were few rumours, no scandal. While Henry and his friend, Thomas à Becket, roistered their way through taverns and brothels she remained almost anonymous. In the 600 detailed pages of Warren's *Henry II* she is mentioned just twice and briefly.

She was not accused of greed like the avaricious Alice Perrers. She was not publicly led through the streets of London in disgrace like Jane Shore. She did not dance merrily about the court like Nell Gwynne. Instead, she lived quietly in her hunting lodge. Only almost at the end was she brought to the palace and the eyes of the world.

There had been one piece of gossip and it was mistaken. It claimed that she had two sons by Henry II: Geoffrey, Archbishop of York, born around 1151–2 and William Longsword, Earl of Salisbury who died in 1226. Both are improbable children of hers, as she would only have been about 10 years old at the time of their births. The real mother, claimed Walter Map, Archdeacon of Oxford, in his 1192 anecdotal *De nugis curialium* 'Of Courtiers' Trifles', was Ykenai, 'a common harlot', 'a bawd whose name was Hikenai'.[9]

The one fact upon which every contemporary agreed, was that Rosamund was exceptionally lovely and attractive, 'a masterpiece of nature'.

> Most peerlesse was her beautye founde,
> Her favour, and her face;
> A sweeter creature in this worlde
> Could never prince embrace.
>
> (Deloney, 'The Ballade of Fair Rosamond', lines 5–8)

Thomas Deloney was a prolific Elizabethan pamphleteer but not greatly esteemed by his contemporaries. 'A balletting silk-weaver of Norwich,' wrote Thomas Nashe, and derisively, his work was described as 'such trivial trinkets and threadbare trash,' by Robert Greene. Yet picking scraps of fact and rumour from earlier writers Deloney wrote his long, inaccurate but dramatic ballad of 'Fair Rosamund', posthumously published in 1607. Later it was included in Bishop Thomas Percy's compendium, *Reliques of Ancient English Poetry*, of 1765.

The poem told that the King had a hiding place for her near Oxford to protect her from the vengeful Eleanor of Aquitaine and how the Queen discovered her:

Henry's grandfather, Henry I, had built a lavish hunting lodge, his favourite, there in the middle of a forest near Woodstock.[10] It stood in a royal deer park surrounded by 7 miles of wall. In the park was a splendid pavilion of many rooms and so many passageways and corridors that it seemed like a maze.[11] Around it were three ponds, a stream and a cultivated orchard. The isolated, comfortable residence 'formed a rural retreat which was the setting of their dalliance'.

After Rosamund's death rumours flourished that she had been kept hidden there in a secret chamber.

The Tudor historian Robert Fabyan, sheriff of London in 1493, gathered scraps of tittle-tattle and in *The New Chronicles of England and France* of 1516, he wrote of a 'howse of wunder working or Daedalus' werke which is to mean . . . an house wrought lyke unto a knot in a garden called a *maze*,' and went on, 'the common fame tellyth that lastly the quene wane to her [Rosamund] by a clewe of threde or sylke and delte with her in such maner that she lyved not long after'.[12]

'Discovery' of the non-existent labyrinth was enhanced by later writers who fantasised that Queen Eleanor had found Rosamund's secret chamber by following a trail of thread that her quarry had dropped.

Dissatisfied with simplicity fiction grew into fable. Eleanor of Aquitaine's revenge developed story by story into blunders and torture. The kings changed from Henry the Second to the Third. Rosamund was to be bled to death in a hot bath. That being unsatisfying, sadism was added. Eleanor had her victim stripped naked, roasted over two fires, had venomous vampire toads planted on her breasts and cackled as they sucked out her blood.[13]

Such increasingly murderous attempts made popular reading. Like Hollywood scriptwriters recreating medieval history any mundane fact was omitted. Rosamund's true story did end in sadness but not through any act of Eleanor of Aquitaine's.

"Alas! Alas", a low voice, full of care
Murmur'd beside me, "Turn and look on me,
I am that Rosamund, whom men call fair,
If what I was I be
Would I had been some maiden coarse and poor,

O me, that I should ever see the light!
Those dragon eyes of anger'd Eleanor
Do hunt me day and night"

(Tennyson, 'Dream of Fair Women', verses 62–3)

Yea, Rosamonde, fair Rosamonde,
Her name was called so,
To whom our queene, dame Ellinor,
Was known a deadlye foe.

(Deloney, lines 17–20)

The Queen's opportunity for revenge arrived when Henry departed on one of his many visits to France:

For when his grace had past the seas,
And into France was gone;
With envious heart, queene Ellinor
To Woodstocke came anone.

(Deloney, lines 133–6)

Cast off from thee those robes, she said,
That riche and costlye bee;
And drinke thou up this deadlye draught,
Which I have brought to thee.

(Deloney, lines 151–4)

Rosamund pleaded for mercy. There was none.

But nothing could this furious queene
Therewith appeased bee;
The cup of deadlye poyson stronge,
As she knelt on her knee

She gave this comelye dame to drinke;
Who tooke it in her hand,
And from her bended knee arose
And on her feet did stand:

And casting up her eyes to heaven,
Shee did for mercye calle;
And drinking up the poison stronge,
Her life shee loste withalle.

It was a long ballad, 48 quatrains, almost 200 lines, and in the *Reliques* it was followed by an anonymous ballad in which on her deathbed Eleanor confessed to poisoning Rosamund and attempting to poison the King, her husband.

Over the years the murderous tale became more and more lurid, gruesomely embroidered for popular reading and hawked cheaply in the streets as a 'penny dreadful' pamphlet. It had the enticing title, *The Life and Death of Fair Rosamond, Concubine to King Henry the Second: who was Poisoned by Queen Eleanor.*

There was retribution for Rosamund. Confronted by her furious husband the queen confessed not only to that crime but to another.

> The next vile thing that ever I did,
> To you Ile not denye,
> I made a boxe of poison strong,
> To poison king Henrye.

('Queen Eleanor's Confession', lines 45–8)

She failed and was judged by her husband. 'She being a foreign princess, her life was spared', but she was condemned to life imprisonment and when 'she died her body should not be buried, but left to moulder to dust'.

The tawdry chapbook provided bloodthirsty reading but such romantic inventions ignored the conventions of noble life in the twelftfh century. The majority of well-bred wives overlooked their husbands' adulteries, tolerated it almost with a shrug of 'men will be men', their indignity eased by troubadour songs of illicit love.

Women also, of course, could be women. Eleanor's own grandmother, Dangerosa, Viscountess of Châtellerault, had been a notorious adulteress. Eleanor herself was not blameless, accused of affairs with her uncle at Antioch; and perhaps also with Geoffrey of Anjou, Henry's father. Walter Map wrote that as Queen of France she had 'cast glances of unholy love' on Henry and of 'the charge secretly made against her that she had shared Louis's bed with Henry's father, Geoffrey'.[14]

A French biographer of Eleanor's first husband, Louis VII, was even more vindictive. She was a devourer of men, *'fille incontinente et corrompue'* who *'ne pouvait vivre sans hommes'*. Another historian, Aubrey de Trois Fontaines, commented contemptuously on the 'promiscuity of the woman, who did not conduct herself like a queen, but offered herself almost as common property'. It was unjust, uncorroborated, unlikely. But it was Eleanor's reputation.[15]

Like so many wives of that time her life disproved the myth that women were no more than breeding machines and the acquiescent chattels of their husbands. Some were independent. After the Christmas of 1166 Eleanor went to Poitiers and its glittering court where troubadours sang of carefree love and happiness.

It was perhaps because of the infidelities of her second husband that Eleanor encouraged her sons, Henry, Richard and Geoffrey to rebel against their father. She was imprisoned in 1174 for the treason. By then Rosamund was well known at court.

Gerald of Wales, despising her, made mocking Latin puns on her name and nickname. Henry II had 'long been a secret adulterer, now flaunted his paramour for all to see, not Rosamunda but *rosa immunda*, the unclean rose – and not "rose of the world", *Rosa-mundi*, as some vain and foolish people called her, but *rosa-immundi*, the rose of filth or unchastity'.[16]

In 1176 Rosamund retired to the nunnery of Godstow near Oxford, perhaps in bitterness that after so many years her fickle king had taken yet another mistress, the Capetian princess Alais, sister to Philip of France. The girl was already engaged to Henry's son, Richard. In 1176 she was 16, about the same age as Rosamund Clifford had been so many years earlier.

Rosamund Clifford died that year, not yet 30, and was buried in her nunnery. Her father and Henry endowed Godstow richly for her soul. Her tomb, being so royally endowed, was placed in the middle of the choir in front of the altar. It was sumptuously adorned with tapestries, lamps and wax candles.
The epitaph on her tomb was characteristic of the medieval fascination with the corruption of death.

Hic jacet in tumba Rosa mundi, non rosa munda;
Non redolat, sed olet, quae redolere solet.

Here in this tomb lies the rose of the world, not a clean one,
Not fragrant but stinking as is commonplace.

Around 1190 Hugh, Bishop of Lincoln, a stern Carthusian, appalled at the near-sacrilege of an immoral woman being so honoured, ordered the tomb to be moved from the choir to the chapter house outside. 'Remove her from here, for she was a harlot, and that love between her and the king was unlawful and adulterous! And bury her with the other dead outside the church, lest the Christian faith come into disrepute, and for that to be an example for other women outside to guard against illicit and adulterous intercourse'.[17]

Later Eleanor's youngest son, John, King of England, endowed Godstow's nunnery with an annual revenue so that 'these holy virgins might releeve with their prayers, the soules of his father King Henrie, and of Lady Rosamund there interred'.[18]

More than 300 years later on his long itinerary around England between 1535 and 1543 the Tudor antiquarian John Leland visited Oxfordshire and went to Godstow. He described what had happened to her tomb during the iconoclastic years of Henry VIII's lucrative destruction of the monasteries.

Rosamundes tumbe at Godestow nunnery was taken up a late. It [had] a stone with this inscription, *Tumba Rosamundae*, her bones were closid in lede, and with yn that the bones were closid in lether. When it was openid there was a uery swete smell cam owt of it' from the herbs and spices upon which her body had been laid.[19]

Almost 30 years after Rosamund's death Eleanor of Aquitaine died on 31 March 1204.She had outlived both her husbands and four of her five sons. William, the first, perished as an infant in 1156. Henry, the Young King, contracted a mortal fever in 1183. Three years later Geoffrey, even in full armour, was trampled to death when he fell from his horse during a chivalrous tournament. Infection from a crossbow bolt killed Richard in 1199. Only the youngest son, the feckless John, survived his mother.

What his father and his martial brother had gained and secured in France that inadequate king systematically squandered through vacillation and ill-judged whims, antagonising allies by his egotism and avarice. He also shamefully neglected Eleanor even though he had depended on her advice for survival. Only her death forced him into brief reality.

> . . . What! Mother dead?
> How wildly then walks my estate in France![20]

Eleanor of Aquitaine was buried in the crypt of Fontevrault abbey, resting in a fine marble tomb amongst others of her royal family. On her sarcophagus was a full-length painted effigy of her, crowned, her wimpled face with the faintest of smiles. She held a book open before her but whether it was a holy missal or a volume of the troubadour *cansos* she had loved is debateable.

During the proletarian carnage of the French Revolution the crypt was savaged in 1793, the graves desecrated and their bones scattered irretrievably around the neighbourhood.

The abbey was converted into a prison and remained so until 1963 when the abbey was restored. Excavations in the 1990s removed the slabs of the emptied tombs to the south transept of the abbey, weathered, shabbied, colours almost gone, but still elegantly recognisable.

Eleanor's rests there alongside Henry's and in front of Richard's. It remains a handsome monument, of better quality than the others, the Queen's image perhaps sculpted by the master craftsman of the transepts of Chartres cathedral. Eleanor of Aquitaine survives.

But of Rosamund Clifford? Godstow nunnery has gone. Today it is reduced to a walled rectangle around emptiness. There is no house, no church, no tomb, just the mouldering remnants of her chapel in the south-east corner of the enclosure.[21]

That fragment where she was finally buried, and the ruins of the castle where she was born, are the only tangible relics that survive of her life.

Notes

Chapter One

1. The reality of Courts of Love? Bumke, 408–9. Capellanus: J.J. Parry, *The Art of Courtly Love*, Columbia University Press, New York, 1990; A. Hopkins, *The Book of Courtly Love. The Passionate Code of the Troubadours*, HarperCollins, New York, 1994; P. Porter, *Courtly Love in Medieval Manuscripts*, British Library, London, 2003.
2. Ovid, *Ars Amatoria*, Books I–III, P. Green, trans. *Ovid. The Erotic Poems*, Penguin, London, 1982.
3. Ovid, *Ars Amatoria*, Book I, lines 270–1.
4. Ovid, *Ars Amatoria*, Book II, line 717; Book II, line 725.
5. 'aetas Ovidiana': Parry (Note 1) 6.
6. Supremacy of the woman: An 'enticingly unavailable mistress'; Green (Note 2) 70. See also: Bumke, 301–2.
7. Pure and Mixed Love in Capellanus: Parry (Note 1) 8th Dialogue. 122–3.
8. Seducing a nun: Parry (Note 1) 143.
9. Forcing a peasant woman: Parry (Note 1) 150. Forcing a well-bred woman: Ovid, *Ars Amatoria*, Book I, 673–7.
10. Jean de Nostradamus: *Jehan de Nostredame. 'Les Vies des Plus Célèbres et Anciens Poétes Provensaux'* (1575), eds C. Chabaneau and J. Anglade, Honoré Champion, Paris, 1913. Monk des Îles d'Or: *ibid*, 148–51.
11. Chaucer's ransom: M. Chute, *Geoffrey Chaucer of England*, Robert Hale, London, 1951, 35–6.
12. Chaucer's spurious poem, 'The Court of Love': H.S. Bennett, *Chaucer and The Fifteenth Century*, Clarendon Press, Oxford, 1961, pp. 136–7. Chaucer's 'Troilus and Criseyde': Hopkins (Note 1) 20, 25, 30–2, 46, 72–3.
13. A *tenson*: A debate in which two combatants maintained in turn, by similar couplets, and terminated with similar rhymes, opposite opinions on questions of love, chivalry, morality. If they could not agree the question was referred to an impartial judge. Bonner, 22, Chaytor, 1912, 21.
14. De Mauléon a powerful lord; Chaytor, 1939, pp. 3–61; Lindsay, pp. 86–7; Boutière & Schutz, 'Savaric de Malleo', no. XXVIII, pp. 220–8; Pillet & Carstens, poet 432, pp. 386–7.
15. Supported Arthur of Brittany against John: Chaytor, 1939 (Note 14), 12–13.
16. Murder of Arthur of Brittany: Warren, 1974, 81–4; Tyerman, 281, 313.
17. North and south English dialects: M. Schmidt, *Lives of the Poets*, Phoenix, London, 1999, 20. La Langue d'Oc: Wolff, 32, 45, et seq.
18. De Mauléon on the Fifth Crusade: S. Runciman, *History of the Crusades*, III, 161, Cambridge, 1950; Chaytor, 1939 (Note 14), 38–41.
19. 'Willing help': Shirley, *Song of the Cathar Wars*, 39 (*Laisse 61*).
20. 'Stay calm . . .': Shirley (Note 18), 54 (*Laisse 103*).
21. Vaux-des-Cernay: Sibly & Sibly, 130 (Section 254); Savaric de Mauléon as a poet, Pillet & Carstens, poet 432, pp. 386–7.

22. Kidnapping of Raymond VI's son: Sumption, 148.
23. Executor of John's will: Warren, 1974, 254–5.
24. *In triclinio . . .*, A. Burl, Catullus. *A Poet in the Rome of Julius Caesar*, Constable & Robinson, London, 2004, 132, 183.
25. Ben Jonson, *Discoveries* 1641, 85–106; *Conversations with William Drummond of Hawthornden*, 1619, 2–28, p. 13, ed. G.B. Harrison, Edinburgh University Press, 1966.
26. N. Murray, *Andrew Marvell. World Enough and Time*, Abacus, London, 2000. Palgrave, 3; the poem, 88–92.
27. Age of marriage: Parsons, 66–7, in: Parsons et al, 1998; Labarge, 22.
28. The unknown trobairitz and her husband: trans. Bruckner et al, 130–3; The nameless trouvère and hers: trans. Doss-Quinby et al, *Rondeau 50*, 184–6.
29. 'Lives' of Faidit and la Bacalairia: Boutière & Schutz: 'Gaucelm Faidit', no. XVIII, 167–195; *ibid*, 'Uc de la Bacalaria', no. X XVI, 218. Farnell, 167–78.
30. The précis of the *tenson*: Chaytor, 1939 (Note 14), 88–93; Farnell, 203–5.
31. Uc's statement: Burgwinkle, in Gaunt & Kay, 259.
32. The 'Book': Burgwinkle (Note 31), 'The *chansonniers* as "books"', 246–62 (254).
33. Uc's *Vida*: Boutière & Schutz: no. XXXIII, 239–49; *Vida, Razos* x 2; Pillet & Carstens, poet 457, pp. 410–17, forty-four poems plus six doubtful. Farnell, 208–9; Akehurst & Davis, 188.
34. Haughty and superior ladies: Porter, 27.
35. Cercamon: Bonner, 43. Boutière & Schutz, 'Cercamon', no. II, 9. Pillet & Carstens, poet 112, pp. 102–4. Poem *Qu'eu*, Akehurst & Davies, 86.
36. 'Elaborate joke': Hopkins, 14; 'satire': Porter, 28.

Chapter Two

1. Robert Graves and Omar Ali-Shah, *The Rubaiyyat of Omar Khayaam*, Penguin, 1972, 8, 45. The forgery: Garrard, 100–4. For Khayyam's life, see: H. Lamb, 1943, 278–88.
2. From 'The Battle of Finnsburh'. Fr. Klaeber, *Beowulf, and the Fight at Finnsburg*, Heath, London, 1941, 245–49. See also: M. Swanton, *English Poetry before Chaucer*, University of Exeter Press, Exeter, 2002, 50–4.
3. Battle of Brunanburgh, 'Parker Chronicle (A): M. Swanton, *The Anglo-Saxon Chronicle* Dent, 1996, 106–10. The poem: Bradley, S.A.J. (1982) *Anglo-Saxon Poetry*, Dent, London.516–17; Swanton (Note 2), 180–1.
4. A possible site of Brunanburh is the village of Brinsworth, SK41.90., on the southern outskirts of Rotherham A. H. Burne, *More Battlefields of England*, Methuen, London, 1952, 55–9.
5. Tennyson and 'Brunanburh'. His translation was first published in the *Contemporary Review* of 1876.
6. The 'Brunanburh' quotation: G.N. Garmonsway, *The Anglo-Saxon Chronicle*, Everyman, London, 1954, 106, 108.
7. S.A.J. Bradley, *Anglo-Saxon Poetry*, Dent, London, 1982, 528, lines, 320ff.
8. Maldon: P. Marren, *Battles of the Dark Ages*, Pen & Sword, Barnsley, 2006, 147–60. Danegeld: Corèdon & Williams, 98; Swanton (Note 2), 179–90.
9. Byrhtnoth's burial: P. Meadows and N. Ramsay, eds, *The History of Ely Cathedral*, Boydell, Woodbridge, 2003, 28, 56, 126–8. See also, *ibid*, S. Keynes, 401–4; J. McSween, Byrhtnoth. Anglo-Saxon Warrior, Ely Cathedral, 191.
10. *Beowulf*. The earliest known copy is a manuscript of *c.* 1000. It was a composite poem accumulated from earlier stories written in the first half of the eighth

century. But mythical events in it came from heroic exploits as early as AD 450–550

11. S. Heaney, *Beowulf*, Faber & Faber, London, 1999, 50; L.J. Rodrigues, *Beowulf and the Fight at Finnsburgh*, Runetree, London, 2002.
12. Hildeburh: G. Bone, *Beowulf*, Blackwell, Oxford, 1945, 38–41.
13. Juliana: *The Battle of Maldon*, ed. E.V. Gordon, Methuen, London, 1937, 182–96; Bradley (Note 7), 301–20, 'little to start the emotional response of the audience'.
14. 'Judith': R. Hamer, *A Choice of Anglo-Saxon Verse*, Faber & Faber, London, 1970, 136–9. *The Apocrypha. New Revised Standard Version*, Cambridge University Press, Cambridge, 1998, 'Judith', 24, Chapter 13; Swanton (Note 2), 166–78.
15. Few Assyrians escaped: Hamer (Note 14), 159.
16. Capestanh: Boutière & Schutz, no. XCIV, 530–6; Pillet & Carstens, poet 213, pp. 179–81.
17. Concentration of the audience: *Song of Roland*, trans. J. Shirley, Felinfach, Llanerch, 1996, v.
18. Roland refused to blow the horn: Shirley (Note 17), 83, 4–5.
19. Ganelon's death: Shirley (Note 17), 296, 3–11.
20. Gérald Béchade: Gareyte, 2007, 6–8, 67–520, Fragments 1–88; Runciman, I, 332; see also: Chaytor, 1946.

Chapter Four

1. Guilhem of Poitiers: Lindsay, 3–24; Wilhelm, 2–59; Pillet & Carstens, poet 183, pp. 155–8; Cholakian, 12–41.
2. NO NOTE
3. 'Life': 'Lo Coms de Peiteus', Boutière & Schutz, no.1, 7–8.
4. Aénor, Dangereuse, and Eleanor of Aquitaine: Meade, 16–17; Seward, 18; Weir, 13–14.
5. *Pus vezem . . .* B. Duisit, *Les Cansos del Coms de Peiteus*, Alpha CD 505, 2003. His numbers for the poems, 1, 2 and 4–12, are not those of Pillet & Carstens, nor, differently, of Jeanroy's, I–XI. Duisit's 1 = Jeanroy's I; 2 = III; 3 = 'Interlude'; 4 = VI; 5 = II; 6 = VII; 7= IX; 8 = IV; 9 = VIII; 10 = X; 11 = V; 12 = XI.
6. Women's clothing: F. & G. Gies, *Daily Life in Medieval Times . . .*, Grange, Rochester, 2005, 59; Reeves, 1997, 49–56.
7. Accomplished Moorish female singers: Briffault, 53, 247, note 78.
8. Influence of Moorish music and verse: Briffault, 43, 44.
9. His character: Topsfield. 1; Lindsay, 15.
10. The sons of William the Conqueror: Poole, 1955, 97–108.
11. Louis I: William of Malmesbury, II, 62, 307.
12. Assassination of Janah-al-Dawla: B. Lewis, 2001, 4–6, 100; F. Daftary, *The Assassin Legends. Myths of the Isma'ilis*, Tauris, 2001, 64.
13. Death of William Rufus; Peterborough Chronicle (E): *The Anglo-Saxon Chronicle*, trans. M. Swanton, Dent, 1996, 235.
14. The mystery of the king's death: E. Mason, 2005, 218–31; R. Castleden, *Infamous Murderers*, Timewarner, 2005, 260–8.
15. Guilhem and Toulouse: Wilhelm, 27. Ezra Pound, 21.
16. Peter the Hermit: Sumption, 1, 113–15, 121–33. Turks at Nicosia: Finucane, 1983, 176.
17. Prostitutes at Acre: F. Gabrieli, ed., *Arab Historians of the Crusades*, trans. E.J. Costello, Dorset Press, New York, 1969, 123; G. Hindley, 1976, 157.
18. Eclipse of the moon: E. Bradford, *The Sword and the Scimitar*, Pen & Sword, Barnsley, 2004, 64.

19. 'Chastity belt': *Wikipedia* encyclopaedia, 1.

20. Women on crusades: G. Hindley, *The Crusades. Islam and Christianity in the Struggle for World Supremacy*, Constable & Robinson, London, 2003, 109–10.

21. The siege of Acre and women crusaders: Finucane, 1983, 177.

22. The ambush at Heraclea: William of Malmesbury, 118, §382.

23. Margravine: Wilhelm, 33, quoting from the *Historia . . .* of Albert of Aix., *ibid*, 209, note 45.

24. Tancred and the Assassins: B. Lewis, Note 12, 102; Daftary, Note 12, 64–5.

25. *Copa Surisca . . .*: H. Waddell, *Mediaeval Latin Lyrics*, Constables, London, 1933, 3. From the *Appendix Vergiliana*.

26. William of Malmesbury, 162, §438.

27. Bonner, 241.

28. *Jeu de Sainte Agnès* music: Rosenberg, Switten & Le Vot, 35.

29. Duisit (Note 5): forty-third page of the unnumbered pages in his booklet.

30. Keats: 'Ode to a Grecian Urn', II, 1, 2,

31. *Sol ramium fervens . . .*, B. Stock, *Medieval Latin Lyrics*, Godine, Boston, USA, 1971, 54–7.

32. 'Two horses': Hopkins, 1994, 65.

33. The pun on horses: Jean de la Tournelle, Bonner, 242.

34. *Chansons de geste* and Poitiers: Chaytor, 1946, 12–16.

35. Moorish influences: Chaytor (Note 32), 17–18.

36. Guilhem of Poitier's use of the *Conductus*: Lindsay, 6; Riot, 30.

37. *Conductus*: Hughes, 93, 171; Reese, 201; Aubrey, 75, 206. The surviving melody: Aubrey, 6.

38. Marlowe's classical translations: *The Poems. Christopher Marlowe*, ed. M. Maclure, Methuen, London, 1968 (Ovid, 105–217; Lucan's 1st Bk, 219–54); A.L. Rowse, *Christopher Marlowe. A Biography*, Macmillan, 1964, 37–43; P. Honan, *Christopher Marlowe. Poet and Spy*, Oxford University Press, 2005, 91–5. The tenth-century love poem: in Waddell (Note 25), 144–7.

39. The poems of Catullus, even in a corrupt state, were not circulated until the early fourteenth century in Verona. A. Burl, *Catullus. A Poet in the Rome of Julius Caesar*, Constable & Robinson, 2004, 259–66.

40. John of Salisbury: P. Whigham, *Letter to Juvenal*. 101 Epigrams from *Martial*, Anvil Press, 1985, 18.

41. *Martial. Epigrams*, D.R. Shackleton Bailey, trans., three volumes, Harvard University Press, 1993: Galla: Vol. II, Satire IX, line 4. Cornelia et al, Vol. III, Satire XI, 104. *Cunnus*: Vol. I, Bk 1,77, 6; Bk 2, Bk III, 93, 13; 34, 3; Vol. II, Bk VII, 35, 8; Bk IX, 37, 7; Bk X, 90, 1; Vol. III, Bk XI, 61, 9.

42. 'Folen': J.N. Adams, *The Latin Sexual Vocabulary*, Duckworth, 2002, 75.

43. Martial and *cunnus*: Adams (Note 42), 80–1. Catullus: XCVII, 8.

44. William of Malmesbury, 162–3, §438.

45. Boccaccio, *Decameron*, Third Day, Story One: G.H. McWilliam, trans., *The Decameron*, Penguin, 1995, 192–9.

46. *Futuo*: Adams (Note 42), 118–22; Martial, *Epigrams*, Bk III, XI, 20, Bailey (Note 39), Vol. III, pp20–1. Catullus, poem XXXII, 8.

47. A. Jeanroy, *Les Chansons de Guillaume IX, duc d'Aquitaine* (1071–1127), Classiques Français du Moyen Age 9, 2nd ed., Paris, 1927, Poem V, verses I–III. Duisit (Note 5), poem 11.

48. Verse IV: Topsfield, 16–17.

49. Verses V–VI: Bonner, 35.

50. Verse VII: L. Kendrick, *The Game of Love: Troubadour Wordplay*, University of California, Berkeley, 1998, 130. '*foc*' was the Occitanian rendering of the Latin *foculus*, 'vagina', Adams (Note 40), 86.
51. 'Pepper thick', *pebr'espes* or 'pubic hair': U. Malm, '*Dolssor Conina*'. *Lust, the Bawdy and Obscenity in Medieval Occitanian Troubadour Poetry*, Uppsala University Press, Uppsala, 2001, 144, note 32.
52. Verses IX, X, XI: Wilhelm, 40.
53. *Fotei*: Latin *futuo*, Adams (Note 42), 118. Martial, *Epigrams*: XI, 20; Catullus, poem XXXII, 8.
54. Verses XII–XIV: Lindsay, 10–11.
55. Verse XV: Lindsay, 11. For *malaveg* read *mal a veg*, 'pain in the prick', and for *mal me fes* read 'after-pains' Malm (Note 51), 149.
56. Apocryphal 'kill cat', Verse XVI: Malm (Note 51), 144.
57. Poem X, Bonner, 38–9.
58. Eblo's 'school': Lindsay, 122.
59. Brémule: Hillister & Frost, 2001, 64.
60. Eleanor of Aquitaine's birth: Meade, 17–18; Weir, 14. Bernart de Ventadorn: Boyd, 138–40; Rosenberg, 165–72.
61. Omar Khayyam and Edward Fitzgerald: G.F. Maine, ed. *Rubáiyát of Omar Khayyam. Rendered into English Verse* by Edward Fitzgerald, Collins, 1954; Garrard, 80–1.
62. Winfield: Omar Ali-Shah, in R. Graves and O. Ali-Shah, *The Rubáiyát of Omar Khayyam*, Penguin, Harmondsworth, 1972, 36–7.
63. Failure of Fitzgerald's first edition published by Quaritch in 1859: P. Avery and J. Heath-Stubbs, trans.: *The Rubáiyát of Omar Khayyam*, Allen Lane, London, 1979, 25.

Chapter Five

1. References to Rudel's poems, some with several variations, are to be found in Pickens, 1978. It is his Provençal lines that are quoted. See also: Pillet & Carstens, no. 262, pp. 238–42.
2. Marcabru and immorality: Meade, 39; Gaunt, Harvey and Paterson, Poem XI, 152–7; Cholakian, 42–82.
3. Matilda: R.H.C. Davis, *King Stephen*, 1977, 35–6, 54–67, 136–43.
4. Rudel's writing: Pickens, 1978, 4–5. Songs and melodies: Aubrey, 7; Rosenberg, Switten & Le Vot, 54–5.
5. Furnell, 32.
6. Rudel's *Vida*: Boutière & Schutz, no. V, 16–19; Pillet & Carstens, poet 262, pp. 238–42; Cholakian, 83–116.
7. Rudel's complexity: Bonner, 62; Press, 28–9.
8. Odierna, her sisters and daughter: Barrington, Tables I, 67; II, 94; and III, 120. Assassination of Raymond II: Lewis, 109, the Assassins' first victim.
9. *Jongleurs*: Sumption, 29. Goliards: Waddell, 1934, 102 et seq. to 260; the Arch Poet, Waddell, 1933, 176–7, 338–40; Waddell, 1982, 259–70.
10. Cercamon's poem: Aubrey, 28; Bonner, 41–2.
11. Poem I. Five versions are known. The quoted verse is twice cited as no. 2, once as no. 3, and twice no. 4: Pickens, 70–87.
12. Unwanted nunnery *motet*: Doss-Quinby et al, 244–7.
13. Guiraut de Borneil: Press, 142–3.
14. *Chanson*: Doss-Quinby et al, Grimbert, Pfeffer & Aubrey, 2001, 153–4; Rosenberg, Switten & Le Vot, 181–2.

15. Adulterous love: Press, 28.
16. Jaufré Rudel castrated?: Bonner, 62.
17. 'Linking of love and distance': Rosenberg, Switten & Le Vot, 56–7.
18. 'The back of her leg': Bonner, 100.
19. Lombarda, the intimate lady of Toulouse: Boutière & Schutz, no. LX, pp. 416–19; Pillet & Carstens, trobairitz 288, 254.
20. Vitry-sur-Marne: Meade, 57–8; Owen, 18–20.
21. The infatuated Louis VII: William of Newburgh, *The History*, Llanerch, Felinfach, 1996, Book I, chapter xxxi, 442.
22. Eleanor the Amazon: Meade, 72.
23. 'Married a monk': William of Newburgh (Note 21), I, xxxi, 442.
24. Camp attack and march to the ships: Rosenberg, 92–100.
25. The luxuries of Antioch: Seward, 48–9.
26. The chroniclers: Suger, Weir, 70; John of Salisbury, M. Chibnall, ed., *The 'Historia Ponitificalis' of John of Salisbury*, Nelson, London, 1956, xxiii, 52–3; Richard of Devizes, Weir, 67; William of Tyre, Meade, 100. Cercamon, Harvey, 131–2, 235, n.39. Marcabru: Boutière & Schutz, no. III, 10–13; Furnell, 22; Bonner, 44. Geoffrey of Anjou: Warren, 2000, 119, note 3.
27. Marcabru, Poem XV: Press, 60–1; Gaunt, Harvey & Paterson, 204–5.
28. Raymond of Antioch and William of Tyre, Boyd, 103. Eleanor and Bernard of Clairvaux, Meade, 64–5.
29. Adultery or no adultery: Weir, 68.
30. The abduction of Eleanor: William of Tyre, Weir, 70.
31. Henry of Huntingdon and the crusaders: Weir, 71.
32. Consanguinity: Kelly, 61; Meade, 108–9; Weir, 43–4.
33. The divorce: Hindley, 81.
34. The battle of Inab: Hindley, 88; Runciman, II, 326.
35. Rostand: Wilhelm, 89. Browning, 'Rudel to the Lady of Tripoli'; Swinburne, *Triumph of Time*; verses 41–2; 'a masterpiece in lyric'. Bonner, 61.
36. Seasickness: Hopper, 2002, 103. Conditions at sea: Hopper, 2006, 127.
37. Lengths of voyages: Ohler, 1989, 98–9.
38. The *planh*, Rosenberg, Switten & Le Vot, 128–9.
39. Faidit and the sea: Berry, 43, 1 – 44, 2.
40. Drowning: Hopper, 2006, 145–6
41. Fates of Rudel's companions: Runciman, II, 280–1, 287; Barrington, 64–5.
42. *Vida* V: Boutière & Schutz, 16–19. There are several translations of this passage. The one quoted is from Smythe, 1929, 11. See also: Bonner, 61; Furnell, 33–4; Topsfield, 42; Wilhelm, 89–90.
43. News of Tripoli: Pickens, 1978, 1.
44. *Petrarch*, 1912, 257

Chapter Six

1. M. Costen, *The Cathars and the Albigensian Crusade*, Manchester University Press, Manchester, 1997, 11–14, 43–7, Fig. 13.
2. Cathars: Sumption, 32–52; Lambert, 1998, 60–76.
3. Cathars: Lambert, 1998, 43–4.
4. Roux, 2004, 44; Lambert, 1998, 40.
5. O'Shea, 30.
6. Sumption, 46–7; Lambert, 1998, 42.
7. Montanhagol: Poem I, stanza 3, Ricketts, 1964, 44; Lindsay, 24.
8. Figueira: Zuchetto & Gruber, 209–13; Lindsay, 243.

9. Cardenal: Press, 290–1.
10. Gormonda: Bruckner et al, xlvi, 182–5; Paterson, 1993, 241.

Chapter Seven

1. Richard I's poem: *Ja nuns hons pris ne dira sa raison* . . . On compact disc: 'Richard Coeur de Lion', Alla Francesca, LC 5718, 1992, track 3, pp. 16–19. Pillet & Carstens, poet 420, pp. 379–80, poem 2. 'Richard I, von England'. *Je nuis hom pres no dira sa razo.*
2. Edward Fitzgerald. *Rubaiyat of Omar Khayyam*, ed. G.F. Maine, Collins, Glasgow and London, 1954, 60, quatrain 16. *The Rubaiyyat of Omar Khayaam*, trans. R. Graves and O. Ali-Shah, Penguin, Harmondsworth, 1967, 16, stanza 17.
3. Hostility to non-Christians: *The History of William of Newburgh, 1066–1197*, trans., ed. J. Stevenson. 1856. Facsimile reprint, Llanerch Press, Felinfach, 1996, 500–1, 508.
4. Eleanor of Aquitaine's imprisonment: Boyd, 2004, 217, 222; Meade, 1997, 274–7; Owen, 1993, 47, 72–3; Seward, 1978, 137–47; Weir, 2000, 245.
5. Bertran de Born and the death of the 'Young King': Press, 168–9.
6. Richard's capture and imprisonment: D. Boyle, *Blondel's Song. The Capture, Imprisonment and Ransom of Richard the Lionheart*, Penguin Viking, London, 2005, 97–239; A. Bridge, *Richard the Lionheart*, Grafton, London, 1989, 194–209.
7. Eleanor's letter to the Pope: A. Crawford, ed., *Letters of the Queens of England, 1100–1547*, Sutton, Thrupp, 1994, 43.
8. Blondel: Charles Dickens, *A Child's History of England*, Chapter XIII, 'England under Richard the First, called the Lion-Heart' (1853), Chapman & Hall, London, n.d., 116.
9. Versions of Blondel's story: R. Barber, 1978, 114; Boyle, 2005, 166–7.
10. Blondel's and Richard's shared song: Boyle, 169–71; Chaytor, 1923, 56–8.
11. The *Syrens*, T. Browne, *Hydriotaphia*, Chapter 5; Homer, *The Odyssey*, XII, ll, 184–91.
12. Blondel's music: Rosenberg, Switten & Le Vot, 239–40. One of his songs is on a compact disc: *L'amour dont sui espris* . . . . *A Mediaeval Banquet, Music from the Age of Chivalry*, Martin Best Mediaeval Consort, Nimbus, NI 1753, 1999; Disc 2, Track 8. see also: Goldin, 1983, 364–73.
13. Espionage: see: Boyle (Note 9), 166–79; P. Chaplais, *English Diplomatic Practice in the Middle Ages*, Hambledon & London, London, 2003.
14. Forewarnings: The Plantagenet chronicler, Roger of Wendover, *Flowers of History, comprising The History of England from the Descent of the Saxons to AD 1235*, I, 1 – II, 2, 1235, trans. J.A. Giles, Llanerch, Felinfach, 1995, II, 1, 129.
15. Blondel's death? 1197–1200. Rosenberg, Switten & Le Vot, 239; Second half twelftth century: Goldin, 1983, 364; 1220, Boyle (Note 9), 290.
16. Death of Richard I: Roger of Wendover (Note 14), II, 1, 178.
17. Faidit's *Vida*. Boutière & Schutz, poet no. XVIII, 167–95; Pillet & Carstens, poet 167, pp. 138–47.
18. 'Marueill': Akehurst & Davis, 5.
19. Arnaut de Mareuil's *Vida*: Boutière & Schutz, no. VII, 32–8, 'Maroill'; Pillet & Carstens, poet 30, pp. 32–7, Songs 1–25, and five love letters, I–V.
20. 'Burlatz' and Castelnaudary: Briffault, 1965, 146.
21. The 'Letters': P. Bec, *Les Saluts d'Amour du Troubadour Arnaud de Mareuil*, Edouard Privat, Toulouse, 1961.
22. The four stages of seduction: Rosenberg, M.V., 1937, 157.

23. The *Razo*: Boutière & Schutz, no. VII, 36–7.
24. Mareuil's songs: R.C. Johnson, *Les Poésies Lyriques de Troubadour Arnaut de Mareuil*, Slatkin, Geneva, 1973, no. 25, 148–52.
25. Alphonse II: C. Chabeneau, *Les Biographies des Troubadours en Langue Provençale*, Privat, Toulouse, 1885, 13, note 1.
26. Crowded castles and intimacy: Bogin, 25.
27. *Na donzela* . . .: Bogin, 152–5; Bruckner et al, 92–3.
28. Maria de Ventadorn and Gui d'Ussel: Bogin, 98–101; Bruckner et al, 38=41.
29. Marcabru and lust: Gaunt et al, 390–5, poem XXXI, 46–54.
30. Bernart de Ventadorn, *Vida*: Boutière & Schutz, no. VI, 20–31; Pillet & Carstens, poet 70, pp. 50–60, forty-five poems.
31. Marcabru, poem XXXI, verse 9.
32. The information board: Merwin, 2002, 85.
33. Ezra Pound, Canto VI, 41–6.
34. Guilhem de Capestanh: Vida, Boutière & Schutz, no. XCIV, 530–55; Pillet & Carstens, poet 213, pp. 179–81.
35. Ezra Pound, Canto IV, 17–36.
36. Bernart de Ventadorn at Poitiers: Boutière & Schutz, no. VI, 20–1.
37. Nostradamus: 'De Bernard de Ventadour', Chabaneau & Anglade, no. XVII, 47–8.
38. Villon A. Burl, *Danse Macabre. François Villon: Poetry and Murder in Medieval France*, Sutton, Thrupp, 2000, 140–1.
39. Eleanor as Guinevere: Swabey, 2004, 75.
40. The court: Seward, 1978, 113.
41. The score of poems with music: Rosenberg, Switten & Le Vot, 59. For the musical output of Bernart de Ventadorn there is no comprehensive English translation of the poems. Accompanying the original Occitan Goldin provides translations of eight, Press six. Good critiques of his work can be found in: Goldin, 108–25; Topsfield, 111–36; and Wilhelm, 107–30. Several of the songs have been recorded on compact discs. The most popular is no. XLIII *Can vei la lauzeta mover* . . .'When I see the lark beating with joy . . .'. For his music there are instrumental renditions of *Can l'erba frescha* . . . 'When the fresh grass . . .', no. XXXIX; and *Ai tantas bonas* . . ., no. VIII.
42. Lovers and madmen: Shakespeare, *A Midsummer Night's Dream*, V, I, 4–6.
43. Campion's *Rose-cheeked Laura*: M.M. Kastendierk, *England's Musical Poet Thomas Campion*, Russell & Russell, New York, 1963, 86–7.
44. Bernart de Ventadorn ordered to England: Kelly, 35–7; Weir, 106–7.
45. His lament: Chaytor, 1923, 35–6.
46. Eleanor in Poitiers: Seward, 110–11.
47. Bernart de Ventadorn's supposed 'death' in 1223 at Montmajour: Nostradamus, Life XVII, 48.

Chapter Eight

1. *Vida*, Peire d'Alvernhe: Boutière & Schutz, no. XXXIX, 263–6. Pillet & Carstens: poet 328, pp. 278–83.
2. *Trobar clus*: Bonner, 241. Perfect diction: Press, 91, 93.
3. Puivert castle: Tisseyre, 1982.
4. Peire Rogier, *Vida*: Boutière & Schutz, no. XL, 267; Pillet & Carstens, poet 356, pp. 311–13; Cheyette, 6–10.
5. Guiraut de Bornelh, *Vida*: Boutière & Schutz, no. VIII, 39; 242; Pillet & Carstens, poet 242, pp. 202–14.
6. Jeanroy: Bonner, 115.

7. The two Alamandas: Smythe, 125–7.
8. Raimbaut d'Aurenga, *Vida*: Boutière & Schutz, no. LXVIII, 441–4; Pillet & Carstens, poet 389, pp. 346–51.
9. Raimbaut d'Aurenga and troubadours: Topsfield, 137–58. Raimbaut d'Orange Pattison, 2–37. 'Punch on the nose': Poem, XX.
10. Pattison, 134–5. Naked in bed: *ibid*, Poem XXVII, 161–2.
11. *Planh* of Guiraut de Bornelh: after Topsfield, 158.
12. Monk of Montaudon: Boutière & Schutz, no. LXVI, 307–10; Pillet & Carstens, poet 305, pp. 268–72.
13. *Autra vetz . . .*: Bonner, 183–5; Lindsay, 206–8. For an overview of the Monk's poems, see: Michael J. Routledge, *Les Poésies du Moine de Montaudon*, Centre d'Études Occitane de l'Université Paul Valery, Montpellier, 1977.
14. Guillem de Saint-Leidier: Boutière & Schutz, no. XLI, 271–83; Pillet & Carstens, poet 234, pp. 194–7.
15. Raimon Jordan, viscount of St Antonin: Boutière & Schutz, no. XVII, 158–66; poet 404, pp. 365–7.
16. Raimon de Miraval: Boutière & Schutz, no. LVIII, 375–407; Pillet & Carstens, poet 406, pp. 367–74; P. Andraud, *La Vie et l'Oeuvre . . . de Raimon de Miraval*, Émile Bouillon, Paris, 1902; Topsfield, 219–37.
17. Peirol: Boutière & Schutz, no. XLV, 303–4; Pillet & Carstens, poet 366, pp. 325–30.
18. Guillem Ademar: Boutière & Schutz, no. LVI, 349–50; Pillet & Carstens, poet 202, 169–171.
19. Arnaut Daniel: Boutière & Schutz, no. IX, 59–62; Pillet & Carstens, poet 29, pp. 27–32.
20. Arnaut Daniel: Dante, *Purgatoria*, XXVI, 116–19, trans. Dale, 248; Petrarch, *Trionfo d'Amore*, trans., Topsfield, 197.
21. Three poems by Arnaut Daniel: Pillet & Carstens, nos. 8, 10 and 14.
22. Salh d'Escola: Boutière & Schutz, no.X, 64; Pillet & Carsens, poet 430, p. 385; Guilraut le Ros, Boutière & Schutz, no. LVI, 345; Pillet & Carsens, Poet 240, pp. 200–1.
23. Folquet of Marseilles: Boutière & Schutz, no. LXXI, 470–84; Pillet & Carstens, poet 155, pp. 125–32.
24. Peire Vidal: Boutière & Schutz, no. LVII, 351–74; Pillet & Carstens, poet 364, pp. 125–32.

Chapter Nine

1. Esclarmonde at Pamiers: *Corinthians*, 1, 14, 34–5. Paterson, 1993, 249.
2. Blanche of Castile described by Guillaume de Nangis: Labarge, 55.
3. Héloïse: for her story see McCleod, 1938.
4. Marie de Ventadorn: *Vida*, Boutière & Schutz, no. XXIII, 212–14, Bogin, 168–9; Pillet & Carstens, poetess 295, pp. 263–4.
5. Guy d'Ussel: Bogin, 98–9; Bruckner et al, 38–9; Rosenberg, Switten & Le Vot, 152–3.
6. Ermengarde of Narbonne: Capellanus' four judgements: Parry, 171. Peire Rogier: Boutière & Schutz, no. XL, 267–70; Cheyette, 6–10.
7. Peire Duran: and his domna: Bruckner, 64–5.
8. Male obedience: Bruckner et al, xxxiii–xxvii.
9. Capellanus, *The Art of Courtly Love*, Precept V, Parry, 81. Also, Muir, 47–8.
10. Verse 4, Bogin, 156–9.
11. Countess of Die: Bogin, 88–9; Bruckner, 110–11. Boutière & Schutz, no. LXIX, 445–6; Pillet & Carstens, poetess 46, 'Beatritz de Dia', pp. 41–3; five poems.

12. Castelloza, Lady of: Bogin, 118–29. Pillet & Carstens, poetess 109, p. 101. Three songs.
13. Clara d'Anduza: Bogin, 130–1; Bruckner, 30–1. Boutière & Schutz, no entry; Pillet & Carstens, poetess 115, p. 104, one poem.
14. Female spendthrift apparel: Meade, 5–6; Sumptury laws: Comte, 45.
15. Nuns: Bumke, 153.
16. The forbidden blouse: Bruckner, 102–5.
17. *Aube*: Doss-Quinby et al, 147–9, Poem 29.
18. 'Ah, God! . . .' Bergin, I, 259; Bruckner, 134–5; Smythe, 183.
19. William Shakespeare, *Romeo & Juliet*, Act III, Scene 5, 1–36.
20. Bieris de Romans: Bogin, 132–3; Bruckner, 32–3; T. Sankevitch, in Gaunt & Kay, VII, 113–26. Boutière & Schutz, no entry; Pillet & Carstens, poetess 93, p. 88, one poem.
21. 'Probably unique': Bogin, 75. 'So personal', *ibid*, 18.
22. Jean de Nostradamus, 1575, Life IX, 31–2.
23. Adhemar and the Monk of Montaudon Zuchetto & Gruber, 168; Bonner, 186.
24. *Vida*, Countess de Die: Boutière & Schutz, no. LXIX, 445–6; Pillet & Carstens, trobairitz 46, pp. 41–3, 'Biatritz de Dia'. Five poems.
25. Raimbaut d'Aurenga's *Vida*: Boutière & Schutz, LXVIII, 441–4; Pillet & Carstens, poet 389, 346–51.
26. His philandering nature: Rutherford, 1873, 152–4.
27. The *tenson*: Pattison, Poem XXV, 155–7. The belief that the debate was between Beatritz and Raimbaut: A.H. Smith, 1899, 1, 102–3; Chaytor, 1912, 30, 64–6. For a clear translation, see: Wilhelm, 134–6.
28. Lindsay, 1976, 186–8.
29. 'The Provençal Sappho': Rutherford (Note 26), 169–70.
30. The mistaken identity: Smith (Note 27), 1, 429–30, note 3. Sernin Santy, Jeanroy, 1964, 47, no. 48. Schutz-Gora, *ibid*, 37, no. 10. Title: *Die Provenzalischen Dichterinnen, Biographieen und Texte . . .*, Leipzig, 1888.
31. No Beatritz or Countess of Dia: Wilhelm, 134.
32. Similarities between her poem 4 and his *tenson*, poem 3: Bogin, 88–90; *tenson*, Pattison, *Tenson*, XXV, 155–8.
33. Poem III, *quar no m'en puesc*: Pattison, 156.
34. Candidates for the role of Countess of Die: Pattison, 27–29.
35. Raimon d'Agout in the *Vidas*: Pattison, 29, note 38; Boutière & Schutz, pp. 188–91.
36. Dia of Montdragon: Pattison, 30; Bruckner et al, xxxix.
37. The *Vida* of Raimbaut d'Aurenga: Boutière & Schutz, no. LXVIII 441–4. It is almost ten longer than that of the Countess of Die. Pillet & Carstens, poet 389, pp. 346–51, forty-one poems.
38. The six compact discs containing Die's Poem II: (Appendix One). The longest performance with *Vida* added is Clemencic Consort's *Troubadour*, track six.
39. A sympathetic study of the poems and problems of the Countess of Die can be read in 'The Countess of Dia, "The Sappho of Provence"', in Wilhelm, 131–42. The music to Poem II and a photograph of the original manuscript is printed in Rosenberg, Switten & Le Vot, 98, 99.

Chapter Ten

1. Robin Hood: there are many recent 'histories' of the outlaw. For doubts about his link with Richard I, see: J.C. Holt, *People's Hero or Lawless Marauder?* Thames & Hudson, London, 1982, 37, 41; G. Phillips and M. Keatman, *Robin Hood. The Man Behind the Myth*, O'Mara, London, 1995, 51–4.

2. Bertran de Born's *Vida*: Boutiére & Schutz, no. XI, 65–139; Pillet & Carstens, poet 80, 67–77. There are editions of his poems in: C. Appel, *Die Lieder Bertran de Born*, Niemeyer, Halle, 1932; and G. Gouiran, *Le Seigneur-Troubadour de Hautefort, l'Oeuvre de Bertran de Born*, University of Provence, Aix-en-Provence, 2nd edition, 1987. Recordings of his music are rare. Perhaps because he was singing of war rather than romance he is a rarity on compact discs. To the writer's knowledge there are only three songs, all in *A Mediaeval Banquet*, Disc 4 (Appendix One).

3. *Es autresi . . .* see: Goldin, 244–6; Wilhelm, 155–6.

4. Warren, 2000, 578.

5. The court at Argentan: Warren (Note 4), 603.

6. The *Razo*: Boutière & Schutz, *Razo 37*, 72; translated by Bonner, 139.

7. The lively young rabbit: Poem 'Rassa', *Tan cries e monta e poia*, Stanza 2, see also: Bonner, 139–41; Press, 156–7.

8. Gerald of Wales's opinion of Eleanor's morality: Bartlett, 79.

9. Oc-et-Non: in poem beginning, *No puosc mudar un chanter non esparja*.

10. *Razo*, no. 44: Boutière & Schutz pp. 88, 122.

11. Bertran de Born's intriguing: Warren (Note 4), 576–8.

12. Geoffrey of Vigeois: Wilhelm, 145.

13. Peter Dale, *Dante. The Divine Comedy*, 1996, 114, *Hell, Canto 28*, 119–42.

14. *Razo*, no. 21, Boutière & Schutz, pp. 103–4.

15. The 'incestuous' family war: L. Clédat, *Du Rôle Historique de Bertran de Born (1175–1200)*, Paris, 879, 52.

16. Richard's ruthlessness: Warren (Note 4), 593. Death of the Young King: Barber, 2001, 208–9.

17. Bertran de Born's threnody: *Razo*, no. 26, Boutière & Schutz, pp. 114–15. There are translations in: Bonner, 147–8; Press, 168–71; and Rosenberg, Switten & Le Vot, 106–7.

18. The *sirventes* against Alfonso: *Puois le gens terminis floritz . . .*: Pillet & Carstens, no. 32.

19. *Razo*, no. 32, Boutière & Schutz, 107.

20. The release of Bertran de Born: *Razo*, no. 32, Boutière & Schutz, 107–8.

Chapter Eleven

1. Raimon de Miraval: Boutière & Schutz, *Vida LVIII*, 375–407; Pillet & Carstens, poet 406, pp. 367–74. M.L. Switten, *The Cansos of Raimon de Miraval. A Study of Poems and Melodies*, Medieval Academy of America, Cambridge, Mass., 1985; L.T. Topsfield, ed., *Les Poésies de Raimon de Miraval*, Nizet, Paris, 1971, 236.

2. Sirvente XXXVIII: Topsfield, 1971, 313–15.

3. Topsfield, 1975, 'Raimon de Miraval and the Joy of Court', 219–37, 236. For general background material, see: P. Andraud, *La Vie et l'Oeuvre . . . de Raimon de Miraval*, mile Bouillon, Paris, 1902.

4. *Razo C*, Boutière & Schutz, 384.

5. Loba and Raymond-Roger, Count of Foix: *Razo C*, 385; Burl, 2002, 98–9.

6. Nostradamus: Life XIII, 38–40.

7. Poem 3: Switten, 152–3.

8. The king's conquest: *Razo D*, Boutière & Schutz, 393.

9. Lindsay, 88; Topsfield, 1971, Poem XLI, 325–9.

10. The farcical wedding at Miraval: *Razo B*, Boutière & Schutz, 380.

11. J. Lindsay, *Song of a Fallen World. Culture during the Break-up of the Roman Empire (AD 350–600)*, Andrew Dakers, London, 1948.

12. Arnaud Amaury: Wakefield, 197; Burl, 2002, 243, n. 17
13. Gormonda: Bruckner et al, 106–19, 182–5.
14. Riquier's lament: the English text for this unaccompanied poem can be heard on a compact disc, Disc 6, Track 1, of *A Medieval Banquet*, 1–6.
15. Modern accounts of the Albigensian Crusade, *inter alia*, alphabetically: Burl, 2002; Oldenberg, 1961; O'Shea, 2000; Sumption.
16. Tudela's successor: Shirley, 1996, 2.
17. Raymond-Roger's refusal: Sismondi, 21; Sumption, 99.
18. Evacuation from Carcassonne: Vaux-de-Cernay, [98], 54; de Tudela, *Laisse 33*, 26.
19. Simon de Montfort's religious scruples: Phillips, 2004, 137, 194.
20. Battle of St-Martin-Lalande: William de Tudela, *Chanson, Laisses 103–4*, Meyer, 103–4; Shirley, 54.
21. Miraval's poem XXXVII: Topsfield, 1971, 301–9; 'Audiart': Switten, 68.
22. Death of the king of Aragon: Anonymous, *Chanson, Laisse CXL*, Meyer, 137; Shirley, 70. The battle of Muret: Sibly & Sibly, 213, n. 54; Sumption, 167.
23. Miraval's retirement to Lerida: *Vida*, Boutière & Schutz, 376.
24. *Laisse 165*: Meyer, 197–8; Shirley, 99.
25. Hanged on an olive tree: *Laisse 161*: Meyer, 167; Shirley, 94.
26. *Laisse 171*: Meyer, 213; Shirley, 105.
27. 'Morning dew': *Laisse 187*, Meyer, 203; Shirley, 131.
28. *Chanson*, 342, lines 8448–54; Meyer, 343–4; Shirley, 172.
29. Guy of Cavaillon as the 'anonymous' poet who continued the work of William of Tudela: Francesco Zambon, *Cathares 2004, Pyrénées Spéciale, Les Témoins de Pierre*, Toulouse, 2004, 18–20.
30. His *Vida*: Boutière & Schutz, LXXXII, 505–7; Pillet & Carstens, poet 192, 162.
31. *Paretge: Laisse 154*; Meyer, 166; Shirley, 84–5.
32. The poem: Boutière & Schutz, 505–6.
33. Elias Barjol: Boutière & Schutz, XXVI, 215–16; Pillet & Carstens, poet 132, 113–15.
34. Garsenda, a trobairitz in a world in which women were adored: Bogin, 64, 75; Bruckner et al, xxxvii, xxxix-xl; 163.
35. The *cobla*: Bogin, 108–9; Bruckner, et al xxvi, 54–5
36. Marmande massacre: *Laisse 212*, Meyer, 373; Shirley, 188, 189.
37. Louis' army: *Laisse 212*, Meyer, 371; Shirley, 187.
38. The end of the *Chanson: Laisse 214*, 9562–78: Meyer, 383–4; Shirley, 193–4.
39. Thomas Gray, 'Elegy Written in a Country Church-Yard', verse 15; Sir Thomas Browne, *Hydriotaphia or Urn-Burial, Everyman*, London, 1937, 135.

Chapter Twelve

1. Bernard Sicart de Marjévols: Topsfield, 241. He has no *Vida*.
2. Blanche of Castile, Burl, 2002. 192; exhumation of Cathar burials: Burl, *ibid*, 175; Wycliffe, *Chambers Biographical Dictionary*, Edinburgh, 1990, 1587; Tyndale, *ibid*, 1484–5.
3. The massacre at Montségur: Puylaurens, XLIV, 186–7; Burl, 2002, 192–6; Oldenbourg, 340–64.
4. Peire Cardenal: Boutière & Schutz, *Vida L*, 335–7; Pillet & Carstens, poet 335, 291–300.
5. *Orgue portatif*: Montagu, 36–7; Riot, 95.
6. Other troubadours: Aimeric de Belenoi: Boutière & Schutz, XXXVI, 255–6, Pillet & Carstens, poet 9, 5–6; Guilhem de Montanhagol, Boutière & Schutz, C,

518–19, Pillet & Carstens, poet 225, 187–9; Sordello, Boutière & Schutz, XCVIII, 562–8, Pillet & Carstens, poet 437, 394–400; Dante, *Purgatory*, Cantos 6, 7, 8, 9; Sayers, *Divine Comedy*, 2; Purgatory, 115, note.

7. St Mary: Lavaud, XXXVIII, 232–8; Pillet & Carstens, poem 70; Goldin, 297–301.
8. Jeanroy and Cardenal's protectors: Bonner, 193.
9. Kings and grasping subjects: Poem *Mon chanter . . .*: Lavaud, LX, 388–97; Pillet & Carstens, poem 57.
10. Lavaud, XXIX, 170–7; Pillet & Carstens, poem 31.
11. *Tartarassa ni voutor*: a poem already quoted in Chapter Six: Lavaud, LXXIV, 490–3; Pillet & Carstens, poem 55.
12. Villon and the Carmelites: Burl, 2000, 108; P. Dale, *Poems of François Villon . . .*, Anvil Press, London, 2001; *The Legacy*, 32, 255–6.
13. *Monge solon . . .* Lavaud, XXXIV, 216–15; Pillet & Carstens, poem 64. There are translations in English by Bonner, 107–8; and Press, 296–9 with the original Occitan text.
14. *El seran . . .*: Note 13, third full verse.
15. Guiraut Riquier: Pillet & Carstens, poet 248, pp. 225–34, listing eighty-nine poems and Epistles I–XV; albas, nos. 2, 70; *pastorelas* (Note 19). See also: Bonner, 223–31, 307–8; Goldin, 316–27; Press, 306–25. Forty-eight melodies: Aubrey, 24.
16. Uc de Saint-Circ as a biographer: Zuchetto & Gruber, 199.
17. The loss of the Languedoc: Runciman, III, 268–9, 274, 'Alfonso of Poitou'.
18. Riquier's distinction between troubadours and jongleurs: Lindsay, 119, 128–9.
19. Cholakian, 155–80; *Pastorelas*: nos. 15, 22, 32, 49, 50, 51.
20. Pastorela One: *L'autra jorn m'anava . . .* Pillet & Carstens, poem 49; Hill & Bergin, 1, 248–50; Bonner, 224–31.
21. Pastorela Six: *A san Pos de Tomeiras . . .* Goldin, 318–24; Pillet & Carstens, poem 15.
22. Marcabru's two *pastorelas*: *L'autrier, a l'issida d'abriu* and *L'autrier jost' una sebissa*; Pillet & Carstens, poems 29 and 30.
23. Riquier's lament: *Be.m degra de chantar tener . . .*: Goldin, 316–27; Press, 306–25; Rosenberg, Switten & Le Vot, 172–3. Pillet & Carstens, poem 17.
24. The last group of Cathar Good Men: Burl, 2002, 209–10; Weis, 2000, 239–40.

Appendix Two

1. The assassination of the vizier: Daftary, 2001, 35; B. Lewis, 2001, 47.
2. Known facts of Khayyam's life: Lamb, 1943, 281–3.
3. Name and pen-name: Graves, R. and Ali-Sham, O., trans. *The Rubaiyatt of Omar Khayaam*, Penguin, Harmondsworth, 1972, 19, 32.
4. The revised calendar: Edward Gibbon, *The Decline & Fall of the Roman Empire, 1776–88*, Vol. VI, Chapter LVII, 382; Avery & Heath-Stubbs, 23–4.
5. Khayyam as a mathematician: Avery & Heath-Stubbs, 20.
6. Original stanzas: Graves and Ali-Shah (Note 3) 23, 32; 'Sensualities': *ibid*, 23.
7. An unreliable Sufi: Avery & Heath-Stubbs, 13, 17, 25.
8. The 'wondrous paraphrase': Lamb, 1943, 288. For a readable and scholarly account of the publishing history of Fitzgerald's *Rubaiyat* as a 'publishing phenomenon', see Garrard, 2007.
9. Blossom on the tomb: Avery & Heath-Stubbs, 20.
10. Desecration: Lamb, 295: For other translation of the *Rubaiyat* see: Doxey, W., *Rubaiyat of Omar Khayyam, the Astronomer-Poet of Persia, Rendered into English Verse by Edward Fitzgerald*, 5th edition, Doxey's, New York, 1900; Heron-Allen,

E., trans., Edward Fitzgerald's *Rubaiyat of Omar k Khayyam, from Their Original Persian Sources*, Quaritch, London, 1899; Maine, G.F., ed., *Rubaiyat of Omar Khayyam*, rendered into English verse by Edward Fitzgerald (1st, 2nd and 5th editions) intro. L. Housman, Collins, Glasgow and London, 1954; Whinfield, E.H., trans., *The Quatrains of Omar Khayyam*, London.

Appendix Three

1. Vernacular love poems in northern France: by men: Rosenberg, Switten & Le Vot, 1; Thibaut, 305; Guy, 249; Blondel, 239. By women: Doss-Quinby et al, 1–26; words and music, Rosenberg, Switten & Le Vot, 4.
2. Muscadet: F.S. Wildman, *A Wine Tour of France*, Cassell, London, 1976, 271–4.
3. The learning of Héloïse: as a child at Argenteuil, Ward & Chiavaroli, in Wheeler, ed., *Listening to Héloïse. The Voice of a Twelfth Century Woman*, Macmillan, Basingstoke, 2000, 58–62. Héloïse: as a young woman, Mews, 2005, 59. Abelard the intellectual: Clancy, 15–118; G.R. Evans, *Fifty Key Medieval Thinkers*, Routledge, London, 2002, 86–91. For the story of Héloïse and Abelard see Burge, 2003, Mews, 2005. For Abelard's career, Clancy, 1997. For Héloïse the most readable account is McCleod, 1938. See also Hamilton, 1966; Pernoud, 1973. Only fervent feminists will gain much from the turgidities of Wheeler, ed., 2000. For the long series of later letters the most accessible is Radice, 1974. There is an attractive Folio Society edition of 1974 but, being Folio, there is no Index. For the earlier letters written in Paris, see Mews, 2001.
4. Abelard's calculated seduction: Radice, 1974, 66.
5. Her pleasures: Radice, 1974, 115, 117–18.
6. The lost correspondence: There are two sets of letters, the earliest written in Paris and not discovered until c. 1471 by Johannes de Vepria, a monk, at Clairvaux abbey: Mews, 2001, 8–15, 190–289, Letters 1–113. The second was a long correspondence between Héloïse and Abelard when she was abbess of the Paraclete nunnery. A copy was found by the poet, Jean de Meung, some time before 1278: Mews, 2001, 29–30; Radice, 1974.
7. Héloïse to Abelard: Mews, 2001, Letter 92, 272–5.
8. Her pregnancy: Burge, 2003, 270; Hamilton, 1966, 136–8. Astralabe: Burge, 2003, 270; Hamilton, 1966, 136–8. Clisson, *ibid*, 30–4.
9. Héloïse as whore rather than wife: Radice, 1974, 114, Letter 1; Mews, 2001, 260–3, Letter 82.
10. Jean de Meung's satire: *Roman de la Rose*, lines 999–1023. Sorbonne Library, Robertson, *Abelard and Héloïse*, Purnell, London, 1972. 149–53.
11. Argenteuil convent: Héloïse's pretence to be a noviate nun: Radice 1974, 74, from Abelard's *Historia calamitatum*, see also: Muckle, J.T. *The Story of Abelard's Adversities. A Translation with Notes of the Historia Calamitatum*, preface. Gilson, Pontifical Institute of Mediaeval Studies, Toronto, 1964.
12. Fulbert's Old Testament enactment: Deuteronomy, 23, 1; Lloyd, 80.
13. Castration: Radice, 75, *Historia calamitatum*; Burge, 2003, 132–5; Robertson (Note 10) 55–6.
14. Héloïse, a reluctant nun: Her quotation of Cornelia's lament: The Roman poet Lucan's *Pharsalia VIII*, V, 94. McCleod, 1938, 77–80; Pernoud,1973, 81.
15. Her protestation of love: Radice, 1974, 113, Letter 2.
16. The *Carmina Burana*: Russell, C. and Pickett, P., *Carmina Burana*, Printer in the Rye, UK, 1978; P.G. Walsh, *Thirty Songs from the Carmina Burana*, University of Reading, 1976, 1–8.

17. Poem 169, *Hebet sydus . . .*: Mews, 2001, 90; P. Dronke, *Mediaeval Latin and the Rise of the European Love-Lyric*, 1, 2, Oxford University Press, Oxford, 1968, 1, 313–18.
18. The Paraclete: Burge, 174–5.
19. St Gildas-de-Rhuys: Abelard, *Historia calamitatum*, Radice, 1974, 103.
20. Suger and the closing of Argenteuil: Mews, 2005, 145–6. Also, Burge, 186–7.
21. Héloïse the abbess: Abelard, *Historia calamitatum*, Radice, 1974, 97.
22. 'Lovely Douette': Rosenberg, Switten & Le Vot, 187, verse 8.
23. Héloïse to Abelard: Letter I, Radice, 1974, 113.
24. Abelard to Héloïse: Letter VII, Radice, 1974, 196.
25. Héloïse to Abelard: Letter 3, Radice, 1974, 133.
26. The long letters: Radice, 1974, 109–271.
27. *Requiescat a labore . . .*, McCleod, 282–3, n. 195.
28. The legend: McCleod, 226; 240–1, n.224.
29. The crypt at the Paraclete: Hamilton, 143–6.
30. The chapel: McCleod, 234–41.
31. The peregrinations of the burials of Héloïse and Abelard: McCleod, 229–42. Visitors to Père Lachaise can find the tomb at the lower end of the slope in square N10 of the graveyard map obtainable from florists outside the spacious cemetery. Epitaph on the tomb: Burge, 276.
32. Héloïse to Abelard: Letter 1, Radice, 1974, 117.
33. Waddell, 1933, 168–9. Corrigan (see Waddell, 1982), 7–14, 280–1.

Appendix Four

1. 'Fair Rosamond' by Thomas Deloney, balladeer and pamphleteer, *c.* 1543–1600, in: *Reliques of Ancient English Poetry, I–III*, compiled by Thomas Percy, ed.: H.A. Wheatley, Allen & Unwin, London, 1885. Volume II, 154–64. 'Queen Eleanor's Confession', *ibid*, anonymous, 164–8. For a short biography of Rosamund de Clifford see: Tyerman, 2001, 196–7.
2. Henry and Rosamund first met in 1165–6: Meade, 1977, 234; Owen, 1993, 114; Seward, 1978, 108; Weir, 2000, 171.
3. Born, *c.* 1140 or before: Owen, 1993, 114; Gerald of Wales (*Giraldus Cambrensis*): Meade, 1977, 171.
4. Earlier mistresses of Henry II: Rohese: Weir, 2000, 97, 180; Avice: Barber, 2003, 66; Pernoud, 1967, 135.
5. Clifford castle: A. Mee, *Herefordshire*, Hodder & Stoughton, London, 1938, 43–4; N. Pevsner, Herefordshire, Penguin, London, 1963, 27, 101,
6. Gifts to her father: *Compact Edition of the Dictionary of National Biography, I, II*, Oxford University Press, 1975, 1, 389.
7. 'Installed her with regal honours in Eleanor's apartments': Meade, 1997, 237.
8. An unusual affair: Meade, 1977, 235.
9. Her unlikely children: Owen, 1993, 120. The true mother, Ykenai: Walter Map, F. Tupper and M.B. Ogle, *Master Walter Map's Book, De Nugis Curialium (Courtiers' Trifles)*,Chatto & Windus, London, 1924, 99, 309.
10. The hunting lodge: Hollister & Frost, 2001, 316, n. 140.
11. The 'maze': Barber, 2003, 62; Meade, 1997, 236; Weir, 2000, 172.
12. Robert Fabyan: Owen, 1993, 118–19.
13. Vampire toads: Meade, 1997, 235.
14. Walter Map: Tupper & Ogle (Note 9), 297; Gray, R., *The King's Wife. Five Queen Consorts*, Secker & Warburg, London, 1990, 25.

15. Adulteresses: Eleanor's grandmother: Meade, 1997, 237. Eleanor: Warren, 2000, 119; the biographer of Louis VII: Owen, 1993, 111. Trois Fontaines; Gray, 1990 (Note 14), 4.

16. Gerald of Wales' puns: Boyd, 2004, 182.

17. The Bishop of Lincoln: Owen, 1993, 115.

18. King John's endowment: Percy's *Reliques of Ancient English Poetry*, II, 157.

19. Leland at Godstow: *The Itinerary of John Leland in or about the years 1535–1543, Parts I–III*, ed. L.T. Smith, Southern Illinois University Press, Carbondale, 1964, I–V, Godstow, I, 328–9.

20. Death of John's mother: Shakespeare, *King John*, IV, 2, 127–8.

21. Godstow's chapel: A. Mee, *Oxfordshire*, Hodder & Stoughton, London, 1942, 108–10; J. Sherwood and N. Pevsner, *Oxfordshire*, Penguin, London, 1974, 852.

Bibliography

Akehurst, F.R.P. and Davis, J.M. eds (1995) *A Handbook of the Troubadours*, University of California Press, Berkeley

Anonymous. See: Shirley; Tudela

Aubarbier, J.-C. and Binet, M. (2001) *Le Pays Cathars*, Éditions Ouest-France, Sarlat

Aubrey, E. (2000) *The Music of the Troubadours*, Indiana University Press, Bloomington

Avery, P. and Heath-Stubbs, J., trans. *The Rub'aiyat of Omar Khayyam*, Allen Lane, London, 1979

Barber, R. (1978b) *The Devil's Crown. A History of Henry II and His Sons*, Book Club Associates, London

—— (2001) *Henry Plantagenet*, Boydell, Ipswich

Barrington, M. (1953) *Blaye, Roland, Rudel and the Lady of Tripoli*, Bennett, Salisbury

Bartlett, R. (2006) *Gerald of Wales. A Voice of the Middle Ages*, Tempus, Brimscombe Port

Bec, P. (1961) *Les Salus d'Amour du Troubadour Arnaud de Mareuil*, Privat, Toulouse

Begg, E. (1996) *The Cult of the Black Virgin*, Arkana, London

Benton, J.R. (2004) *Medieval Mischief. Wit and Humour in the Art of the Middle Ages*, Sutton, Thrupp

Bergin, T.G. (1975) *Anthology of the Provençal Poets, I, II*, Hill, R.T. and Bergin, T.G, 2nd edn, rev. T.G. Bergin, Yale University Press, New Haven and London

Berry, A. (1961) *Anthologie de la Poésie Occitane*, Libraire Stock, Paris

Boccaccio, G. (1350–?) *The Decameron*, Cohen, M. (trans) *Tales from the Decameron*, New English Library, London, 1962

—— *The Decameron*, McWilliam, G.H., trans, Penguin, London, 1972

—— *The Decameron*, Waldman, G., trans, Oxford World's Classics, Oxford, 1993

Bogin, M. (1976) *The Women Troubadours*, Paddington, New York and London

Bonner, A. (1973) ed. and trans. *Songs of the Troubadours*, Allen & Unwin, London

Boutière, J. and Schutz, A.H. (1973) *Biographies des Troubadours. Textes Provençaux des XIIIe et XIVe Siècles*, 2nd edn, by J. Boutière, trans. from Provençal into French, I.-M. Cluzel, Nizet, Paris

Boyd, D. (2004) *Eleanor of Aquitaine. April Queen of Aquitaine*, Sutton, Thrupp

Boyle, D. (2005) *Blondel's Song: the Capture, Imprisonment and Ransom of Richard the Lionheart*, Viking, London

Bradford, E. (2004) *The Sword and the Scimitar. The Saga of the Crusades*, Pen & Sword Military Classics, Bradford

Briffault, R.S. (1965) *The Troubadours*, ed. Koons, L.F., Indiana University Press, Bloomington

Bruckner, M.T., Shepard, L. and White, S. (2000) eds and trans., *Songs of the Women Troubadours*, Garland, New York

Bumke, J. (2000) *Courtly Culture. Literature and Society in the High Middle Ages*, trans. T. Dunlop, Overlook Dunlop, Woodstock, New York, London

Burge, J. (2003) *Héloïse & Abelard. A twelfth century love story*, Profile, London

Burl, A. (2002) *God's Heretics. The Albigensian Crusade*, Sutton, Thrupp

Chabaneau, C. and Anglade, J. eds (1913), *Jehan de Nostredame. 'Les Vies des Plus Célèbres et Anciens Poètes Provensaux'* (1575), Honoré Champion, Paris, 1913

Chanson de la Croisade contre les Albigeois (Song of the Cathar Wars), see: Meyer, 1875; Shirley, 1996

Chaytor, Revd H.J. (1902) *The Troubadours of Dante*, Clarendon Press, Oxford
—— (1912) *The Troubadours*, Cambridge University Press, Cambridge
—— (1923) *The Troubadours and England*, Cambridge University Press, Cambridge
—— (1939) *Savaric de Mauléon. Baron and Troubadour*, Cambridge University Press, Cambridge
—— (1946) *The Provençal 'Chanson de Gest'*, Cumberlege, Oxford University Press, London

Cheyette, F.L. (2001) *Ermengard of Narbonne and the World of the Troubadours*, Cornell University Press, Ithaca

Cholakian, R.C. (1990) *The Troubadour Lyric: a Psychocritical Study*, Manchester University Press, Manchester and New York

Clanchy, M.T. (1997) *Abelard. A Medieval Life*, Blackwell, Oxford

Comte, S. (1978) *Everyday Life in the Middle Ages*, trans. D. Macrae, Minerva, Geneva

Corédon, C. and Williams, A. (2004) *A Dictionary of Medieval Terms and Phrases*, Brewer, Woodbridge

Daftary, F. (1995) *The Assassin Legends. Myths of the Isma'ilis*, Tauris, London

Dale, P. trans. (1996) *Dante. The Divine Comedy*, Anvil, London

Dante Alighieri. See: Chayter, 1912; Dale; Lewis, R.W.B.; Reynolds; Rubin; Sayers

Doss-Quinby, E., Grimbert, J.T., Pfeffer, W. and Aubrey, E. eds (2001) *Songs of the Women Trouvères*, Yale University Press, New Haven and London

Duvernoy, J. (1996) trans., *Guillaume de Puylaurens. Chronique 1145–1275*, Péregrinateur, Toulouse

Eco, U. (2002) *Art and Beauty in the Middle Ages*, Yale University Press, New Haven and London

Farnell, I. trans. (1896) *The Lives of the Troubadours*, Nutt, London

Fénié, B. and J.-J. (1997) *Toponymie Occitane*, Sud Ouest Université Presse, Rennes

Finucane, R.C. (1983) *Soldiers of the Faith. Crusaders and Moslems at War*, J.M. Dent, London

Fleming, A. (1952) *The Troubadours of Provence*, Maclellan, Glasgow

Gaunt, S., Harvey, R. and Paterson, L. (2000) *Marcabru. A Critical Edition*, Brewer, Cambridge
—— and Kay, S. eds (1999) *The Troubadours. An Introduction*, Cambridge University Press, Cambridge

Gareyte, J.-F. (2007) *L'Aube des Troubadours. La Chanson d'Antioche du chevalier Béchaude*, La Lauze, Périgueux

Garrard, G. (2007) *A Book of Verse: The Biography of the Rubaiyat of Omar Khayyam*, Sutton, Thrupp

Goldin, F. (1983) *Lyrics of the Troubadours and Trouvères. An Anthology and a History*, Peter Smith, Gloucester, Mass

Green P. see: Ovid

Hamilton, E. (1966) *Héloïse*, Hodder & Stoughton, London

Harvey, R. (1989) *The Troubadour Marcabru and Love*, Westfield Publications, London

Henry of Huntingdon (c. 1135–48) *The Chronicle*, trans. T. Forester, 1853. Llanerch reprint, Felinfach, 1991

Hill, R.T. and Bergin: see: Bergin, T.G.

Hindley, G. (1976) *Saladin*, Constable, London

Hollister, C. W. and Frost, A.C. (2001) *Henry I*, Yale University Press, New Haven and London

Hopkins, A. (1994) *The Book of Courtly Love. The Passionate Code of the Troubadours*, Harpers, San Francisco
—— (1997) *Most Wise and Valiant Ladies. Remarkable Lives of Women of the Middle Ages*, Past Times, Oxford
Hopper, S. (2002) *To Be A Pilgrim, the Medieval Pilgrimage Experience*, Sutton, Thrupp
—— (2006) *Mothers, Mystics and Merrymakers. Medieval Women Pilgrims*, Sutton, Thrupp
Hueffer, F. (1878) *The Troubadours*, Chatto & Windus, London
Hughes, A. ed. (1955) *Early Medieval Music up to 1300*, Oxford University Press, Oxford
Jeanroy, A. (1964) *Bibliographie Sommaire des Chansonniers Provençal . . .*, Librairie Honoré Champion, Paris
—— (1974a) *Anthologie des Troubadours XIIth – XIIIth Siècles*, A.-G. Nizet. Paris
—— (1974b) *Bibliographie Sommaire des Chansonniers Français du Moyen Age*, Librairie Honoré Champion, Paris
Johnston, R.C. (1973) *Les Poésies Lyriques du Troubadour Arnaut de Marueil*, Slatkin, Geneva (reprint of 1935)
Kelly, A. (1950) *Eleanor of Aquitaine and the Four Kings*, Harvard University Press, Cambridge, Massachusetts
Labarge, M.W. (2001) *Women in Medieval Life*, Penguin, London
Lamb, H. *Persian Mosaic. An Imaginative Biography of Omar Khayyam Based upon Reality in the Oriental Manner*, Robert Hale, London, 1943
Lambert, M. *The Cathars*, Blackwell, London, 1998
Lewis, B. (2001) *The Assassins. A Radical Sect in Islam*, Weidenfeld & Nicolson, London
Lewis, R.W.B. (2002) *Dante. A Life*, Phoenix, London
Lindsay, J. (1976) *The Troubadours and their World of the Twelfth and Thirteenth Centuries*, Frederick Muller, London
Lloyd, R.B. (1947) *Abelard. An Orthodox Rebel*, Latimer, London
Malm, U. (2001) *'Dolssor Conina'. Lust, the Bawdy and Obscenity in Medieval Occitan . . . Troubadour Poetry . . .*, Uppsala University Press, Uppsala
Martin, W.H. and Mason, S. (2007) *The Art of Omar Khayyam. Illustrating Fitzgerald's 'Rubaiyat'*, Tauris, London and New York
Mason, E. (2005) *William II. Rufus, the Red King*, Tempus, Brimscombe Port
Massey, A. (1986) *The Fire Garden*, Agenda, London
Matthew Parris. See: Vaughan, R.
McCleod, E. (1938) *Héloïse. A Biography*, Chatto & Windus, London
Meade, M. (1977) *Eleanor of Aquitaine. A Biography*, Phoenix, London
Merwin, W.S. (2002) *The Mays of Ventadorn*, National Geographic, Washington
Mews, C.J. (2001) *The Lost Letters of Héloïse and Abelard*, Palgrave, New York and Basingstoke
—— (2005) *Abelard and Héloïse*, Oxford University Press, New York
Meyer, P., ed. and trans. (1875) *La Chanson de la Croisade Contre les Albigeois, I, II*, Renouard, Paris
Miller, D. (2003) *Richard the Lionheart. The Mighty Crusader*, Weidenfeld & Nicolson, London
Montagu, J. (1979) *The World of Medieval & Renaissance Musical Instruments*, David & Charles, Newton Abbot
Nostradamus, Jean de, see: Chabaneau & Anglade
Ohler, N. (1989) *The Medieval Traveller*, trans. C. Hillier, Boydell, Woodbridge
Oldenbourg, Z. (1961) *Massacre at Montségur*, trans. Green. P., Weidenfeld & Nicolson, London
O'Shea, S. (2000) *The Perfect Heresy. The Life and Death of the Cathars*, Profile Books, London

Ovid (Publius Ovidius Naso) (1982) *The Erotic Poems: The Amores; The Art of Love; Cures for Love; On Facial Treatment for Women*, trans. P. Green, Penguin, London

Owen, D.D.R. (1993) *Eleanor of Aquitaine. Queen and Legend*, Blackwell, Oxford

Parry, J.J. (1960) ed. and trans. *The Art of Courtly Love. By Andreas Capellanus*, Columbia University Press, New York

Parsons, J.C. ed. *Medieval Queenship*, Sutton, Thrupp, 1994

Paterson, L.M. (1993) *The World of the Troubadours. Medieval Occitan Society, c. 1100–c. 1300*, Cambridge University Press, Cambridge

Pattison, W.T. (1952) *The Life and Works of the Troubadour Raimbaut d'Orange*, University of Minnesota Press, Minneapolis

Pélhisson, Guillaume de (1229–c. 1250) *Chronicle*. See: Wakefield, Appendix 3, 207–36

Pernoud, R.(1967) *Eleanor of Aquitaine*, Collins, London

—— (1973) *Héloïse and Abelard*, Collins, London

Petrarch (Francesco Petrarca) *The Sonnets, Triumphs and Other Poems*, various translators, Bell & Son, London, 1912

Phillips, J. (2005) *The Fourth Crusade. And the Sack of Constantinople*, Pimlico, London

Pickens, R.T. *The Songs of Jaufré Rudel*, Pontifical Institute of Mediaeval Studies Toronto, 1978

Pillet, A. and Carstens, H., *Bibliographie der Troubadours*, Niemeyer, Halle, 1933

Poole, A.L. *From Domesday Book to Magna Carta, 1087–1216*, Clarendon Press, Oxford, 1955

Porter, P. (2003) *Courtly Love in Medieval Manuscripts*, British Library, London

Pound, E. (1996) *The Cantos of Ezra Pound*, New Directions, New York

Press, A.R. (1985) ed. and trans. *Anthology of Troubadour Poetry*, Edinburgh University Press, Edinburgh

Puylaurens, Guillaume de. See: Duvernoy, 1976

Radice, B. trans. (1974) *The Letters of Abelard and Héloïse*, Penguin, Harmondsworth

—— (1977) *Abelard & Héloïse. The Story of His Misfortunes and the Personal Letters*, Folio Society, London (no Index)

Reece, G. (1940) *Music in the Middle Ages. With an Introduction on the Music of Ancient Times*, Norton, New York

Reeves, C. (1997) *Pleasures and pastimes in Medieval England*, Sutton, Thrupp

Reynolds, B. (2006) *Dante. The Poet, the Political Thinker, the Man*, Tauris, London

Ricketts, P.T. ed. (1964) *Les Poésies de Guilhem de Montanhagel, Troubadour Provençal du XIIIe Siècle*, Pontifical Institute of Medieval Studies, Toronto

Riot, C. (1998) *Chants et Instruments. Trouveurs et Jongleurs au Moyen Age*, Rempart, Cahors

Robertson, D.W. (1972) *Abelard and Héloïse*, Book Club, London

Rosenberg, M.V. (1937) *Eleanor of Aquitaine. Queen of the Troubadours and of the Courts of Love*, Hamish Hamilton, London

Rosenberg, S.N., Switten, M. and Le Vot, G. eds (1998) *Songs of the Troubadours and Trouvères. An Anthology of Poems and Melodies*, Garland, New York

Roux, J. ed. (2004) *The Roads to Santiago de Compostella*, MSM, Vic-en-Bigorre

Rowbotham, J.F. (1895) *The Troubadours and Courts of Love*, Swan Sonnenschein, New York

Rubin, H. (2004) *Dante in Love. The World's Greatest Poem And How It Made History*, Simon & Schuster, New York

Runciman, S. (1965) *A History of the Crusades, I–III*, Peregrine, Harmondsworth

Rutherford, J. (1873) *The Troubadours. Their Loves and their Lyrics*, Smith, Elder, London

Sayers, D.L. (1949) *The Comedy of Dante Alighieri, the Florentine, I, Hell*, Penguin, London

Sayers, D.L. (1955) *2, Purgatory*, Penguin, London

—— (1962) *3, Paradise*, Penguin, London

Seward, D. (1978) *Eleanor of Aquitaine. The Mother Queen*, David & Charles, Newton Abbot

Shirley, J. (1996) trans. *The Song of the Cathar Wars. A History of the Albigensian Crusade*, by Guillaume de Tudela, *[Laisses 1–13]*, and Anonymous *[Laisses 132–214]* (*c.* 1220), Scolar Press, Aldershot

Sibly, W.A. and M.D. trans. (1998) *Historia Albigensis*, by Pierre des Vaux-de-Cernay (*c.* 1212–18), Boydell, Woodbridge

Smith, J.H. (1899) *The Troubadours at Home. Their Lives and Personalities, Their Songs and Their World, I, II*, Putnam's Sons, New York and London

Smythe, B. (1911) *Trobador Poets. Selections from the Poems of Eight Trobadors translated from the Provençal. With Introduction and Notes*, Chatto & Windus, London

Song of the Cathar Wars. see: Meyer, 1875; Shirley, 1996

Sumption, J. (1999) *The Albigensian Crusades*, Faber & Faber, London

Swabey, F.F. (2004) *Eleanor of Aquitaine, Courtly Love and the Troubadours*, Greenwood, Westport, CT and London

Switten, M.L. (1985) *The Cansos of Raimon de Miraval. A Study of Poems and Melodies*, Medieval Academy of America, Cambridge, Massachusetts

Tisseyre, J. (1982) *Le Château de Puivert*, Archéologie du Midi Médiéval, Carcassonne

Topsfield, L. (1975) *Troubadours and Love*, Cambridge University Press, Cambridge

Tudela, Guillaume de and, Anonymous. See: Shirley, 1996

Tyerman, C. (2001) *Who's Who in Early Medieval England, 1066–1272*, Stackpole, Mechanicsburg, Philadelphia

Vaux-de-Cernay, Pierre des. See: Sibly & Sibly

Wace (*c.* 1160–*c.* 1175) *The History of the Norman People (Roman de Rou)*, trans. G.S. Burgess, Boydell, Woodbridge

Waddell, H. (1933) *Mediaeval Latin Lyrics*, Constable, London

—— (1934) *The Wandering Scholars*, Constable, London

—— (1982) *Songs of the Wandering Scholars*, ed. F. Corrigan, Folio Society, London (no Index)

Wakefield, W.L. (1974) *Heresy, Crusade and Inquisition in Southern France 1100–1250*, University of California Press, Berkeley

Walsh, P.G. ed. (1976) *Thirty Poems from the Carmina Burana*, Department of Classics, University of Reading, Reading

Warren, W.L. (1974) *King John*, Book Club Associates, London

—— (2000) *Henry II*, Yale University Press, New Haven and London

Weir, A. (2000) *Eleanor of Aquitaine. By the Wrath of God, Queen of England*, Pimlico, London

Wellesz, E. (n.d.) *Music of the Troubadours. Six Songs in Provençal by Bernart de Ventadorn*, Oxford University Press (Music Department), New York and London

Wheeler, B. ed. (2000) *Listening to Héloïse. The Voice of a Twelfth-Century Woman*, Macmillan, Basingstoke

Wilhelm, J.J. (1970) *Seven Troubadours. The Creators of Modern Verse*, Pennsylvania State University Press, University Park

William of Malmesbury (*c.* 1135–40) *A History of the Norman Kings, 1066–1125*, trans. J. Stephenson, 1854. Llanerch reprint, Felinfach, 1989

Woolff, P. (2003) *Western Languages. AD 100–1500*, trans. Patridge, F., Phoenix, London

Zuchetto, G. and Gruber, J. (1998) *Le Livre des Troubadours, XIIIe et XIVe Siècle Anthologie*, Éditions de Paris, Paris

Index

Bold indicates an important reference.
Italic refers to a *map*, a *foreign word*, or a *photograph*.